ORIGINAL DISCONTENTS:
COMMENTARIES ON THE CREATION OF CONNECTICUT'S CONSTITUTION OF 1818

Edited by Richard Buel Jr. and George J. Willauer

The Acorn Club
2007

Thirty-fifth Publication of
The Acorn Club
c/o The Connecticut Trust for Historic Preservation
940 Whitney Avenue
Hamden, CT 06517-4002

Designed by Teri Prestash, Red Barn Studios
Copyright © 2007 by The Acorn Club
ISBN 0-615-13437-8
Library of Congress Catalogue No. 2006936419

Dedicated to the memory of
Ralph Gregory Elliot
For many years secretary and treasurer of
The Acorn Club

CURRENT MEMBERS
OF THE ACORN CLUB
January 1, 2007

Elizabeth Brown, Guilford – 1997

Richard Buel, Jr., Essex – 1993

Gerald N. Burrow, Hamden – 2006

Christopher Collier, Orange – 1986

Carolyn Cooper, Guilford – 2006

Milton P. Devane, Hamden – 1997

James F. English, West Harford – 1981

Bruce Fraser, Middletown – 1986

Eugene Gaddis, Hartford – 2001

Ellsworth S. Grant, Bloomfield – 1986

Helen Higgins, Hamden – 2000

William Hosley, Enfield – 1998

Howard R. Lamar, North Haven – 1998

Warner Lord, Madison – 2006

Richard C. Malley, Simsbury – 2002

J. Bard McNulty, Glastonbury – 1980

David Franklin Musto, New Haven – 1987

Brian Rogers, Mystic – 1986

Judith Ann Schiff, New Haven - 1995

John W. Shannahan, Suffield – 1998

Edward Sloan, Madison – 1986

George J. Willauer, Lyme – 1998

Walter W. Woodward, West Hartford – 2006

Honorary member

Donald B. Engley, Bloomfield – 1953

TABLE OF CONTENTS

BACKGROUND COMMENTARIES

PRE-CONVENTION COMMENTARIES

POST-CONVENTION COMMENTARIES

APPENDIX

Acknowledgements

The Acorn Club's thirty-fifth publication of materials relating to Connecticut's history complements volumes 17 and 18 of the Connecticut State Records edited by Douglas Arnold and published by the Connecticut State Library. The State Records volumes include the legislative record and the debates of the Constitutional Convention. Largely missing is the polemical debate that took place in the public press relating to the framing and adoption of the Constitution of 1818. The Acorn Club therefore decided that a selection of newspaper and pamphlet commentaries about the constitution would be helpful in illuminating the political process surrounding the formation of the constitution.

Under the editorship of Richard Buel Jr. and George J. Willauer, who were assisted by a committee consisting of James F. English, David F. Musto, and Brian Rodgers, 25 separate commentaries were selected for inclusion in this anthology. In response to Walter Woodward's recommendation, texts of the Fundamental Orders of 1639, Connecticut's Charter of 1662, and the Constitution of 1818 are included in an appendix. The wording in that last document that survives in the state's 1965 Constitution is printed in bold. The Acorn Club hopes this volume will be of interest to the state's constitutional lawyers as well as useful to all students of Connecticut's past.

Individual members of the Club cheerfully shouldered the task of verifying the accuracy of the transcription of the texts to disk made by a Wesleyan work-study student, Michael A. James. The Acorn Club gratefully acknowledges the assistance of the Return Jonathan Meigs (1740-1823) Fund administered by the History Department of Wesleyan University, which provided the funds needed for the transcription. The Fund was created by Dorothy Mix Meigs and Fielding Pope Meigs, Jr., in memory of the soldier of the Revolution whose home was in Middletown, Connecticut from 1740-1787. The Connecticut Humanities Council, the law firm of Tyler, Cooper, where the late Ralph G. Elliot was a partner for many years, and the Meigs Fund all generously contributed to helping the Club meet the costs of printing this volume.

HISTORICAL BACKGROUND

In 1662 Charles II issued a charter uniting the settlements on the Connecticut River and eastern shoreline with those of the New Haven Colony. Prior to 1662 the Connecticut River and eastern shoreline towns had governed themselves under the Fundamental Orders of 1639. The new charter unified two colonies into a single autonomous republic within the first British Empire. Because Connecticut possessed no gateway port comparable to Boston, Philadelphia, or New York, the British government paid little attention to it. A few customs officials represented the Crown in New London and New Haven, but they were powerless to insist on more than token compliance with imperial regulations. Officials in London were content to have their agents in Connecticut ignored because the colony's overseas commerce focused on the West Indies. The Privy Council sent instructions to Connecticut's governors, but they pleaded inability to comply whenever the instruction was not to the colony's interest or liking. Internally, Connecticut was left to do pretty much what it wanted throughout the colonial period.

The situation changed dramatically at the conclusion of the Seven Year War, when Parliament tried to extract revenue from its North American possessions. Connecticut protested the Sugar Acts of 1764 and 1766, the Stamp Act of 1765, and the Townshend Duties of 1767, but not just because of the revenue these acts threatened to raise. After 1750 Connecticut had begun to export people to the less settled north and west because there was nowhere else to turn in establishing new family farms. Britain's new revenue measures competed for the capital required to finance this emigration. Connecticut's peripheral position in Britain's commercial empire allowed it to escape primary responsibility for resisting Britain's new taxes, which proved to be an advantage in radicalizing the colony. In 1774 Connecticut joined Massachusetts in the vanguard of the revolutionary movement, and in 1775 Connecticut responded faster than any other colony in complying with the Second Continental Congress's call for troops after Lexington and Concord. The colony's commitment to the Revolution in turn helped the governor's son, Joseph Trumbull, win appointment as commissary general of the continental army. By the spring of 1776, when escalating hostilities had eliminated reconciliation as a political option, Connecticut was fully mobilized for war. That presented its leadership with an option shared only with Rhode Island, which had a royal charter similar to Connecticut's. Instead of framing a new state constitution to replace the existing royal government, both colonies pursued the easier course of continuing with their charters after eliminating the few words referring to the Crown.

Connecticut's leaders were confident that the war would be fought elsewhere, won quickly, and that victory would give the state access to lands beyond her recognized borders. Instead, the war went on for eight years, bringing with it grievous suffering. Connecticut labored to maintain its initial commitment to the continental army throughout the struggle. But Washington's insistence that the state's Line regiments be deployed to secure strategic objectives in New Jersey and the Hudson River Valley left Connecticut's coastline exposed to attack. So long as the British controlled Long Island, Connecticut could not defend herself against enemy incursions. The enemy's naval supremacy enabled the British to attack when and where they chose along the state's 120- mile shoreline. At the same time Connecticut could not give up trying to defend its shoreline without abandoning it to enemy control.

Increasing pressure from loyalists based on Long Island worsened the situation after 1779. Many shoreline denizens found that the best protection against targeted kidnappings was to trade with the enemy. The state government could do little to prevent the illicit commerce beyond licensing the loyal to prey on the disloyal, which had the effect of compounding civil strife along the shoreline. By the end of the war Connecticut was as economically exhausted as it was politically demoralized. Congress's 1782 award of disputed lands on the Upper Susquehanna River to Pennsylvania, which the state had hoped to reap as a spoil of war, darkened Connecticut's future prospects. The absence of any gateway ports resembling those in Massachusetts, Rhode Island, and New York also emerged as a liability. Not only was Connecticut barred from taxing imports, the most politically acceptable way to raise revenue, but her people found themselves paying the debts of other states when they bought foreign goods that entered through New York, Boston, or Providence.

Postwar demoralization invited challenges to the state's revolutionary leadership. The colonial charter had concentrated power in a Council of twelve assistants which doubled as an Upper House of the legislature. Its supremacy derived from the continuity of its members in office and the veto they exercised over most of the General Assembly's actions. The procedure for selecting the assistants almost guaranteed that once elected, one would remain in office until either incapacity or death intervened. Only twice during the colonial period had the electorate dismissed incumbent Council members from office. The most recent case had occurred in 1766 when five assistants in addition to the governor had failed to win re-election because the former had administered to the latter an oath required by the Stamp Act. In 1783 a group of dissidents, regarded as lukewarm to the Revolution, tried to organize a similar challenge in what became known as the Middletown Convention. Though the attempt narrowly failed, it did succeed in putting the state's revolutionary leadership on the defensive. The exclusion of American vessels from most of Britain's West Indian trade, so crucial to the state's previous prosperity, exacerbated the effects of a postwar recession and further weakened the leadership. During the 1780s Connecticut's government showed no inclination to join Massachusetts in demonstrating how the states might provide for the revolutionary debt and restore public credit. Though Connecticut escaped Shays's Rebellion that Massachusetts brought upon itself during 1786-1787, Connecticut's inaction measured how far its former revolutionary activism had dissipated.

Shays's Rebellion did influence the Connecticut legislature belatedly to name delegates to the Philadelphia constitutional convention. And by all accounts the Connecticut delegation played a pivotal role in brokering the compromise whereby the equal representation of the states in the Senate was traded for proportional representation in the House. The state was also one of the first to ratify the new government, doing so without significant opposition. By the end of the 1780s many realized that Connecticut's best chance for economic recovery lay in a national government able to bargain effectively with Europe's commercial empires for trading privileges and empowered to lay a national tax on imports known as an impost. But Connecticut was not rewarded for its tardy conversion to federalism until the early 1790s.

The keystone of Hamilton's plan for funding the revolutionary debt lay in merging the interests of the state and federal creditors through the assumption of most state debts. Though this created a larger debt for the new government to service, it insured that all importers would have a common interest in collecting the new duties. Merchant assistance was vital because wrapping the tax into the retail price of goods helped insure its payment. Shays's Rebellion had been sparked in part by direct taxes, which everyone had to pay whether or not they were willing or able. An impost was less likely to be resisted because only those who choose to purchase the dutiable goods paid the tax. Though the initial yields from the national impost proved insufficient to cover all the liabilities Hamilton had assumed, the plan enhanced the credit worthiness of the Republic sufficiently to allow the government to borrow the remainder in Europe's capital markets.

Access to foreign capital became more difficult after the French Revolution ignited a general European War in 1792. Nonetheless that conflict proved to be a commercial boon for the United States because neutrality allowed its vessels to take over most of the colonial trade of the European powers. The invisible earnings from this trade in turn enabled merchants to expand their imports from overseas, which swelled the yields from the impost to the point where they more than covered the costs of debt service. Connecticut prospered from these developments to a degree not seen since the late colonial period. But the European war also made it impossible for the United States to have good relations with Britain, from whom most of the imports came, without having bad relations with France. Washington reluctantly chose an accommodation with Britain in the Jay Treaty in 1795-1796, thus assuring the success of Hamilton's funding policy but at the cost of France's increasing hostility. Most people in Connecticut thought bad relations with France were a price worth paying. Though it eventually led to a limited naval war between the two countries between 1798 and 1800, Connecticut's merchants and her people benefited from the informal alliance with Britain that provided American vessels with access to the West Indies as well as the benefit of British convoys. The commercial advantages of aligning with Britain in turn confirmed the Federalist identity of Connecticut's leadership.

A limited war with a great power like France involved the risk that it would escalate into a full-scale conflict. Given the sectional divisions that had arisen over the Republic's foreign relations, such an escalation threatened national disintegration. President John Adams accordingly sought to negotiate an end to the Quasi-war with France in 1799. His diplomatic initiative, undertaken despite uncertainty about the stability of the French government and against the objections of a majority of his cabinet, eventually proved successful. But it also divided the Federalist Party on the eve of the election of 1800. Though Adams had succeeded in restoring peace between the United States and France, this division doomed his re-election. Rapprochement with France instead benefited Thomas Jefferson's candidacy because Jefferson was a known partisan of France. Some members of the Electoral College, not to mention members of the House of Representatives responsible for breaking the electoral tie between

Jefferson and Burr, would have been reluctant to vote for him had the Quasi-war with France continued or escalated into a full-scale conflict.

New England's Federalist leaders looked upon Jefferson's victory as a disaster with ominous implications for the Republic. They were jealous of the support Jefferson and his followers commanded in the expanding South and West and attributed the Republicans' victory to France being more popular with Americans than Britain. Some Federalists had hoped war with France would purge the American public of the anti-British prejudices acquired during the Revolution. Now that was no longer a prospect, they were pessimistic about the political future.

Connecticut's Federalist leaders shared these attitudes but responded to the changed political landscape after 1800 much as they had during the Revolution and its aftermath. They dug in for the duration in the expectation that eventually the rest of the nation would come around to seeing things as they did. Two circumstances reinforced their intransigence. First, their control of the state government seemed unchallengeable. Though Jefferson's election allowed him to appoint Republicans to federal offices in Connecticut, the state had had enough experience with isolating royal officials during the colonial period to know how to stymie their influence. Republican appointees were discredited as venal office seekers and their supporters prosecuted in the state courts. In 1802 a Republican editor, Seth Wetmore, was convicted of seditious libel for advocating universal suffrage. But to make sure it remained immune to Republican challenges a Federalist controlled General Assembly added a stand-up provision to the law regulating nominations for the Council. After 1801 the written ballots formerly cast in the September freemen's meetings were replaced by raising one's hand or standing up. This permitted closer supervision by the presiding "authority," which was comprised of the justices of the peace appointed by the General Assembly rather than locally elected town officials. The new electoral law reinforced the procedures followed in the April freemen's meetings for winnowing twelve councilors from the list of nominees. Each freeman still had twelve ballots, but the candidates were voted on in order of their seniority rather than the number of votes they had won the previous September. To vote for someone who was not already an assistant required a freeman to withhold at least one ballot or more and then publicly cast it for a newcomer. Few had either the temerity or patience to do so. Unchallengeable local dominance also conferred on the Federalists total control over the state's representation in the federal Congress.

The state's Federalist leadership celebrated the stability the Council communicated to Connecticut's government as exemplary of an ideal republic. In doing so they exploited the spectacle that France provided by way of contrast. Though the French Revolution had begun with noble sentiments articulated in the Declaration of the Rights of Man, its subsequent course had been anything but ideal. Initially it was possible to attribute France's missteps to a monarch who betrayed the Constitution of 1791 he had sworn to uphold. But after France became a republic in 1792, such an apology was no longer available. Instead of peace and prosperity, republicanism in France brought war and terror. Under the pressure of both developments a nation, previously renowned for its high culture and refinement, not to mention technical proficiency and pretentious grandeur, transformed itself into a military dictatorship that plundered its continental neighbors under the pretense of liberating them from monarchical oppression. In 1804 Napoleon openly crowned himself "emperor."

Connecticut's Federalist ideologues joined those of Massachusetts in regarding the evolution of France towards dictatorship as embodying a tendency to which all republics were prone. They equated resisting that tendency in their domestic adversaries with the patriotism the revolutionary leadership had displayed in resisting Britain. So deep was Federalist anxiety and so advantageous their posturing, especially in recruiting the support of the Congregational clergy, that the Federalists took to portraying their Republican adversaries as embryonic Napoleons. Though it was stretching things to cast either Jefferson or Madison in this light, the fertility of the Federalist imagination, reinforced by the instability of the world they inhabited, was up to the task. In the leadership's eyes Connecticut became an example of what a republic had to be to avoid France's fate. Such an ideological identity reinforced commercial considerations that had initially shaped the state leadership's preference for aligning the United States with Britain.

That preference became even more urgent after 1806 when both of the principal belligerents established their supremacy in a separate domain, Britain on the sea and Napoleon on continental Europe. Since the new state of affairs made it difficult for either power to attack the other, both attempted to deny their adversary the benefits of America's neutral commerce. Jefferson responded by asking Congress for an embargo that withdrew American ships and produce from the world's oceans. In addition to buying time, Jefferson hoped the even-handedness of such a policy would preserve national unity until Congress could determine against which of the belligerents the nation should declare war. He believed unity to be a republic's strongest suit in war and that it would be much easier to achieve by acting defensively.

The New England Federalists attacked the embargo with the intention of subverting it. Though there was an element of opportunism in their actions since the embargo injured regional commercial interests, they justified their behavior on the grounds that the embargo was a French measure designed to complete Napoleon's Continental System and as such risked precipitating a war between Britain and the United States. Modern commentators have ignored this pretext because it seems so preposterous. They have also failed to appreciate that the embargo as an alternative to war commanded more support at that time than it would today. Most Americans remembered the revolutionary war and were anxious to avoid the devastation so much of Europe was experiencing. Few were entirely dependent on overseas markets for their livelihoods despite the lingering colonial nature of the economy. Connecticut's government nonetheless followed the lead of the Massachusetts Federalists, who urged those most affected by the restrictions to defy them. Connecticut officially refused to place the state's militia at the disposal of federal collectors as required by the Enforcement Act of 1809, going one step beyond Massachusetts which still had a Republican governor.

The resistance of the New England Federalists eventually forced Congress to modify the embargo so that it only applied to Britain and France. This was really a capitulation to Britain, given her naval supremacy, since Britain would have access to American produce in other countries that she could deny to France. Napoleon understood a modified embargo this way and retaliated by sequestering all American vessels that entered the continental ports he controlled. The British minister in Washington, David Erskine, sought to consolidate what he construed as the surrender of the nation's strict neutrality by promising that Britain would lift its restrictions against American commerce if the United States removed hers against British commerce. The only condition he imposed was that the United States maintain an embargo against France. Madison accepted Erskine's terms and lifted the prohibitions against trading with Britain only to learn that the British government rejected the agreement on the grounds that their minister had exceeded his instructions. Britain then sent a new minister to Washington who insinuated that the Madison administration had known full well Erskine was acting without authority. The Federalist opposition in New England echoed that claim, but took it one step further by asserting that Madison had purposely entered the agreement to provoke a war between the United States and Britain.

The Federalists' insistence on taking Britain's side against their own government convinced the Republicans that the nation confronted not just a foreign adversary bent on humiliating them, but a domestic faction in league with that adversary seeking domestic political advantage from those humiliations. The Republicans were concerned about the long-term effect these humiliations might have on the loyalty of the next generation of Americans to republicanism. When the time came for the current leaders to retire from the scene, they wanted to make sure their successors had not lost faith in either the nation's Revolution or its republican institutions. Though they were worried about the damage a war might do to the Republic, eventually they decided accepting war was preferable to allowing the nation to be dishonored without a fight.

Connecticut did not play a conspicuous role in the national drama leading up to the declaration of war in 1812. In 1810 the state recalled its most prominent national figure, James Hillhouse, from Congress to manage its school fund. In doing so, the state signaled that it put greater stock in tending to its ideal republic than in the fortunes of the national Republic. However, once war was declared, Connecticut's Federalist government abandoned its former restraint, taking the lead in resisting the Madison administration's attempts to put detachments of the state's militia under federal command. Connecticut Federalists also actively resisted recruitment of young men into the United States army, first by enlisting the most promising youths into a state force that paid its rank and file roughly twice what the United States army paid; and secondly by harassing federal recruits and serving their recruiters with writs of habeas corpus to recover enlistees.

The tension between Connecticut and the federal government briefly abated when the British blockaded Stephen Decatur's squadron in New London during 1813. That gave federal and state authorities a common interest in resisting a possible repetition of Benedict Arnold's raid in 1781. But all cooperation between the two governments collapsed in 1814 after the April 8 British raid on Pettipaug Point. This was the direct outgrowth of a dispute between federal and state authorities about who should pay for Connecticut's defense. The federal government refused to do so unless the troops were placed under federal command. That proved unacceptable to the state which then allowed a key post at the mouth of the river to disband.

Fear of repeating the Connecticut's revolutionary war experience helped shape Federalist intransigence, but the conviction that the United States was capitulating to Napoleonic tendencies in waging war against Britain remained the lynchpin of Federalist opposition to the national administration throughout 1814, even surviving Napoleon's abdication in April. That obsession led to Connecticut's biggest misstep at the end of the year when its government agreed to host a convention of southern New England states that assembled in Hartford. The summons to this meeting originated with the Massachusetts legislature in early October after the outrageous terms Britain had demanded at the beginning of the negotiations at Ghent convinced its leaders that an immediate, negotiated conclusion to the war was no longer possible. Instead of rallying to the nation's defense against a foreign enemy, though, these leaders sought to extract sectional political advantage from the common peril. They knew that a large expeditionary force of veteran soldiers was making for New Orleans, and they assumed that a British seizure of that port would place the future development of the Republic at Britain's mercy.

The Hartford Convention framed a set of constitutional amendments designed to enhance the power of New England in the federal union and coupled them with the threat to conclude a separate peace with Britain if these amendments were not accepted by the other states. When Britain unexpectedly offered to terminate the conflict by reverting to the status quo ante bellum and Andrew Jackson managed to defeat Wellington's veterans at New Orleans, the Hartford Convention appeared to the rest of the nation like a nest of traitors bent on blackmail. It did not help that commissioners deputized by the legislatures of Massachusetts and Connecticut to accept the national government's surrender appeared in Washington simultaneously with receipt of the news of the Peace of Ghent and Jackson's victory at New Orleans. That left the commissioners with little alternative but to retire in disgrace.

Subsequent efforts by the Federalists to exonerate themselves backfired when they argued that the war had achieved none of its stated objectives at the expense of a crushing debt. At the end of 1816 the yields from the impost were large enough so that Madison could predict, accurately it turned out, that the nation would be debt free by the 1830s. Being regarded by the rest of the nation as moral traitors was a far cry from the way Connecticut had been accustomed to view itself during the Revolution. It also contradicted the pretense of patriotic virtue the Federalists had consistently made in claiming an exclusive association with Washington. Many Federalists began to have doubts about their former commitments at the same time dissidents, emboldened by the disgrace the state had brought upon itself during the war, united in attempting to replace a regime that had failed its people so badly. Early in 1816 the dissidents tested the political waters with a series of "Aristides" essays in Hartford's

American Mercury that attacked the Federalists for the "shame, mortification and regret" they had caused by committing "the whole management of our concerns with the government of the union, to the unlimited control of an unprincipled faction in a neighboring state."(2/20/16) Subsequent numbers in the series concentrated on the policies the state had pursued during the war, describing them as "little short of a series of overt acts of rebellion." (3/19/16).

The Reform or Toleration Party's candidates did far better than anyone had expected in the April 1816 freemen's meetings. Though their candidate for governor, Oliver Wolcott Jr., failed to be elected, their nominee for lieutenant governor, Jonathan Ingersoll, defeated a Federalist, Calvin Goddard, who had participated in the Hartford Convention. The challengers' decision to abandon the designation of "Republican" for "Reform" and "Toleration" sent two important messages to the freemen of the state. Former Federalists would be welcome in the new coalition, as the candidacies of Wolcott and Ingersoll made clear, and the reformers were committed to working within the structure of the existing state government to change it. The latter point was of particular importance because of the fate of a prior attempt by the Republican opposition in 1804 to call a constitutional convention.

The call had issued from a New Haven convention of Republican delegates representing 97 towns who unanimously resolved that the state lacked a constitution. The Convention's address to the people began with the preamble to the Declaration of Independence affirming governments derived "their just powers" from the people and the people's right to "alter or to abolish...and institute a new government" when necessary. The state's Federalist leadership construed the document as "sounding the trumpet of sedition" for a French-style revolution and subjected the five state magistrates who had attended the New Haven meeting to a political trial before the General Assembly. They were found guilty by a large partisan majority and deprived of their commissions. William Judd, who had chaired the New Haven meeting, died shortly afterwards. He left a written statement protesting that the convention had never claimed Connecticut lacked a legitimate government, though he remained adamant that the state did not have a proper republican constitution. The constitutionalists thus acquired a martyr, but at the cost of political immobilization.

The reformers of 1816-1818 were determined to avoid the misstep of allowing themselves to be portrayed as seditious even though they had to win a majority of the Council where the Federalists were strongest to gain their end. That meant deferring framing a constitution until after they had gained political control of the existing state government. The reformers had the advantage of exploiting the full range of political grievances that had accumulated since well before 1804. These included the tax system, the court system, the militia system, and the state's treatment of religious minorities. Though objections were voiced about how councilors, congressmen, and presidential electors were chosen, as well as about the suffrage, the reformers regarded the disgrace the Federalists had brought on the state during the recent war as their trump card.

The Federalists helped their adversaries make the most of that asset with the so-called Appropriation or Bonus Bill they passed during the October 1816 General Assembly. This measure proposed distributing $145,000 Connecticut claimed from the Federal government for its defense outlays during the War of 1812 among the state's religious groups in quantities proportional to the presumed number of their communicants. While designed to head off reform pressures, the Methodists, who would receive the least, were especially critical of the proposal. The following March the second Methodist Society at Ashford questioned the legislature's constitutional right to make such an appropriation and instructed its clerk to correspond with other religious societies about petitioning the legislature to have the appropriation declared unconstitutional under the charter of Charles II. They thereby wedded widespread objections to the appropriation to the state's lack of a regular constitution. The reformers also predicted that the state would receive none of the money from Congress because it had failed to put the state's troops under federal command. Though Congress did eventually recompense Connecticut for some of its costs, the episode conveniently fused religious with patriotic grievances against the Federalists.

In April 1817 Oliver Wolcott, Jr. was elected governor, and the Tolerationists emerged with a decisive majority in the General Assembly. That still left the Council under Federalist control, but a powerful attack by "Cato" on the Council's political sins in the previous autumn's _Mercury_ had begun to make Federalist members of that body very uncomfortable. "Cato" had held the Council responsible for the state government's "disgusting" behavior during the war in making "treason law, and the violation of the laws a virtue." (8/29/16) He lambasted it for perpetrating a system of "DECEPTION." "When they call themselves the 'friends of order,' they mean a faction which nearly produced the disorder of civil war."(10/10/16) Faced with what promised to be a hard battle to retain their former places, some Federalist members of the Council voluntarily withdrew while others failed to garner enough votes in the September freemen's meetings to qualify in the nomination list. Only the five Federalist candidates who had also been endorsed by the Reform Party were among the twenty from whom the next Council would be selected the following April. With little standing in the way of the reformers taking control of the Council in the spring, the Tolerationists used their newly won political leverage to secure the repeal of the Stand-up Law. The Federalists acquiesced, belatedly concluding that it was doing them more harm than good. But in the wake of its repeal two of the Federalists previously endorsed by the reformers failed to be elected to the Council in April, 1818.

With all branches of the government in their control, the reformers used the May legislative session to reform parts of court system, liberalize the suffrage, and issue a call for a constitutional convention. The towns were instructed to elect delegates on July 4, 1818, who would assemble at Hartford on August 26. The sponsors of the Convention assumed that the majority of delegates would be Republicans and that by drawing on the example of the other states and the federal Constitution, they could make quick work of drafting a frame of government. The people of the towns, though, chose more former Federalists as delegates than the reformers had bargained on. That resulted in a protracted convention--it met for three weeks--as well as a more conservative document than might otherwise have been framed. The Constitution of 1818 retained many features of the charter government that the reformers had complained about. Thus the upper house of the legislature continued to consist of twelve men elected by a state-wide vote instead of from separate districts. Only the September nominating election was eliminated. And all judicial appointments below the Supreme and Superior courts would continue to be appointed annually by the legislature. Finally, the executive was denied all but a token check on the legislature. Nonetheless, Governor Wolcott's success in presiding over the Convention and mediating between Federalist and reform extremists showed that the lack of formal empowerment need not preclude the exercise of real influence. And the new Constitution did disestablish the Congregational Church, provide for the separation of the legislative, executive, and judicial branches, and give constitutional status to the recent liberalization of the suffrage.

Because the reformers wanted the process completed before the next legislature assembled, the May General Assembly had specified that approval or rejection of the new constitution would occur within one to three weeks of the Convention's rising. Though the Convention opted for a nineteen-day interval, some Federalists objected to the haste and used it to question the legitimacy of the new constitution. On the other side, several delegates who had championed changing the state's political system did not think the Convention had gone far enough. They had voted against endorsing the document that was presented to the people. But the ratification process took place despite these objections without serious incident, and the constitution was accepted by a majority of those voting. While that majority was far from overwhelming, no one seriously tried to undo what had been accomplished. The Constitution of 1818, albeit with numerous amendments, remained the fundamental law of the state until the Supreme Court mandated a revision in 1965. Even today some of the language and features of the constitution of 1818 survive in our existing frame of government. Now as then steady habits seem to prevail, making the achievements of the early nineteenth-century reformers relevant to all who are interested the the state's past and present.

INTRODUCTION
TO THE COMMENTARIES

The documents republished in this volume are divided chronological-
ly into sections. The first section contains commentaries appearing prior
to the legislature summoning a constitutional convention. These texts illu-
minate the political context during the year and a half before June 1818
and comprise the bulk of the volume. The selections in the second section
include commentaries published during the two-month interval between
the calling of the convention and its meeting at Hartford on August 26,
1818. The third section contains commentaries about the merits of the
constitution drafted by the convention together with assessments of the
ratification process.

All the documents exemplify themes shared with numerous other political essays at the time. Those republished here were chosen for the contribution they make to telling a coherent political story. All but one of the
texts initially appeared in the state's newspapers, and portions of that one
pamphlet, attributed to George H. Richards, were republished in a newspaper. As was customary at the time, all the authors employed pseudo-
nyms. Variants of "Freeman" were most frequently chosen because only
freemen could participate in the political process.

Though the state had fifteen newspapers at one time or another during the controversy over the constitution, the selections contained in
this volume come from only four of them. Two are Hartford papers, the
Connecticut Courant—published by George Godwin & Sons and founded in 1764; and the *Times*—published by Frederick D. Bolles & Co. and
established January 1, 1817; and two are New Haven papers, the
Connecticut Journal— published by Sherman Converse and established
in 1767; and the *Columbian Register*—published by Joseph Barber and
established in 1812. The centrality of Hartford and New Haven newspapers to the debate over the Constitution of 1818 reflects the role both
towns played as seats for the state government. New London had only
one paper, the *Connecticut Gazette*—published by Samuel Green and
established in 1770 until the *Republican Advocate* began appearing in
February 1818. This may have made Green reluctant to provide an out-
let for those challenging the legitimacy of the existing political order,
forcing Richards, who was a New Londoner, to publish initially in pamphlet form.

As might be expected, the older newspapers defended the Federalist
status quo while the younger papers emerged as its leading challengers.

Hartford's *American Mercury*, established in 1784, had launched the reform movement during 1816 with its "Aristides" and "Cato" series. But thereafter it failed to contribute much of quality to the debate besides a series that ran from January 6 to March 10, 1818, under the penname "Reform." New Haven's *Connecticut Herald*, founded in 1803, had also provided a mouthpiece for the Republican opposition before the *Columbian Register* appeared in 1812. Subsequently, it tried to find a special niche for itself by straddling the partisan divide, though with indifferent results. It did publish two short series on the constitutional question in the year preceding the convention as well as a recommendation to the "Freemen of New Haven County" that they vote to ratify the convention's handiwork. But the *Herald* resembled the *Mercury* in its willingness to let the younger Republican papers take the lead after 1816. Texts from Hartford's second Federalist paper, the *American Mirror*, are not included because it published little besides repetitive rants against democracy reflecting the lingering influence of its former editor and principal contributor, Theodore Dwight, who had been the secretary of the Hartford Convention.

Despite the dominant role exercised by the four newspapers represented in this volume, every freeman in Connecticut who so desired would have had access to the texts reproduced below because of the preferential rates newspapers enjoyed under the Postal Act of 1792. The four Federalist and Republican papers in Hartford and New Haven that dominated the debate sometimes republished each other's commentary, further discouraging papers outside the Hartford-New Haven axis from duplicating their efforts. The editors have tried to note when and where copies of the texts included in this volume were reprinted. With the exception of "Judd," VII in the *Times*, September 15, 1818 and the introduction and last part of the "Freeman" series in the *Hartford Courant*, August 4, 1818, all texts are reproduced in their entirety as they first appeared. Archaic forms of spelling have been retained, though a letter or word is occasionally inserted between brackets for clarity, significant errors committed by printers are followed by [sic], and anomalies in the spacing of punctuation marks have been brought into conformity with modern expectations.

BACKGROUND COMMENTARIES

MICHAEL SERVETUS, "THE AGE OF IMPROVEMENTS," HARTFORD *TIMES* FEBRUARY 25-APRIL 1, 1817

With the initiation of the seven-part Servetus series on February 25, 1817, the Hartford *Times* launched the political movement that would eventually terminate in a state constitution. Servetus conducted a devastating canvass of Federalist policies that concluded on April 1 just before the freemen went to the polls to elect the governor and the Council for the following year. The initial essay was erroneously numbered II. Extracts from numbers VI & VII in the series were republished in the *Columbian Register* on April 5.

The author of the series remains unknown. For his pseudonym he chose a sixteenth-century Spanish physician and theologian notorious for his critique of the Trinity and his advocacy of a strict separation between church and state. John Calvin supported Servetus's prosecution for heresy, and he was burned at the stake on October 25, 1553. By adopting the pen name Servetus the author of this series underscored his opposition to the state's religious and political establishment and his call for the reformation of both.

THE AGE OF IMPROVEMENTS,
OR,
CONSIDERATIONS ADDRESSED TO THE PEOPLE OF CONNECTICUT, OF BOTH POLITICAL PARTIES, ON THE NECESSITY OF A REFORM IN THE GOVERNMENT OF THE STATE.

" *Those who employ their pens on political subjects, free from party rage and party prejudices, cultivate a science, which of all others, contributes most to public utility, and even to the private satisfaction of those who addict themselves to the study of it.*" —Hume[1]

NO. II. (FEBRUARY. 25)

Prejudice, governmental patronage and interest, the support of the administration of our Rulers, and the great obstacle to all improvements—some views of these matters—that it is useless to reason with those who are under the influence of prejudice or interest.

In an enquiry after truth, it is important, above all things, that the mind be free from prejudice. It is morally impossible to make any impression upon the mind of a person who is under this influence. A jaundiced eye cannot convey to the mind any just idea of colours, neither can a prejudiced understanding be a test of truth, or a medium of rational con-

---

[1] The Scottish philosopher David Hume was known for his religious skepticism.

viction. Prejudice consists in our having adopted opinions without consideration, and in adhering to them without reason, and even against the clearest reasons. We can all of us perceive the prejudices of others, and are often astonished at their blindness; but we cannot perceive our own, although perhaps the most conspicuous. We can discern the smallest mote in the eye of our neighbours, when at the same time we do not perceive the beam, obstructing all light to the understanding, which may be in our own.

The writer is very sensible that the views which he proposes to unfold, with relation to the administration of the government of this State, may be subjected to the imputation of proceeding from a prejudiced mind, depending upon party feelings, or from interested views. This may be the fact, but if it is, he is insensible of it. He has no interest connected with this subject, other than what is felt in common with his fellow-citizens, for a just administration of the government, the reputation of the State, and the honor and prosperity of our common country. But whether the writer is subject to the influence here spoken of, or not, he is aware that there is probably no section of the union where religions and political prejudices are so general and so obstinate, as in this State. This observation, however, is not to be considered as a reflection upon the State. Prejudice does not suppose ignorance, but false education. There can be no doubt but that the great body of our citizens are as well educated in this State, as in any in the union; but it is from this circumstance, of a general and systematic common education, which is wholly under the control of our rulers, and the dominant clergy, which is nearly the same thing, as they are united for the mutual support of each other, thereby giving them unity of interest, that we are to ascribe those obstinate prejudices upon religious and political subjects, which are so prevalent among us.

To those who are under the influence of *violent* prejudices, the writer does not address himself. He would consider it as a useless waste of time to attempt to operate upon the minds of such men, either by facts or arguments. No, it is to the *candid* of both parties, that he proposes to offer some facts and considerations tending to show that there is a necessity for a REFORM in the government of this state. He would here beg leave to premise that he sincerely hopes that all who may take the trouble to notice his observations, will view them in the same light in which they are written, viz. as though there was no existence of political parties in the state.

But *prejudice*, as obstinate and as blind as it is, is not the most formidable obstacle to those improvements in our system, which the lights of science, the progress of moral and religious sentiments, the development of new interests, and the results of experiments, have rendered necessary. No; *interest* is a more active principle, and a more efficient support of the absurd system of "steady habits," which prevails in the state. No one who has not particularly reflected upon the subject, can be sensible of the extent of this influence. Would any person at first view believe that there was or could be *an extensive government* PATRONAGE in this state? What is there that can authorize or render necessary such a state of things? Is not the form of our government simple? Is not our territory circumscribed? Is not our population, compared with most of the other states, inconsiderable? Are not our citizens possessed of a "moral and religious character"? Such is claimed to be the fact. Do we not derive many facilities towards preserving order and social regularity from the superior advantages of a common education, which are enjoyed by our citizens? Have we not with relation to all social and political purposes, the advantages of an indigenous population only? Is not the whole State divided into ecclesiastical corporations, (a regulation peculiar to N. England) for religious purposes, which, according to the doctrine of our rulers, tends to promote good order in society? And in addition to all these considerations, are there not scores of societies, religious, moral and social, all calculated, as it is said, to promote order and strengthen the authority of government? When these things are considered would any one believe it possible that the administration of the government of this little state could have acquired an extensive patronage? But is not this the truth. If any one doubts it let him attend to the facts of the multiplicity and the multiplying of public offices in the state. Let any person who has the least knowledge of civil polity or political affairs, look at our judicial system—the organization of our Courts—the corps of between seven and eight hundred justices of the peace—the numerous civil and military offices in the state, whose appointments depend upon the government, and then say whether he does not think there is government patronage—whether he can believe that all these civil and judicial officers are necessary to a due administration of justice. Is it not apparent, and indeed has it not been admitted, by a few candid men among our rulers, that one half, and probably one fourth part of the judicial officers in the state, would be more than adequate to all the purposes of a due administration of the laws. But we shall consider these matters more in detail hereafter, as they are noticed here only to shew the extensive patronage the government has acquired, and the *interests* which it has combined.

Yet it is a fact that there are double, and even quadruple, the judicial officers that are necessary for a due administration of justice. From what cause has proceeded this multiplication of officers? Can there be any conceived but patronage and the creation of government interests? But, could there be any doubt upon this subject it would be removed from a view of their *political characters*. If 800 judges, (and it is believed that including justices of the peace, there is more than that number in the state) were necessary for the administration of justice, and if they were appointed for that purpose *only*, their political characters would form no part of their qualifications. But is it not a fact that the *politicks* of a candidate for any of these officers is made an indispensable requisite? Since the commencement of party politicks, there has not been at any time any one of the nine judges of the Superior Court, but what has been orthodox in his political creed, and very few but what have been orthodox in their religious creed. Neither has there been any one of the 40 judges of the several county courts, excepting one or two who were appointed before and were continued in, but what has been of the orthodox creed; and the 30 Judges of Probate have during all this time of near twenty years, been all of them orthodox in politicks and religion, excepting some two or three, who having been appointed at an earlier period, have been *suffered* to continue in office. And out of about 720 justices of the peace, the whole number in the state, there may be at this time about the number of six, who are republicans; but according to the best information I have been able to obtain, there is out of the 720 justices in the state the solitary number of one republican who was known to be such at the time he was first appointed. We will not ask whether this is not liberality— whether it is not magnanimity—but we would enquire whether the fact that *all* our magistrates, from the highest to the lowest, are selected with reference to their politics, taken in connection with the circumstance that their number is probably *four fold* what is necessary for the due administration of justice, does not prove incontestably that they are appointed with a view to extend the patronage of the government, and thereby combine a strong *interest* to support our rulers in power, whether right or wrong. *Interest*, then, is the strong support of our rulers, and the great obstacle to all improvements; an obstacle, however, which we trust will soon be broken down by the united good sense of our citizens. This is but a very imperfect view of the extensive *interests* which our rulers have combined to support their authority, in despite of the will of a great majority of our citizens. We may consider these matters more minutely hereafter—we have not even noticed the most powerful interest of all which our rulers have enlisted for their support, the multiplicity of the "State clergy," posted like faithful sentinels in every town in the state, not more to guard the morals than the politics of our citizens. To all of these, and thousands of others who have become *enlisted* from interest, to support the present order of things and oppose all improvements and reforms, however the public good may require them, the writer does not address himself. As he considers it useless to combat *prejudice*, it is equally useless to oppose *interest*. If a prejudiced person cannot be convinced *at all*, an interested one cannot be persuaded to any *purpose*

A man convinced against his will

Is of the same opinion still.

No. III. (MARCH 4)

Our relations with the national government—that the State has lost its influence in the national councils, and its character abroad, &c.—a reform only can restore them.

In examining the conduct of our rulers, and noticing the considerations which disclose the necessity of a reform in the administration of the Government of this state, we would propose to observe that methodical arrangement, which may tend to render our views the most clear and distinct. From the complex and peculiar structure of the government of this country, the constitutional authorities of the States, although in some respects independent, must, as it regards all the essential attributes of sovereignty, be deemed *subordinate* to the national government. The efficiency of the national authority, the security of the union, and the stability and perpetuity of the Government depend most essentially upon a due observance of those constitutional relations which exist between the national and state authorities.

The political duties of the officers of the State Governments arise from the relation in which they stand to the national Government, and the relations existing between them and their constituents. In pursuance of these principles, deducible from the structure of our Government, we will consider—1st. The conduct of our rulers as it respects the relations of this State with the national Government—and 2d, As it respects their relations with their constituents, or the people of this state. But although we adopt this arrangement of the subject for the sake of perspicuity, yet we do not propose to detail the disgusting catalogue of acts and measures which have characterised the *hostile* relations which our rulers have maintained with the authorities of the nation. These matters are still fresh in the recollection of every body. The sober and reflecting part of the community can never forget the awful crisis that our public affairs had assumed in December, 1814. The clouds of faction which had been gathering in our political horison since the year 1806, had at the aforesaid period become so highly charged with the electric fire of party spirit, as portended such a storm in the political elements as threatened with desolation all that is dear to the friends of liberty in the civilized world. As it is not necessary to our purpose, neither is it consonant to our feelings to go into the particulars of these matters. Suffice to say, that the leaders of faction in the New-England States were actually concerned in a conspiracy for the unhallowed purpose of prostrating the government of this country, when engaged in a war with the most powerful nation on earth. Immediately after the declaration of war a coalition was formed for the purpose of putting down the administration by *force*. The famous declaration of Josiah Quincey,[2] that the administration must be put down, "peaceably if we can, and forcibly if we must," was the principle of this coalition. Having thus assumed the principle of forcing the administration from their ground, all their measures were directed to this object, as undeviatingly as the measures of the national government were directed to a prosecution of the war. The whole weight of the Government of this state was in effect thrown into the scale of Briton, which rendered it practically an Ally in the war. If this State had been a colony of Great-Britain, the leaders of these violent proceedings could not have rendered her more effectual service than they have done—in that situation they would have been an open enemy, and would have had no opportunity of embarrassing the government of the country, of obstructing the execution of the laws, of destroying public credit, and of scattering among the popular elements of society the firebrands of discord and civil war. In these declarations the writer speaks advisably, and trusts he shall not be accused of illiberality. Were not the people of this state, from the mad policy of ambitious & factious men placed upon British ground, in the late war?—were not the proceedings of these men eulugised at Montreal, at Quebec, at Halifax, at London?—were not the ministerial papers in England uniform in their praise—the Courier and the Times, the Ledger and the London Evening Post? In speaking of these matters, a writer justly esteemed for his moderation, says "these treasonable operations have served the cause of England more effectually than lord

---

[2] Josiah Quincy, a Massachusetts congressional representative from 1807-1813.

Wellington could have done with thirty thousand of this bravest troops."[3]

Now these things were not transacted in a corner; they are not concealed from the world. Do not the people of the middle, the southern and western states, know that the men who managed our affairs have done all in their power to obstruct the laws made for the support of public credit and for the prosecution of the war?—to paralise the national efforts, and defeat the success of our arms?—and consequently that they had assumed *British ground*, and that their cause was identified with that of a public enemy, whereby it "rose as the country sunk," and flourished upon the national calamities.

Now, without extending these views, (for I wish to give no false colourings) let me ask the sober, the candid and the inteligent part of the citizens of Connecticut, whether at this day, when the pulse of party feeling has happily lost its fever beat, they can in conscience approve of the conduct of their rulers during the war—we would ask whether, on a cool review of these matters, they will not admit that they have brought disgrace upon the state; forfeited its influence in the national councils, destroyed its national character, and rendered its very name infamous throughout the U. States. If there are any who concur in these sentiments, (and we trust there are many) we would ask whether they believe that it is expedient to continue the same men in power—whether this course will be likely to retrieve the tarnished character of the state, or wipe away its disgrace—whether by continuing their confidence in the men who have so grossly abused it, they do not subject themselves to the imputation of having adopted their conduct as their own—have these men undergone any change favourable to their patriotism and political character—have they renounced their errors, abandoned their prejudices, divested themselves of their anti-republican principles, of their anti-American feelings, and above all of their dangerous personal ambition. We have no evidence that they have undergone any change in any of these particulars. But will the people believe that although the ambition of these men remains the same, yet that it may be safe to trust them upon the calculation that their ambition is now directed to more worthy ends, pursuant to the idea that—

The *same* ambition can destroy or save,
And makes a hero, as it makes a knave.

But this sentiment does not much accord with my ideas of human nature. A man who has once forfeited public confidence, cannot with safety be trusted. If there are any who do not consider that the political con-

---

[3] Footnote in text unintelligible.

duct of our rulers, so far as regards their relations with the general government, and their obligations to promote the interests of our country, has been of such a character as to have justly forfeited all their claims to public confidence, I do not know, I must confess, in what language to address them to convince them of their error. They must, we think, be destitute of all *American* feelings, and lost to all ideas of national honor and character. There is a considerable portion of our citizens who we are inclined to believe, do not just appreciate the loss which the state has sustained in the forfeiture of its character for patriotism and nationality, and all its influence in the national councils. If there is any thing that could excite a just sensibility upon this subject it would be a recurrence to former times, when this state stood preeminent in the American family. During the ever memorable period of the revolution, when the voice of indignant freemen first became terrible to tyrants—when the sacred fire of patriotism animated the hearts, aroused the energies and nerved the arms of freemen—when the principle of public conduct was the sacred maxim that "all who are not for us are against us,"—At this proud period of our history, Connecticut, next to Massachusetts, was the most important state in the union.—Her brave and hardy sons, animated by the breath of inspiration, rallied to the standard of liberty and became the firmest champions of American freedom. The soldiers of this state, together with their associates in arms of other New-England states, comprised the bone and muscle of the continental army, which, under the guidance of a Washington, and the guardian angel of American freedom, raised their country to glory and Independence. Connecticut was not then estimated in national affairs upon any mathematical scale—not from the limits of her territory, nor from her numerical weight; no, but from the bravery and valour of her soldiers, the talents of her statesmen, and the patriotism and intelligence of her citizens—and hence she had obtained an elevated rank, a commanding eminence, and a bedizening splendour in that political galaxy, the states of the American union. —"But how are the mighty fallen," and " how has our glory departed from us." Are the inhabitants of this state at the present time a strange race? Are they not descended from "these pious pilgrims," the first settlers of New-England? Does not the lineal blood of the heroes and patriots of the revolution still flow in their veins? Have they not still the enterprise, the valour, and the spirit of their ancestors? Have not our citizens who have become inhabitants of other states, as thousands have by emigration, displayed those attributes, both physical and moral, which characterised our ancestors? Have not the citizens of this state, every where else but at home, been distinguished, not more for their enterprise, their ingenuity, and their talents, than for their public zeal, their bravery, and their patriotism? How then shall we account for these facts?—Why, in a single word, that our destinies have been entrusted to unworthy men.

No. IV. (March 11)

What have our rulers done for the State—The picture of the state of our government and society, which exists in the imaginations of a certain description of our citizens, no way allied to the original—That our rulesr [sic] have promoted no important national or public objects, that add to the honor or interests of the State.

Having in our last number taken a cursory view of the conduct and policy of our rulers, as it respects the relations of the State with the national Government, whereby it was attempted to be shewn that their unfortunate policy had forfeited the character of the State abroad and its influence in the national councils, we would now, pursuant to the course proposed, enter upon the second part of our subject, viz. the policy and conduct of our rulers, as respects their relations with their constituents, or the people of this state. As from a studiousness of brevity we but just touched upon the first division of our subject, we shall also be obliged to hurry over the second; and it is not expected that we shall do any thing like justice to it. Were we to examine with minuteness and attention the various matters which this subject presents for consideration, it would involve a degree of detail which would comprise a volume; we shall therefore notice only some of the most prominent features which have characterised the policy of our rulers as it respects the State and the people. We will enquire, 1st, what our rulers have done for the *State*—2d, what they have *done* for the people, and what they have refused to do—3d, what they have done for *themselves*. 1st. What have our rulers done for this State? This is a very natural enquiry when reviewing the conduct of men who, notwithstanding their extreme *modesty*, have for years made their own praise "the burthen of their song."

If a person who was an entire stranger to the actual character of our government & state of Society should visit the state, & happen to fall into the company of a certain description of our citizens, he would be lost in amazement, and would be likely to imagine that he was in a "region of enchantment," and that there was no *reality* in any of the objects which would present themselves to his senses—He would hear nothing but the 'Syren songs,' extolling the characters of our Rulers & the excellency of our civil & religious institutions. He would be told that Connecticut was the first state in the union—that it had the best Constitution of Government in the world; that this constitution "was made by our pious ancestors near two centuries since," and that during all this period, when revolutions had prevailed every where else, it had undergone no change, and had produced the greatest portion of civil and social happiness that ever fell to the lot of any people on earth. He would be told that our rulers were an extraordinary race of men, that they were more virtuous, more wise, more pious, more moral, and more distinguished, than the rulers of any other country in the world—that they governed by their example, and the salutary influence of a moral and religious education—that such was the integrity and disinterestedness of our rulers, that although according to the constitution the officers of the government are chosen annually, yet from practice it has become a principle that every man who is once placed *into* an office, is permitted to *die out of it*, and that this is what in Connecticut is meant by rotation in office—he would be told that the religion of this state was more orthodox than in any other part of christendom—that our religious institutions are more numerous and respectable, and that our clergy are more learned, more dignified, and more *disinterested*, than those of any other part of the world—he would be told that the people of this state were a *peculiar people*, that they were more religious, more moral, more learned, than any people in the world, and that they enjoyed greater civil and religious privileges, and a greater portion of social happiness, than any other people. These representations and a thousand others of the same stamp, would induce him to believe that the people of Connecticut were *really* a peculiar people, and the genuine descendants of "pious pilgrims;" and although he would discover no *appearances* of this *milleneal* state of society, yet he would be rather inclined to distrust his own senses, than to suppose that all these representations were without any foundation, and the offspring of habitual imagination. But what would be his astonishment when he became actually acquainted with our affairs; when he should learn the principles upon which our government is administered, and the political character of the men who administer it—that the happy government alluded to was the government of a *party*—that this party had acquired a *permanent* character, whereby they became a *practical aristocracy*, and that as such they had ruled the state for near twenty years—that there was one half, or nearly one half, of the freemen in the state, who, during this period have been excluded from all participation in the government, and treated with as much political rigour as the Plebians were by the Patricians of Rome—that all the poor classes in the state, who do not possess property to a certain amount, are denied the right of voting in the election of the officers of the government, and deprived of all *civil privileges* whatsoever, and at the same time are compelled to do military duty, to bear arms, and to pay taxes, although they have no property—that the orthodox religion spoken of was a church establishment, and the dignified and learned clergy were established and supported by the laws of the state, and that all other denominations were compelled to *degrade* themselves or to "pay tribute to Cæsar." What would be the astonishment of this man on being made acquainted with these facts? Would they present to his mind any features of the picture which had been exhibited to his view?

But we beg pardon for this digression.—We would again ask, what have our rulers done for the State? The enquiry is here made as applicable to the State, considered as a commonwealth, and not as respects the individual interests of its citizens. When the pretensions of our rulers are considered; when we consider their policy with relation to the general government, which lead them to oppose all national objects, however closely they were allied with the best interests of our country, it would be natural to suppose that the considerations which led to this policy were founded upon a scrupulous regard to some important State interests, which were in opposition to the interests of the nation.—But what State interests, or State rights, have been promoted by our rulers? Have they acquired for the State any additional political rights, or added to its national importance? Have they elevated its character, exalted its honour, and extended its influence? Our enquires have already shewn that the reverse of this is the fact. Have they enriched the treasury, and augmented the resources of the state? Let those who have paid in taxes, the 145,000 dollars, every cent of which is lost to the state, answer this question.[4] Have our rulers been distinguished for promoting internal improvements, such as canals, roads, bridges, &c.? There are, it is true, some turnpikes in the state. Have they promoted at *home* any great national interests that would be honourable to the state? Have they done any thing to establish and sustain manufactures, which are exciting so deep an interest every where else? If we mistake not the Legislature made a law last spring, exempting the property of certain establishments from taxation! What liberality! Have they done any thing to encourage agriculture? Our hardy yeomanry can answer this question. What important national or public objects, then, have our

---

[4] The sum Connecticut requested as reimbursement from Congress for its expenses during the War of 1812.

rulers promoted? We answer none! Stop; yes, they have given for the "encouragement of literature & religion," one hundred forty-five thousand dollars *which did not belong to them.*

But the important subjects of literature and religion ought not to be treated with levity. Our rulers claim much merit for the provisions which they have made for the support of schools. They are now telling the people that they receive annually from the school fund as much as they pay in the State tax. We very readily admit that those patriotic and public spirited legislators, who provided by law that a certain proportion of all the monies paid into the treasury from taxes, should be appropriated for the support of schooling, deserve to be held in respectful remembrance to the latest posterity. The pen of 'Servetus' can render but a humble tribute to their memories.—And if he was to attempt, in the elevated language of Junius, to raise "recorded honors round their humble monuments," it might be considered only as a reproach upon their successors, as calculated to exhibit their degeneracy in a more conspicuous light. This law originated in very different times, and with very different men, from those who have directed the destinies of the State for fifteen years past. Our present rulers have no merit from these provisions! But have they any merit from the *school fund,* which originated from the western reserve lands? One would hardly suppose that they would have the assurance to claim any thing on this subject; yet such is the fact. It is well known by all who have any knowledge of the transactions, with relation to the sale of those lands, that our rulers *declined* a proposition with the view of favouring speculation and speculators, whereby the school fund has sustained a loss of thousands and tens of thousands of dollars. As to the manner in which this fund has been managed since that period there is little known, as it has been like the rest of our financial concerns, involved in impenetrable secrecy—Yet still there have facts enough come before the public, to enable us to form some idea of the immense sacrifices which the State has sustained. Besides, it is a fact which ought not to be forgotton, that it was owing to the republican influence in the legislature, that the proceeds of the western lands were appropriated for the support of schooling. It was the intention of all the 'high toned' church and State party, that this fund should have been appropriated for the support of the 'established religion,' and to strengthen the adulterous union between Church and State—a union which corrupts the chastity of the one and destroys the integrity of the other—a union which more than any other cause has cast a dark shade over the history of man—stinted the powers of intellect, paralized the efforts of genius, obstructed the progress of improvement—darkened the earth with superstition, given ferocity to the human passions, and overspread the earth with violence. As it respects our Institutions for religious objects, and the higher orders of literature, or Yale College, we may notice them when we come to speak of "what our rulers have done for themselves," for we consider that they fall properly into that part of the subject. After this hasty review, we may with a degree of triumph ask, what have our Rulers done for the State.

No. V. (March 18)

From the order proposed we are now to consider, "What our rulers have done for the People of this State, and what they have *refused* to do." This part of our subject invites to an examination of the primary principles of civil polity, and the more important regulations of society. Society and government are treated as *existing* objects, being general ideas resulting from, or an aggregate of, various particular ideas—yet at the same time are contemplated in the mind, without reference to the particular ideas upon which they depend, and accordingly we ascribe to them various qualities of character, without any application of these qualities to the individual objects from whence the general object arises. Hence we speak of Governments, States, Republicks and Empires, and observe of them that they are wealthy, powerful, honorable and happy, or that they are weak, impoverished and disgraced, without applying any of these ideas to the individuals of which such States, Republicks, &c. are composed. But of what consequence is the wealth and power of a State or Republic, if the *individuals* who compose it are impoverished and oppressed? It is evident that the prosperity of a State or Government is of no importance, and indeed *may* be the greatest misfortune, unless the *people* are prosperous. The primary object of civil institutions, is, or ought to be, to secure the rights, encourage the indust[r]y and promote the happiness of *individuals*. History, experience and philosophy all concur in convincing us that individual security, industry and happiness, depend most essentially upon those principles and features of civil polity, which prescribe and govern the relations in which individuals stand to the governing power and to each other. Every individual ought equally to have his rights of person, of conscience and of property, secure from the invasion of government, and the violence and abuse of individual aggression. Those provisions intended to secure these objects are the most important of civil regulations; upon which we propose to make a few observations, as it respects the government of this state.

It has become very fashionable for some years past with a certain description of politicians, to profess great veneration for the virtues and wisdom of our ancestors. Their motives in this cannot be mistaken. They would have the people believe that the republicans and the friends of improvements treat with disrespect the wisdom, the virtues and the piety of the first settlers of New-England. We shall see presently who has the best claims of respecting our pious ancestors. All reformers and friends of improvements in civil and religious institutions, corresponding with the progress of the human mind, and the refinements of social relations, must have a great veneration for the first settlers of New-England. What was the character of these men? They were reformers—yes; they were the greatest reformers who have ever lived! They did not come to this wilderness country with their heads filled with those notions which have disgraced so many of their degenerate descendants!—they had no veneration for *legitimacy*—for "the most stupendous fabric of human invention," the constitution and laws of England. Did *they* adopt the constitution of *England?*—no! Did *they* import the laws of England?—no! Although subjects of the same empire they chose to make constitutions for themselves, and to adopt such civil and religious institutions as accorded with their ideas of improvement. And although they were trammelled with collonial dependence, and the fiery cloud of royal authority hung in awful and portentious suspense over their heads, yet such was their spirited inovasion [innovation] that their institutions, both civil and religious, were the greatest improvement upon these subjects which have been made at any one period in the history of the world. These institutions it is true, were not perfect. But we hold them in the highest estimation. We revere their authors—They were a noble and in most respects a just foundation of the magnificent and finished fabric which ought to support the social relations. Did the first settlers of New-England, after their arrival in this country consider that they were from *veneration* to the government and laws of England to decline to provide for themselves such political regulations as might consist with their new situation, and their own principles? Were they devotees to "venerable institutions"—to "antique establishments," to "steady habits"? Were they so *alarmed* at the idea of improvement in civil and religious institutions as to adopt those which from their new condition and prevailing sentiments would not have become them? no! What was their language on this subject? They appealed in the true spirit of high minded men, to the source of all authority; to the laws of nature, and of nature's God! They recurred to first principles; they acknowledge the authority of no *positive* laws; no, they chose to make them for themselves. What innovators, what reformers! Yet these are the men who our modern "steady habits" folks profess to consider as moddles [models], and whose memories they profess to revere.

The first institutions of New-England were novel and simple, and in most respects just; but they were unfortunately infected by the spirit of religious fanatacism and intolerance which prevailed among their framers. But even this obnoxious feature may be in a great measure extenuated, with respect to their framers, as at that period the principles of *religious* liberty were not at all understood; it had not then even "entered into the heart of man" that true religion would flourish best when left to itself, or that it could subsist without the aid of law. The only question then was, "what is the true religion," and it was supposed on all hands, that it was proper that this should have the aid of law. Our ancestors supposed that *theirs* was the true religion, they therefore gave it legal support—they supposed also that all other religious creeds were erroneous and heretical, and refused to *tolerate* them. Upon these principles all our primitive laws relating to religion are founded. But notwithstanding the objections here noticed, the primitive institutions of New-England reflect much credit upon our ancestors—they were a great improvement, a noble foundation, and it only remained for their descendents to have given perfection to the system, by correcting errors, expunging false principles, modifying others, to adopt them to the changes of the times—giving sym[m]etry to the parts, and beauty to the structure. We will see how this has been done in Connecticut.

No. VI .(MARCH 25)

The basis of the government of this State is the Charter of Charles 2d. It does not appear that there was any thing like a *regular* government before that time, a period of only about twenty-eight years from the first settlement of the State.[5] The Charter, considered as a Constitution of government contains but a few principles, and these are very simple.

1st. It recognizes or grants the right of self-government to the freemen of the State (then colony) of Connecticut.

2d. This *right* (of self-government) was to be exercised by the General Court or General Assemblies, of which there was to be two every year, composed of the Governor, Lt. Governor, and twelve Assistants, chosen annually, and the deputies of the freemen, not exceeding two, from a town, to be chosen semi-annually.

---

[5] The Fundamental Orders of 1639 initially only involved Hartford, Wethersfield, and Windsor. By 1662 several other towns had joined the founding three under this form of government.

3d. The General Assemblies were empowered to provide for making freemen or admit individuals to the freedom of the State.

4th. The General Assemblies were to make all wholesome laws, &c. to constitute Judiciaries—to appoint Magistrates, designate their titles, to grant commissions for the punishment of crimes, and the imposition of mulcts, &c.

These were, *and are at this day,* the primary, or constitutional principles of the government of this State.

It has been contended "by some visionary theorists" that the "Declaration of Independence," and the ratification of the Treaty of 1783, dissolving our connections with Great Britain, have abrogated the charter, and invalidated the constitution of our government. That these events have destroyed the *authority* of the charter cannot be doubted. Yet still the freemen might recognize and adopt the *principles* which it contained, as the basis of the State government. Have the freemen or have they not, recognized and adopted the principles contained in the charter, as a basis of government? We think they have; by electing the same officers, and organizing the government upon its *principles*, after the treaty of Paris, of 1783, disannulling its authority. The aforesaid principles are therefore at this day the basis of State government.

That these principles are general, and contain the mere outline of a constitution, must be evident to every one. The more minute features of the system have been supplied by the legislature.—It is evident the legislature (and the authority of which for years past, has been only the will of the council) has great and almost unrestrained power. Our rulers cannot say that there have been any constitutional difficulties in the way to their having promoted improvements; they have not wanted *power.* How have they exercised this power? We have not been able to discover that they have done *any thing* for the STATE. Let us see what they have done for the People. Have they promoted or enlarged their *political* rights? These rights consist—

1st. In the free and unrestrained enjoyment of the *electorial franchise.*

2d. In the free and enlarged exercise of this right. Have our rulers manifested a disposition to render the important *"right of suffrage"* more free and easily obtained, or have they subjected it to innumerable restraints, and thrown every obstacle in the way of a free exercise of it? Although this matter falls most properly into the next part of our subject, yet we will here notice some particulars. At an early part of our history, *property* was no part of the qualifications of freemen. All who had "cohabited in the jurisdiction, and been admitted inhabitants by a major part of the town wherein they lived," were permitted to vote in the choice of officers. Afterwards it was provided that none should be made freemen, but those who had fulfilled twenty-one years of age, and were *possessed* (not rated up*on the list*) of a personal estate of thirty pounds. Afterwards twenty pounds on the list were required, exclusive of the poll-list. Passing over various restraints upon the right of suffrage, we come to the origin of the present *property test law*, requiring a freehold estate of forty shillings per annum, or a personal estate of forty pounds. Following up the same course of restriction, this provision has since been altered, requiring a freehold of seven dollars per annum, or a personal estate of one hundred and thirty four dollars in the general lists of estates. The select-men of the several towns had by law long been the board for the examination of the qualifications of freemen; but our rulers thought that this was too *popular* a feature in the government, and in A. D. 1801, made a law taking this power, in a great measure, from the select-men, who are *appointed by the people*, and giving it to the civil authority, who are appointed by *themselves*. In order to give effect to the property test law, there was a statute past in 1812, providing that no person should be admitted to the freedom of the State on any deed or lease unless the same had been recorded at full length in the proper office at least four months preceding the freemen's meeting in which he presented himself. To throw every possible restraint in the way of the right of suffrage, a law was made in 1813, that no person should be admitted a freeman on the account of any real estate which was subject to a mortgage, and also that no person admitted a freeman in one town shall be admitted to vote in any other town, without producing a certificate from the town clerk, and also, that no person admitted a freeman in one town shall be permitted to vote for representatives in any other town, unless he shall have "statedly resided therein" for four months next preceding the meeting. This simple statement of facts gives some idea of the policy of our rulers, and of what they have done for the *people* as respects the important "right of suffrage." "But one half is not told." Let us see, 2dly, what they have done to promote a *free* and *enlarged* exercise of this right.

The law made some years since altering the mode of appointing the assistants and members of congress, is a proof of what our rulers have done to promote the *freedom of elections*. This law commonly called the "stand up law," provides that the Assistants, &c. are first to be chosen into nomination, and afterwards chosen *mechanically* from this nomination. Why this circuity and indirection, but to embarrass and fritter away the right of election, which they *dare not openly invade*. But this is not the worst; the freemen are required to vote by *standing up*. What does this mean? Was it intended to render elections *more free*? No; it speaks a language too plain to be misunderstood? It was intended to give an undue influence to the rich and the powerful; to overawe the poor man and make him silent, or yield his vote in subserviance to their will. It is one important link in the chain which has been fabricated by our rulers to fetter the poor and build up a monied aristocracy in the State. THIS IS, WHITHOUT QUALIFICATION, THE MOST INFAMOUS LAW THAT EVER OUTRAGED THE RIGHTS, OR INSULTED THE UNDERSTANDINGS OF a FREE PEOPLE.

No. VII. (March 25)

1st. But the freedom of elections has been invaded by the *general policy* of our rulers, as well as by particular regulations. We have noticed the "Stand up law" as an instance of the latter kind. We would also notice the *abuse* of the *principle of* ROTATION in office as a proof of their general policy. If there is any one axiom in politics, it is this, "that rotation in office is essential to the security of a free government." The justice of this proposition is too obvious to require any considerations to substantiate it. It is *constitutionally* interwoven into the systems of most of our sister republicks, and it ought to form a constituent part of the texture of the constitution of every free people. But perhaps it is not necessary or expedient that this principle should be very *extensively* incorporated into the constitutional compact; yet it ought to be infused into the spirit of the people. It is not the body, but the soul of a free government. If public offices have either honour or profit attached to them, why not dispense this honor and profit to as great a number of individuals, who are equally deserving of it, as may consist with the public services? But if public offices involve personal sacrifices, and become a burden to individuals, why should one man be burdened to death? But is not the public service promoted by rotation in office? Men, when first engaged in either public or private employment, possess a peculiar zeal and a scrupulous integrity, both of which are very sensibly impaired by time. When public officers are raised directly from, and return frequently to the mass of the people, they are sensible of their dependence upon them, and will not be likely to acquire aristocratic feelings, or to arrogate to themselves peculiar privileges. But the advantages of this principle are too numerous to be noticed here.

But we would ask, what has been the policy of this state? Has the principle of rotation in office been recognized? Has it been acted upon? Does it have any influence in the multiplicity of appointments, which are annually made by the legislature of the state? No; unfortunately a very different policy prevails in Connecticut, and will continue to prevail until there is a *radical reform*. The principle of steady habits has usurped the place of that of rotation in office. It has long been a maxim in Connecticut, that when a man is once appointed to an office, he is to be continued to enjoy it for life, or be removed only for scandalous and immoral conduct. Every effort has been made that ingenuity could suggest, to render the seats of all public offices *permanent*. This is called stability in government. Is not this a most shameful violation of the spirit of our constitution, which requires the appointment of all public officers, even those of the judiciary, to be made *annually*? If this principle is a just one, it ought to have the sanction of *law;* If it is not a just one it ought not to prevail in *practice*. What would our people say at a law of the legislature which should render all the offices *permanent*, and those who hold them removable only for misbehaviour? If such a principle, established by law, would be a great outrage upon the rights of the people, is not such a practice *without law* a greater outrage still?

2d. Another instance of the unwillingness of our rulers, to promote a *free exercise* of the right of suffrage, and to guard against undue influence in elections, is discoverable in their *refusing* to DISTRICT the State for the appointment of the assistants and members of Congress. A regulation of this kind has been adopted in most, if not all of the other states; the propriety and justness of which are most apparent. Why should the Upper House be constituted upon different principles from the House of Assembly? The individual members of the Council are not the representatives of the *people*, but collectively, and as a corporation, they are the representatives of the State in its corporate character. The individual members have no particular constituents, but the whole of them as a body, thrown together so as to destroy their individual capacity, are constituted by the State at large. Is not this calculated to destroy all individual responsibility? But this is not the only objection to this principle; it opens a wide field for political fraud and management, which may nearly destroy the *freedom and fairness* of elections. The freemen at large can know nothing about the character or fitness of the candidates; and an undeserving man is as likely to succeed as a deserving one; it is only necessary to get nominated by the political cabal to get *their* support. But if the assistants were chosen by districts, the candidates would be personally known to most of the voters, and it would be extremely difficult for an undeserving man to get elected; and every member in such case would *know* his constituents, and be cautious how he offended them.

A vast majority, and indeed the whole body of the people, in some sections of the State, may have peculiar and local views and interests; why should they not be indulged in a representation of these local views and interests? But upon the principle which prevails, they cannot be represented at all. Most of the observations which have been made, with respect to the assistants, will apply to the members of Congress.

Is not the general sense of mankind entitled to some respect? Is not the example of every other state worthy of imitation? Are not representatives of congress chosen district-wise every where else? Why then should they not be in Connecticut? Is human nature different here from what it is elsewhere? Are political rights differently constituted here from what they are in the other states? or are our citizens more easily defrauded out of them? Such has been the fact; but we trust that a speedy reform and correction of abuses will soon do away this imputation upon our character.

3d. But what have our rulers done to extend or *enlarge* the important right of suffrage? We have seen that there are no constitutional provisions which restrain or confine the right of election to the appointment of representatives to the assembly, the assistants and the executive; it might and ought to extend to the appointment of sheriffs, who are the principle executive officers in the several counties. This is the practice in Ohio, Pennsylvania, and some of the other states.

But what is a greater evidence of the designs of our rulers to restrain the right of election, and to destroy as far as possible the *popular features* of our government, is the *mode* in which the electors of President and Vice-President of the United States have uniformly been appointed in Connecticut. The constitution provides that the state governments shall *direct* the presidential electors to be appointed, thereby clearly implying that the appointment was not to be made by the state legislatures; but that they were to *provide* for its being done. And, accordingly, in almost every state in the union they have been appointed by the people, either by a general ticket, or by districts.—But in Connecticut they have been uniformly appointed by the legislature; our rulers have wished to save the freemen this trouble. The *people*, therefore, have had no voice in the election of the supreme magistrate of the nation; but only the government, (that is the few individuals and families who form the cabinet council) whose personal feelings and views have alone been consulted upon this important subject.

We have thus very cursorily noticed some of the ["]*political rights*" of our citizens, and the policy of our rulers, with relation to those rights. We have seen in the first place, that instead of facilitating they have thrown every obstacle in the way to the *obtaining* of the "*right of suffrage*"—in the second, that instead of securing the free enjoyment of this right, they have *embarrassed* its exercise, and subjected it to an undue influence—that in the third, instead of enlarging its extent they have *narrowed* its limits and restrained its application.

No. VIII. (APRIL 1)

The writer of these numbers intended to have taken something of a *systematic* view of the politics of this State, and of the policy of our rulers for some years past. But as he proceeded he became sensible that the arrangement of the subject which had been adopted, would lead to an examination of so many matters, and all requiring some degree of minuteness, as rendered it impracticable to go through with the subject within the time contemplated. He therefore had but an alternative either to abandon the subject abruptly and without completing the views contemplated, or resume it at some future period. He has resolved upon the latter course, unless a change of the political auspices of the State should render all discussions of this kind unnecessary—"*a consumation devoutly to be wished.*" He will therefore take leave of the subject for the present by briefly *noticing* some particulars which fall within the scope of its views, and which may be considered at some other time more in detail. We have been through with the first part of our enquiries—of what our rulers have done for the State, and entered upon the second—what they have done, and what they have *refused* to do for the PEOPLE. In this most important branch of the subject we considered firstly the *political* rights of the people, and intended in the second place to have considered their *religious* rights, and in the third their *civil* rights.

1. At the present enlightened period, it cannot we think be seriously made a question, whether it is just and expedient to *force* religion upon society. Religious duties, are no longer considered of that description of obligation, the observance of which are to be *coerced* upon mankind. Law is a rule of *force*, it does not commend and reward that which is right, but prohibits and punishes that which is *wrong*. The question therefore, is not

whether religion and religious services, are a *duty* upon all, but whether an inattention to them is a *crime*. If it is, then the neglect of them ought to be prohibited and enforced by *law*. If this principle is correct, there is also another principle which is just, being inseperably connected with this, (viz.) that it must be decided *by law* which is the *true religion*, for it would be absurd to say, that the law should prohibit and punish the neglect of ostensible religion, without defining of what religion consists; and of course, of adopting one system, as the true religion, and consequently condemning all the rest. *These principles* are the basis of law, religion and of "church establishments." If there are any at this day who justify these principles, we have nothing to say to them. But we would ask whether the laws of this State are not founded upon these principles? We intended to have *examined* this subject, and trust, that we should have been able to shew, that they are; but as we cannot do it, we would recommend the enquiry to the candid and consciencious of all parties, both political and religious.

2. Under the important head of *civil rights*, or the relations of individuals, there are a variety of particulars deserving of minute *discussion*. We can at this time merely *notice* some of the most important. The system of Jurisprudence in this state is simple, concise, and intelligible. It is a most striking evidence of the inclinations of our ancestors for innovation. It has little resemblance to the English system. Most of its principle[s] are founded upon the obligations of natural justice, and the nature and fitness of things. Yet notwithstanding this commendation there are many features in this system, which can hardly be reconciled with the security of private property, or the rights of personal liberty. The *"attachment law"* is founded upon principles that are absolutely incompatible with the security of private property;[6] and the law authorizing the *imprisonment* for *debt* is incompatible with *personal liberty*. However these laws may have been considered, just and necessary, at the time they were adopted, the general sense of mankind seems now to be aroused, and to revolt at such barbarous principles. If we are not much mistaken *both* of these principles exist together in very few, if in any community in the whole world, excepting in this State. In England— in the state of New-York and such of the other States whose jurisprudence is most conformable to that of the English, there are laws authorizing imprisonment for debt; but there are no attachment laws. Of the two evils the attachment law is the worst. It is the law of proscription and the GUILLOTINE of *property*—an ax laid at the root of private credit—an awful and portentious cloud, which hangs over every man of *extensive*—business

---

[6] A plaintiff trying to recover a debt could immobilize most of a defendant's property by asking a court to place an attachment on it.

whatever may be his circumstances, and exposed, from the whim, the timidity, the malice or the sinister view of a single individual, to explode with ten-fold vengeance on his head. Nearly the whole of a man's property may be attached, for a debt of five dollars. Even the breath of suspicion may prove the ruin of a man of business possessed of a handsome estate.

The least suspicion may a mighty mischief wake,

As the small pebble stirs the peaceful lake

And how many are there in society who are *interested* in exciting a suspicion of private credit. This is a spark which soon becomes enkindled into a conflagration. No sooner is there a *suspicion* of a persons credit, than the whole kennel of executive offices collect around him "thick as locusts in the land of Nile," and scarcely less destructive, for they will not fail to "eat out his substance.—It is a trite, but just saying, that it is a "surley dog that *bites* before he *barks*," yet cases frequently happen that individuals are made to *feel* before they are permitted to *see* their danger.

The revenue laws of the State are the most *unreasonable* and *unequal* that can well be conceived of. If they had been framed for the express purpose of rendering them the most unreasonable and unequal *possible*, ingenuity itself could scarcely have been attended with a more successful result. The State revenue arises partly from *indirect* but principally from *direct* taxation. But in neither case is PROPERTY the *principle* of taxation. Of the indirect revenue we will notice one instance only viz. the *duty* upon *writs, appeals, &c.* The policy of this mode of taxation we have never yet heard explained; and we consider it as most unjust and oppressive. Yes, *oppressive* because it is a tax upon the poor and distressed. For it is these discriptions of persons who have to submit to be *"sued at law." Property* we say is not the principle of taxation in this State. But it may be asked that if property is not, what is the principle. We answer, INDUSTRY. Whoever will take the trouble to examine our system of taxation will find that it is founded upon this principle. Every person and every article of property, seem to be taxed, not according to the value of the one, or the pecuniary ability of the other; nor according to their productiveness. We need notice but a few particulars. The *poll* or capitation tax is from the very terms of it, a tax upon *industry*. The *property* of the subjects of this tax is thrown out of the question. A poor man who is not worth one cent in the world must pay this tax because he is *able* to work; whereas, a wealthy man who may be worth hundreds of thousands of dollars, is exempted from it, because he is *unable* to work, when if he was able he would probably be *unwilling*. Land is not estimated in the general lists of estates according to its *value*, nor according to its *productiveness*; neither is personal property estimated according to its real value, or its relative value to real estates. The taxes of personal property, are mostly confined to articles of prime necessity in life, such as family horses, oxen, cows, &c. To show that lands are taxed without any reference to their value, we need notice but a single case; *plow grounds* are estimated on the list at $1,67 per acre. Now is it not certain that there are lands plowed in this State which are not worth FIVE *dollars* per acre, and others which are worth *one hundred* and *fifty* dollars! What manifold inequality! Yet such is the result of this absurd principle of taxation. We will notice one or two other particulars. The taxes upon buildings are most egregiously unequal and unjust. A farmer in the country who has a decent and *finished* dwelling-house worth $1500 and which would not rent for more than $50 per annum, pays as heavy a tax on his house as a landlord in this city does for a house worth TEN-THOUSAND dollars, and which would rent for $1000 per annum. But again, a country farmer pays more taxes for *four cows* which give the marrow to the bones of his children and which might be valued at about one hundred dollars, than the land-holder in this city, does for a building of the above description, worth *ten thousand*, and which would rent for *one thousand dollars*. Such is the *justice*—such the *equality* of the system of taxation in Connecticut. How absurd! How preposterous! Why are not taxes levied upon *property* and not *industry*? Why is not every man compelled to pay taxes according to what he is *worth*? Why are articles of first necessity which ought to be *exempt*, taxed with tenfold vengeance? And why is the poor-man who has no property, taxed *at all*? Are not these matters a part of that system of policy which has long prevailed among us; and intended to depress and oppress the poor, and build up the wealthy? Why then let us ask, are these things *suffered* to be so. The Freemen we trust will answer this enquiry on the 7th of April; which will form a new *era* in the State.

But should not the REFORMATION progress according to our present calculations the public may expect again to hear from
Michael Servetus.

GEORGE H. RICHARDS,
THE POLITICS OF CONNECTICUT (1817)

George Hallam Richards, an attorney from New London, penned the only pamphlet printed during the controversy over framing and ratifying the constitution. He also was the first writer to give primacy to the notion that the state lacked a constitution.

The title page identified the author as a "Federal Republican" and carried the injunction "Come, now, let us reason together." At the end of his essay Richards used the pen name "Hamilton," probably hoping to reach as many former Federalists as possible.

We know very little about Richards other than he was a member of the New London bar and active in the local Masonic lodge. His pamphlet, *The Politics of Connecticut* (Hartford, 1817), was published by the same press responsible for printing the recently established Hartford *Times*, a principal promoter of the constitutional cause during 1817 and 1818. Portions of the Richards pamphlet also appeared in the *Times* on March 11 & 25, and April 1, 1817.

THE POLITICS OF CONNECTICUT: OR, A STATEMENT OF FACTS, ADDRESSED TO HONEST MEN OF ALL PARTIES RELIGIOUS AND POLITICAL IN THE STATE: PARTICULARLY TO THE MASS OF THE COMMUNITY, A BOLD AND HARDY YEOMANRY, WHO COMPOSE THE FLESH AND MUSCLE, THE BLOOD AND BONE OF THE BODY POLITIC.

ADDRESS.

FELLOW CITIZENS—

HE who now addresses you, boasts not of superior patriotism; nor prefers pretensions to dictate.

Persuasion is the mark he aims at, and FACTS his only arrows to hit that mark. To compass the end he has in view, he would deign to wield none but the weapons of argument.

He readily accedes to those, who differ from him in opinion, their claims to fair construction; and whilst he extends charity to them, expects justice for himself.

It is of no moment to the reader, who the writer may be, what his motives, or what his objects. Professions too have long since become stale and suspicious. To gratify, however, a natural and just curiosity, in the present instance, he will not hesitate to declare that he was born on the same soil with yourselves, lives under the same laws, pays taxes, and bears arms in support of the same government, has in all respects the same interests, and trusts the sentiments he feels are common to you all—of *love of Country*, of *respect for the Magistracy*, and of *obedience to the Law*.

Let us then join hands, and put forth an effort to render that country *more worthy* of our love, that magistracy *more worthy* of our respect, and that law *more worthy* of our obedience.

The cause of TRUTH is a common cause. Her interests are the general welfare. She is entitled, therefore, to candid attention. With a voice of reason and persuasion, she invites to fair discussion. It is her right to demand it; it is our duty to grant it.

The *administration* of the government of this State has long pursued its pacific policy, and gone on its way rejoicing, reposing in confident security—not dreaming of change.

The PEOPLE also of this State have been characterized by a ready obedience to established authority. Their submission to the laws springs from a principle, which is the noble attribute of an enlightened community, who understand alike their duties and their rights. Yet singular! this principle has been misconstrued into a tameness of temper that could brook an injury, or suffer an infringement of prerogative.

Taught a precedent in the example of our ancestors, we have been little apt to cavil. The acts of our administration we are accustomed to receive with patient acquiescence and with implicit faith. Our support would still have been freely and unsuspectingly yielded, had it not been sternly demanded, and grossly abused.

Now a spirit of inquiry has awakened and walks forth, unfolding the causes of measures, and calling their authors to account. What has roused this spirit of inquiry, and kindled this fire of indignation? Look for answer, to the glaring contrast between the present times, and those which our Fathers saw and blessed.

Time *was*, when the character of this State towered to a proud eminence, and there stood secure—when the public pulse beat high—when the public breast swelled with strong emotions for the interests of our country—and when the public arm laid bare its energies to uphold the standard of her honor. *That* time was, when the venerable names of [Jonathan] Trumbull, [Roger] Sherman, [William Samuel] Johnson, [Matthew] Griswold, [Oliver] Ellsworth and the Wolcotts [Roger and Oliver Sr.],[1] were the Talisman to lay our passions, and raise our better judgment. Their influence, like the electric fluid, pervaded the air we breathed, and purified it for our health. These men, and their compatriots, worthy associates in a holy cause, were wont to guide, in a steady course, the vessel of state, through seas no chart delineated, no mariner had surveyed. Often, in debate, has their reason flashed the lightning of intelligence, and their eloquence rolled the thunder of conviction through the halls of our national councils. These were, indeed, the Corinthian Pillars that supported the FAIR FABRIC OF OUR PUBLIC GLORY.

To pay the tribute of our acknowledgments to those who have advocated our principles, espoused our interests, elevated our views, and adorned

---

[1] Revolutionary leaders and former governors of the colony.

our name, is an act combining justice, gratitude and patriotism. It cherishes a spirit of emulation—it kindles other minds by the fire of example—it nurtures a laudable pride for the land of our nativity—it makes that land a just cause of boast, and it brings in our judgment to fortify our affection; for we seldom love, where we do not esteem.

In this place, then, we may enjoy a pleasure whilst we discharge a duty, in confessing our admiration of the erudition and accomplishments, of the talents and virtues, of the exertion and services to be found, not only in those whom we have just enumerated, but also in that galaxy, [Timothy] Dwight, [John] Trumbull, [David] Humphries and [Joel] Barlow,[2] men of illuminated minds, whose creative imagination has strewed with richer imagery the paths of poetry; and whose universal genius is distinguished by the vigor of its progress throughout the circle of Science—in religion and philosophy, in diplomacy and in politics, in the useful and in the fine arts.

At the period adverted to, when the Wolcotts and other illustrious worthies ruled our destiny under kinder auspices, we raised our head among our sister republics, and spoke a voice audible and commanding. We exercised a powerful influence, and were weighed in the political balance held in the hand of WASHINGTON, by our intellectual, rather than by our numerical force.

Our internal economy was not less prosperous than our federate relations were respectable. We were indeed "a peculiar people," a pra[c]tical republic—without the baneful distinction on either hand, of licentious opulence, or indigent servility. Our conduct evinced, for the most part, the benign principles of a domestic polity; of a polity that appealed to motives of duty rather than to fear of penalty; that inculcated obedience to the law, and reverence for its minister; that sought to reward the labors, and to husband the fruits of industry and prudence; that graduated merit, not on the scale of family and fortune, but on that only of moral worth and mental endowment; that diffused through all classes the means of education; and that carried to the poor man's door the "bread of life," cheering his mind with the light of religion, soothing his heart with the solace of its promises, pouring its balm into his wounds, anointing his spirit with its sacred unction, and shedding a ray of hope through the deep gloom of his despondency.

This picture, though drawn by the hand of a lover, does not adequately represent the elegance and beauty of the original; and hence it becomes a matter of curious speculation and of profound moment, to discover

---

[2] Prominent religious and artistic figures.

how her features have since been distorted, her colours faded, her expression gone, her spirits wasted, her principles perverted, and her whole frame relaxed. This discovery is the purpose of the present investigation. Obstacles to independent inquiry may here be presented by our education, by our habits, by our partisan feelings, and perhaps by our temperament.

A distinctive trait in our character is a tenacity of the manners and morals, of the principles, and even prejudices of our ancestry. This is laudable, because it shows our gratitude and respect for the memory of our benefactors; but this trait, held in rigidity, would be an eternal bar to improvement. It would, under its crusted coat of age, like the moss-grown rock, shut out the day, which is shed by the sun of science. It would stay the progress of the mind, and muffle the music of its march.

A peculiar immobility also attaches to the mass of our community, which is not mercurial and sublimated, but practical and phlegmatic. This disposition, whilst it throws around us a shield impenetrable by the arts of the demagogue, leaves us exposed to the intrigues of our rulers, who, from the ambush of power, let fly their poisoned shafts, and we see no danger. Alas! it too often induces a reliance on false security, an indifference to public interests, and a want of public spirit.

But neither your veneration for antiquity, nor your solidity of judgment, can reconcile torpidity with patriotism, nor conciliate the hostile elements of *aristocracy* and *freedom*.—No ! you will call to mind the labors and dangers, through which your fathers toiled and fought, to acquire that rich estate of civil, political and religious rights, which they have bequeathed to you; and you will be stimulated by their example to improve your patrimony, to enlarge its bounds, to cultivate its soil, to confirm its title, and to transmit it to your children.

To promote these objects, so worthy the wisdom of a … free people to conceive, and of their energy to execute, we will select, from a boundless prospect, a few points of view, whence we cannot fail to perceive the errors we have committed; the grievances complained of; the means to correct the former, and to redress the latter; and the improvements which offer themselves to our adoption.

The principal points of view to which we will direct our attention, are
The Constitution of the State.
The Rights of Election
The Rights of Conscience.

The System of Education.

The Judiciary.

The Appropriation Act.

The Hartford Convention, and general conduct of this State during the late war.

I. THE CONSTITUTION OF THIS STATE.

We are to consider *first*, the Constitution of government under which this State is *said* to be organized.

The only government of this people anterior to the revolution, was founded on the colonial Charter of Charles II. The Declaration of Independence, which burst the bonds of allegiance that bound us to the parent country, necessarily annulled that charter. Yet that charter continues the only basis of our present government! How continues? Why, it is adopted by a *vote* of the Legislature! What! a legislature enact a Constitution; Direct inversion of the nature of things! In other governments, the legislature is a creature of the Constitution; with us, forsooth, the Constitution is a creature of the legislature! Contradictory as this is in theory, it is in practice not less repugnant to the rights and interests of the people. The legislature, playing the mimick to the Parliament of Great Britain, and fancying itself omnipotent, proceeds, without any convention of the people, without any reference to the body of their constituents, to declare such a bill of rights as they are graciously pleased to grant us.—With their own hands they presume to set metes and bounds to the respective departments of government, and to prescribe the orbit in which they shall revolve on the axis of LEGISLATIVE SUPREMACY.

When they had thus clothed themselves with supreme irresponsible authority, did they exercise it in the formation of a Constitution, calculated to guard, with sedulous care, and with jealous vigilance, our choicest rights and dearest privileges, and to incorporate into itself all the pure principles of civil and religious liberty ? What, as Republicans, who had just been rescued from thraldom, and had gained the prize of independence, what did they do? *They adopted, as their own issue, the royal buntling.* They voluntarily bowed the neck, and passed again under the yoke of *colonial* servitude, imposed by the *Charter.*

You are all acquainted with the provisions of this Charter. We will not now enter into their detail. Its principal feature attracts our attention. We may well be astonished and indignant to find the slavish badge of feudal barbarism still fastened on us, as a livery, by the *republican constitution of our royal charter.* This declares us to *hold* our estates of CHARLES, by the *tenure and services of Soccage.*[3] If so, the subserviency of our polities to British policy is expedient, if not justifiable, and has the plea of interest to excuse its depravity. Our yeomanry, indeed, feel they have a firmer title. Their own arm gained the land, and their own arm shall keep it. We hold our property by the God of nature; neither by *feudal* nor *soccage;* but in *allodium.*[4] We are no vassals—We render homage to no earthly lords—We recognize no servitude, by oath or fealty.

Will it be replied, that this obnoxious feature has been effaced from the Charter? How had it been effaced Was it not a *principle of our "boasted constitution?"* Has there been any convention authorized to approve and ratify the amendment? Or, in fact is our Constitution a molten idol, a waxen image, that the legislature may mould into any figure, and stamp upon it any impression? IT IS.

Every legislature, unchecked by a Constitution, is of equal power. It is idle and absurd, therefore, for that which sat yesterday, to attempt controul over that which will set to-morrow. The legislature which, at a former period, adopted the Charter, may, in its succeeding, sessions, abolish it. The power which creates, can destroy, and if [it can] destroy, [can] modify. The higher power includes the interior, as the whole embraces all its parts. The legislature, warranted by the precedent, themselves have created, may abolish the present form of government, as they abolished the last, or they may adopt the last, as they adopted the present. They may, by analogy with their past transactions, change our republic into a monarchy, or aristocracy. Or, what is merely progressive towards it, declare their sessions triennial, septennial, or perpetual. They are, indeed, our sovereigns, without a fiction of law. They are above our reach. They have no limit to their power, but the moderation of their passions, or the dictates of their judgment.

After this review, it would be an insult to your understanding to enquire, whether the State be organized under a constitution?

Are not our rights and privileges entitled to a sure and sacred protection? Should they not be lodged in a safe and permanent repository? *They want a life-guard, and we must compose it.*

It is contended, that there is danger in agitating the question of a constitution. Can danger arise from security? And may it not spring from insecurity? It is too true, that a strenuous opposition has arrayed itself against the attempt to entrench and fortify our liberties. A numerous and respectable class of citizens, who would take every practicable pledge for the future,

[3] A form of feudal land tenure in which lands were held in exchange for certain agricultural services.

[4] Land held completely free of all feudal dues.

who would have the title deed of their rich inheritance, inscribed an authentic record in the register of fate, and stamped with the seal of immortality, are ridiculed, thwarted and frustrated in their object. Why? Because the accomplishment of this object, not only innocent, but indispensable to guarantee and perpetuate republican institutions, would collide with the narrow views, selfish policy and grovelling ambition of a few artful leaders. A Bill of Rights, a CONSTITUTIONAL CHARTER, embodying a fair expression of the public will, is deprecated as a prelude to reform, and harbinger of liberal government.

THE RIGHTS OF ELECTION

The Elective Franchise is the substratum of freedom. Weaken it, and it totters. Remove it, and it falls. The sacred rights of Election are the radical principles that impart life and vigor, activity and strength to our political system. Yet these, which should be like our other rights, sure and stedfast, moored and grappled to our very soil, by the sheet anchor of a Constitution, are still fluctuating on the wild waves of party politics.

The freedom of election is restrained by various modifications, the evil of which has become almost imperceptible by the blinding influence of custom. The choice of Assistants, who constitute, in effect, the council of the State, is an ingenious and complicated piece of mechanism designed, by the multiplicity of its wheels and springs, of its clogs and checks, to divert from the instrument of government, a direct application of the popular power.

In the month of September of each year, by *Statute*, the freeholders are *privileged* to designate twenty persons to be held in nomination; twelve of whom, at the expiration of seven months, must be, by a certain routine of manœuvre, elected to office. See here, how our power of suffrage is paralysed by delay, and frittered away by division! Thus we cannot appoint, directly, the Assistants, in any case. In September, we select twenty candidates, and in the ensuing month of April, *choose per force* twelve of them. On this point a few pertinent inquiries arise. If we be freemen, why may we not directly appoint to office, instead of *recommending to ourselves a nomination?* Are our passions cooler, and our judgments riper in April than in September, that we may elect to office in the former month, and not in the latter; yet are at liberty to exercise the critical duty of selection in the latter month, and not in the former? What offence have we the people committed, that, in April, we ourselves are not only perfectly ineligible, but incapable even to select our candidates from the great body of the citizens? Our choice must be contained to the *chosen few!*

Are the Assistants of a more sacred character than the Chief Magistrate, that they may not be touched by a vulgar hand, nor be blown upon by the breath of popular censure or applause? Why may we not at once and without circumambulation, appoint our own servants? Why not strike the diameter without running a circle? Why not have a full and direct enjoyment of our positive rights? Why spin them out and intertwine them through all the involutions of a labyrinth, until we lose the clue of them? Why dilute and evaporate their essence, or refine away their substantial parts, by this process of distillation through a political alembic?

A desire has long been entertained by our wisest statesmen, and purest patriots, to introduce a more simple, natural and equitable mode of selection, as regards our House of Assistants, or Senate, and, also our Representatives in Congress, and Electors of President and Vice President of the United States. The mode proposed is as safe and practicable, as the existing plan is hostile and dangerous to our interests, intricate in theory, and of circuitous operation. We are now often constrained to select for office, men beyond the circle of our acquaintance, of whose character & qualifications for their station, we are wholly ignorant; and who possess no sentiments, principles, or interests, in common with their constituents.

The plan of *Districts* is just, as it is simple, and sanctioned by the usage of our sister States. This would remove the evils experienced under the present mode. It would give us representatives, in fact, as well as in name. Instead of voting for strangers, we might bestow our confidence on men whom we know and love, and would delight to honor. Such are the advantages we should derive from a plain amendment of the mode of election.— Why then, is it not adopted? Because it runs counter to the views of our State Cabinet; because it would afford an additional security against intrigue; because it would allow room for the public voice to speak with a clearer and more decided tone; and finally because it would take from the hands of those who now *manage* the elections, their great fulcrum, and moving power, and restore them to the people.

Another limitation of the right of suffrage is of a pecuniary nature. A certain estate is requisite for its exercise. No matter what amount of interest you require, the principle is the same. The rule of authority which disfranchises a citizen for want of a particular estate, may debar him any privilege for want of any other portion of property. If one dollar, or one pound be the requisite qualification, why may not 100, 1000, or 100,000 be the standard, and thus, the dearest privilege of a freeman be vested in those, whose only claim to character is wealth? What! adopt a *mercenary* criterion by which to decide on the *expediency of permitting* a man to enjoy his inherent rights! Give this rule a little wider latitude of construction, and an aristocracy of the worst species is immediately erected. Establish the right to draw this artificial line of distinction between the freeman and the slave, and you may draw the line across the body of our laws, and sever the republic.

It is an axiom in politics, that no man shall be taxed without his consent, that is, without a voice in the imposition of his tax. It is also a political axiom that every man shall be admitted to the enjoyment of the full privileges and immunities of that government, to which he owes allegiance, and in whose defence he bears arms. In violation to these *fundamental axioms*, we compel the laborer, unconsulted about its necessity or propriety, to contribute his pittance in the discharge of the tax, which the capitalist may choose to impose.

Are not the ability to pay taxes and to bear arms, and the performance of these duties, a far nobler title to all the honors and benefits of citizenship than any base pecuniary calculation? Never think, then, to estimate by the pence table, the privileges of an high minded people. Never deny an equality of rights to the brave yeoman, to whom you must look for succor in the crisis of danger; but whose brawney arm, if oppression once have palsied it, can never brace its sinews in your cause.

As this principle of a monied distinction is erroneous, the practice under it cannot be salutary. How absurd an enactment which operates as a *mulct* upon the poor! How pernicious the policy, to make poverty a reproach, and to brand the sorrows of misfortune with the stigma of the law! Because the keen blasts of adversity howl chill through his dwelling, you, less merciful, would expose him shelterless to the storm. The law is a common father, and should extend the shield of his protection over all the members of his family, and embrace them in his arms.

The advocates of this invidious discrimination urge it as necessary to ward off from the opulent classes, encroachments by the indigent. *His suffrage is the poor man's poor defence and only protection against the exorbitance and oppression of the rich; and yet the rich urge that the poor man's exclusion from his solitary privilege, as the only security of* THEIR *property against* HIS *depredations!* Oh, sophistical perversion of the mind and heart!

This exclusive principle is also recommended as a guard against intrigue and bribery. Surely here are presented to our admiration a new feature of a republic, and a novel argument in legislation; as though intrigue and bribery were confined by their gross material nature, to the *vulgar herd*, and not permitted to soar into the etherial sphere of the *higher orders;* and, as though the narrower the limits, within which political rights are confined, the safer and purer their exercise; when all history demonstrates, and were history silent, it were obvious to the sense, that the fewer the members, the more easily influenced by corrupt motives, and that to bribe a whole people to their own injury, is an absurdity in terms—not a plausible paradox, but a glaring solecism. Individuals may thus be corrupted, but a people cannot be. Faction may divide them, and passion give a momentary impulse, yet they will soon revert to the guidance of sober judgment; for they must necessarily wish well to their own interest, and in all essential parts understand it. The most incorruptible repository, therefore, and most vigilant guardianship of the people's rights are to be found in the people themselves.

This opprobrious law, that conspires with misfortune to persecute those whose crime is poverty, does, and must as verily it ought to, fail of its object. How ilusive and nugatory experience shows its provisions to be, need not be suggested to any man acquainted with the qualifications of our *manufactured* voters. The rule has grown into a hiss and a by word. None but laughs at its inefficacy, whilst the practice that creeps in under it, like a crawling snail, disgusts us by its sight, and defiles us with its slime. Away with it, then, altogether. Explode the idle rule from your statute-book, as it is already exploded from the observance of your citizens. Keep no longer open the fountain, whence no purifying stream can issue; for its source is stagnant with putridity. Break down the reservoir, and let out the polluted waters pregnant with disease and contagion.

From this view it appears, 1st, That the right of Election *is unduly restricted.* 2d, That this restriction is *unjust in principle.* 3d. That it is and must be *inefficient in practice.* And 4th, That this, like all other violations of correct principles in politics, is productive of baneful consequences; as in the physical world, deviation from order is confusion, and from health is sickness.

THE RIGHTS OF CONSCIENCE

The next division of our subject leads us to a consideration of the rights of conscience, as enjoyed under, or infringed by, the laws of this State. It is the peculiarity of these rights, that he who deprives us of them, *enriches not himself,* *"but makes us poor indeed."* And yet, perhaps, there are none for which a stern- er, longer and deadlier contest has been waged, since the introduction of Christianity. A bloody, revengeful, and almost interminable croisade has attest- ed *the mercy, the justice, and the policy of persecution. Religious liberty,* therefore, is a dear purchase, and a rich possession.

On this point, our prejudices "most easily beset us;" a double caution, therefore, is necessary to this discussion. Whilst we hold fast "the faith of our fathers," let us not fear to open our eyes to any light which TRUTH may emit. Religion is a pillar of fire to guide us: Superstition a pillar of fire to consume us.

A religious sentiment is inculcated into our hearts, through infancy, and through manhood. It is distilled, like the honey dews, on the earliest bud- dings of our intellect. This sentiment is an happy instruction—a proud dis- tinction; and, under our circumstances, not more natural than just, not more grateful than obligatory; for, LORD, thy right hand hath planted our gates, and thine eye hath smiled peace within our borders.

That the Gospel contains the most beautiful and sublime system of ethics; that it carries within itself conclusive evidence of its high original; and that it breathes from its bosom, which has imbibed it, the spirit of inspiration; no man who understands it, can deny; and all men who have sensibility to feel, and mind to perceive its beauties and excellencies, will advance it a cordial support. But whether its holy cause be not profaned by human alliance; whether it be not independent, in its own strength and resources, of governmental assistance; and whether official patronage do not erect on the basis of the church a colossal throne of human despotism, are questions which ages have solved in the blood of martyrs, and answered by the cries of the inquisition. To emblazon this truth in colors of more crimson hues, the flames of the fagot have shot broad masses of light through the death-like darkness of superstition; whilst the agonies of the rack resound the groans of its victims through the remotest recesses of creation.

The admonitions of history point, in every page, to the dangers of con- nexion between ecclesiastical and civil power. When virtue is wedded to vice, the issue must be monstrous—an unnatural brood of hypocrisy, cru- elty and intolerance. The admixture of human ingredients in the chalice of religion converts its nectar into poison—the chyle of its virtues into the gall of the passions.

We now proceed to inquire, whether we have been guilty of the mingled impiety and impolicy of sanctioning an adulterous intercourse between religion and politics—polluting the chastity of the former by the debauchery of the latter. And to ascertain this point by force of fact, rather than of argument, we will recur to the statute book, adverting briefly to only a few, the more obvious traits of what is termed by the Chief Justice, our "*ecclesiastical constitution.*" If it should appear, that our church and state establishment is not the mere burden of the ballad, and theme of invective, but that they are *by law* incorporated as constituent parts of our system ; our increased liberality, will, no doubt, hasten to amend the imperfections of our ju[r]isprudence.

It is enacted, 1st, That the estates of all ministers of the gospel, and all the polls of their families, shall be exempt from the grand list. They are made an exception from all taxation, whilst every other profession and occupation are duly assessed.

2d. If a town or society have no minister to preach the gospel to them for a year or more, they shall be assessed during that period, such taxes as the legislature may determine; which taxes it is the duty of the County court to see collected and appropriated to the support of the ministry in said town or society.[5]

3d. All the inhabitants of a town are taxable, according to their list, for the support of any minister that may be settled there; but, in the election of the minister, *none* are admitted to vote, unless of certain property, or of full age, and *in full communion with the church* in said town.+

4th. Where a town or society enter into no contract with their minister, and if *he* think the support inadequate, he is to make application to the legislature, who will grant him a competency.+

5th. Every householder is required to "KEEP A SUPPLY OF ORTHODOX CATECHISMS."+

6th. Every person is bound to attend public worship, and is interdicted going from his place of abode on Sundays, except for this purpose."+

7th. The Selectmen are required to see that all parents duly instruct their children in an " *orthodox catechism,*" so as to be able to answer the interrogatories of the minister when he comes to examine them. Parents for neglect of this duty to be presented by a grand jury.+

8th. School societies are required to elect visitors, whose duty is to examine and approve all instructors of such schools, and to inspect the proficiency of the scholars in letters, and " *in some catechism by them approved.*"+

---

[5] References to specific pages in the Statutes of Connecticut in the original pamphlet are omitted in this version, but a + marks all the passages that were annotated in this way.

9th. The "General Association" of ministers, in this state, composed *exclusively* of presbyterians, are erected into a corporation, and invested with all the powers and privileges incident to such an institution, under the NAME of "*the Missionary Society.*"+

10th, The *Dissenters*, so called, must lodge a certificate of their secession from the " ESTABLISHED CHURCH," with the clerk of that church."+

Lastly and principally. Atheism, deism, infidelity, polytheism and *unitarianism*, are classed by the *statute*, under the same head of *felonies:* and it is enacted, " That if any person, &c. shall by writing, printing, teaching, or advised speaking, deny the being of a God . . .; or *any one of the persons in the Holy Trinity, to be God;* or shall assert and maintain that there are more Gods than one ; or shall deny the Christian religion to be true, or the holy scriptures of the old and new testament to be of divine authority; and be thereof *lawfully* CONVICTED before any of the superior courts of this state, shall for the *first offence*, be incapable to have or enjoy any offices or employments, ecclesiastical, civil or military, or any part in them, or profit by them: And the offices, places and employments enjoyed by such persons at their conviction, shall be void. And such person, being a second time *convicted* of any of the aforesaid *crimes*, shall be disabled to sue, prosecute, plead or maintain any action, or information in law, or equity; or be guardian of any child, or executor of any will, or administrator of any estate."+

The preceding view, in abstract of a few features of our ecclesiastical establishment, presents a novel and singular prospect, and brings much matter for reflection.

The author of these pages will never debase his pen, nor the cause he advocates, by an illiberal aspersion upon any man or set of men. He is neither hireling to condemn, nor parasite to flatter; neither zealot of a party, nor bigot of a sect; but as a man will boldly assert and firmly maintain the conviction of his judgment. He cherishes an high respect for the virtue and intelligence of the clergy. He understands the full scope of their agency in the machinery of society, and their importance as an auxiliary to law and to morality. He believes them, as a body, to be an holy priesthood, and, like the ancient Druids, to contain in their minds and libraries a rich and varied store of useful and curious learning. He tenders, them, therefore, a cheerful personal support by a ready contribution of his property, and of his influence; but he wishes that contribution still to be *voluntary;* and his principles compel him to be decisive and strenuous in opposition to the interference of civil authority with matters of religion. Their union is pernicious; for their *natures are distinct.* The one descends from heaven; the other springs from earth. The one is born of God; the other is born of man.

That this union is established, and the interests of the church are carefully interwoven in all its filaments, into the texture of the law, is manifest on the face of the articles just recited from the statutes. The duty of public worship, which indeed is prescribed by natural and divine law, our municipal code recognizes among *civil* obligations, and makes the neglect, or violation of it, *penal.* The ministry also are endowed with ample provision, either by their contracts with their respective societies, or, on their *individual application* to the legislature.

The partiality evinced by a variety of acts towards the presbyterian or "*orthodox church,*" and the anxiety displayed to guard against "*heterodoxy*", or, in other words, against secession from the "Established Church," are too positive to be denied, and too palpable to be palliated." To illustrate the terms "orthodoxy" and "heterodoxy," abundant comment is furnished by the whole context of our jurisprudence, on the subject of religion. The name and the thing were introduced and defined by the Synod[6] that sat at Saybrook, and laid, according to the authority of our Chief Justice, the PLATFORM of our *Ecclesiastical Constitution.*

This marked favoritism towards the established church long exercised the extreme patience of the dissenting persuasions; and at length has entirely alienated their attachment and support. This cause and consequence were naturally to have been expected from a knowledge of our rights, on one hand, and from their violation on the other; from abuse of power in its possessors, and from the spirit of resistance against usurpation, that springs up in the soil of freedom.

The "orthodox" church, not content with the possession of peculiar privileges, arrogate pretensions over other sects, and enhance the odium of their prerogative by its impolitic exercise. This church requires to be deposited with their officer, a certificate from the other sects, as a legal evidence of secession, without which evidence, the "heretics" are assessed in maintenance of the "orthodox" church. This *render of homage* is so gross a perversion of every idea of equal liberty, such a base perversion of worse than feudal bondage, that we are astonished at finding it subsisting under a professedly free republic, and in the enlightened nineteenth century. Its apologists excuse it with ingenious sophistry, and argue, that, indeed, it is quite equitable in theory, and in practice operates no hardship. We answer,

---

[6] A meeting of Congregational religious leaders that took place in 1708.

that in theory, the slightest infringement is as much tyranny, as absolute privation; and that in practice, the former is both precedent and prelude to the latter. Liberty is the freeman's honor, as chastity is the virgin's virtue, and both should remain *untouched*. The very consciousness of not enjoying equal rights, is painful oppression, and this consciousness, in the present instance, is enforced by practical proof.

Take a case. If a man be of peculiar sentiments in religion, and find no denomination within the State, or his vicinity, with whom he can unite in worship; or if any sect exist within the limits of a society who cannot accord in religious principles with that society, and yet are themselves insufficient in numbers and estate, to support a minister of their own sentiments; the individual and the sect, in this case, must sacrifice their independence of feeling and thinking—do penance for their poverty, and yield their hard earned gains to propagate opinions which they conscientiously believe erroneous.

It appears that the General Association are incorporated a Missionary Society! This fact is full of meaning. When we consider the exclusive constitution of that body—the zeal, activity and intelligence of its members—the ardor and concert with which they co-operate for the completion of their plan of action—the connexion they have long sustained with, and the secret influence they have habitually exerted over the administration of our affairs; that they are endowed with perpetual life, extensive resources, and other chartered privileges and immunities; we may well awaken to a sense of its existence, activity, and powers, and anticipate results inauspicious to toleration. It is not here intended to cast positive censure upon the character or conduct of that Society; though the very nature of their combination will glance at them such a reflexion. Many who compose it are of high respectability, whose motives it would be indecorous, if not unjust, to impeach. The Missionary Society may be an instrument of good; and it *may be* an engine of State, to play upon the passions and prejudices of community. Those who know the ways of men, and " *what is in man*," best know the danger of any institution, that throws into the hands of its members, temptation and power to induce and to enable them to deviate from their duty. The funds and authority with which they are invested, may be perverted to the propagation of *sectarian creeds*, rather than devoted to the diffusion of a *gracious gospel*. And this perversion of treasure and of influence may be more readily effected in that association, than in others of the same nominal description; because of the unison of its members in sentiment and design, in exertion and interest, in religion and politics.

A principle illustration of the bigotry and intolerance of the ecclesiastical character, in this State, is exhibited in the *anathema* by which they *denounce* the *herecy*, and in the *ban* by which they excommunicated the *sect of Unitarianism*. Would it not be more conformable to the condescension, and to the meek and forgiving temper of the Saviour—Would it not be more consonant to the example set by God himself, when he was born into the world, and tabernacled in the flesh—Would it not more display that "charity, which is the bond of perfectness," and which the gospel so sweetly, yet forcibly inculcates, gently to reclaim the wandering, and *to pity those weaker brethren who want capacity to comprehend the mystery of the Holy Trinity, rather than to curse and to persecute them?* Yet *Unitarianism* is solemnly declared, by a deliberative assembly of experienced statesmen, holding their consultations under a constitution of republican government, which guarantees to all who live under it, freedom of speech, of person, and of the press,—to be a *statutable offence—a felonious crime*— classed under the *same head* with *impiety, blasphemy, polytheism,* and *atheism,* and subjected to the *same infamous punishment of total and perpetual outlawry*! ! ! This is the spire that crowns the temple of our ecclesiastical establishment. Here, it would seem, the demon of superstition has fixed his encampment, drawn his entrenchments, fortified his ramparts, pointed his batteries, unfurled his banners, and proclaimed an interminable war of *persecution*.

A legislature will never be wanting to forge fetters for a people who can submit to be bound by them.—Will you submit? Have you already submitted? Are you this moment slaves to the worst despotism, which shuts us out from both heaven and earth? No!—You thought, if they ever existed, these laws were buried in the grave of bigotry; nor did you dream that they now sleep in the archieves [sic] of your government, ready to be awakened into action, whenever the emergency shall call them forth from their slumbers. Yet such is the FACT!

Whether to institute a Court of Conscience in matters of religion, and to extend its jurisdiction into the recesses of the breast, and its province into futurity, be prudent and proper; let the common sense of mankind, and the uniform experience of history decide. But whether such institutions do actually exist, and, consequently invalidate the provisions of the FEDERAL COMPACT, and derogate from the authority of that sacred charter, is a subject of judicial cognizance.

The night of ignorance, thank God, is passed away; and the sun of science dawns a new day upon the intellectual world. The darkness is vanished, under cover of which, fanaticism could rule with a rod, her disciples in the school of error. Witches and goblins are divested of their power to fascinate or intimidate; and the watery and fiery ordeals may safely be superseded by regular Courts of Justice.

Toleration, which is *merely not depriving* others of that liberty which we ourselves use in investigating their opinions, is no longer craved as a *favor:* it is demanded as a right. Denied by their legislature the acknowledgement of this and other essential and inalienable rights, the choicest boon of heaven, the people have engraven them, with their own hand, upon the record of their power, *and well know how to cause that record to be respected.*

IV. THE SYSTEM OF EDUCATION.

The system of education adopted in this State, constitutes a just cause of boast. It is fruitful of instruction. It is the informing principle of the public mind. It imparts tone and energy, wisdom and elevation to the character of the State, whilst it forms intelligent and competent citizens for the execution of all the varied functions of civil life.

Our common schools are an original and admirable institution. These reach forth to each individual of every class, the means of understanding the duties which he owes to society, and those which society owes to him. He is taught to ascertain his rank on the scale of moral, social and political being—to appreciate himself in his relative as well as absolute capacity—to perceive the principles and operations of government—and to feel the reciprocal ties of allegiance and protection.

The funds, by which these schools are established, are of competent amount; and judicious in their imposition and collection. They are partially raised by voluntary assessment, and, in part, but permanently charged upon the revenue of the State as part of its civil list. Thus, with the wisest and most magnanimous policy, we acknowledge to be among the necessary expences of government, those which confer the elements of knowledge; and we place education among the primary objects to be defrayed by the Treasury. We know the wants and admit the rights of the mind, as well as those of the person and of property; and, whilst our Courts protect the latter from assault and injury, our schools defend the former from corruption, and free it from the bondage of ignorance.

The beauty of this system of common instruction would have been unsullied and truly lovely, had not, even here, the finger of ecclesiastical intrigue been permitted to intrude, and to insinuate its poison. The handicraft of priestly cunning is always meddling with our fairest works. These schools are subject to the inspection of visiters, whose prescribed duty is to take care of the *"orthodoxy"* of the preceptor, and that he duly instil it into the minds of his pupils. The funds also are under the control and management of ecclesiastical corporations. The proceeds from the sale of a quantity of public lands were given by the legislature, for the benefit of the schools; yet, pursuing the scent of stratagem, and on its usual bent, ecclesiastical policy slides in a provision, that, on petition, these proceeds may be diverted from their original appropriation, " to the support of the ministry."+

Were these pages submitted to you, with a view to foment your passions, and inflame your prejudices, the present occasion would be seized to turn them into the tide that now sets against Yale College; and to swell the sea that rolls upon her sides. In the storm that threatens her, many are the able defenders that will crowd around her, and plant mounds before her, to repel the raging current, and rebuff its billows. Her sons are numerous; who, from gratitude and duty, will be prompt to protect their "Alma Mater," who fostered and reared them up. She tells, among her children, many great and good men, not only in our own state; but in every section of our extensive territory; she may point, with exultation, to men preeminent among the liberal professions, through the branches of science, and in the departments of State.

These honors, which she scatters with an open hand, redound to our common credit; in which we may participate with honest pride. To diffuse the light of science and the love of letters, through the circles of this wide growing empire, is our peculiar praise, and most distinguished honor.

The endowments which an enlightened munificence has granted her, are grudged by the parsimony of some, and condemned on principle by others. It is contended, that resources derived from the people, should be exclusively and faithfully devoted to the benefit of the people. No position can be assumed more just, nor argument advanced more tenable; and, fortunately, they are in point to prove the justice and expediency of encouragement to literature; for the substantial prosperity, as well as brilliant glory of a people is never so judiciously consulted, essentially promoted, and permanently secured, as by the diffusion of knowledge. It is this that gives direction and efficacy to physical force, and developes mines of riches that would otherwise lie unexplored in the bosom of society.

To give birth to literary institutions, and to nurse them with maternal care, is not only compatible with, but necessarily results from, the most expanded liberality of sentiment, in religion and in politicks. *Science is of no party, and of no sect.* She pours a stream of light, whose rays warm the heart whilst they vivify the mind. She smooths the asperity, harmonizes the discordance, brings within the circle of affection the distant members of the human family, and bind[s] them up together in bonds of union.

It is not wished to screen Yale College from censure, if she deserves it. Amend her imperfections—correct her errours—admonish her that she do so no more—if necessary, rescind her charter, and give her a better—but oh! deprive her not of life. If, indeed, this seminary, like the common schools, be polluted by priestly creeds, tests, catechisms and " orthodoxy," then it is high time for a free people to interpose, to assert their independence, and to declare that they will not subscribe to a religion of dictation; nor admit, as standard of orthodoxy, articles of faith prescribed by men and enforced by church authority; then is it high time to efface the slightest vestage, to abolish the mouldering relick, and to dispel the last lingering shadow of ecclesiastical domination. The fountain should at least be pure, that its spring-tide may send forth and spread abroad fertility and verdure.[*]

V. THE APPROPRIATION ACT.

The ruling denomination soon saw that, by one rash act, they had left their assailable points exposed, that a practicable breach had been effected in the bulwarks of ecclesiastical usurpation, and that the soldiers who had valiantly fought for victory over tyranny in every shape, and for the acquisition of equal privileges, were fast entering through the walls. How to repel the assailants, to close the breach, and to adjust a truce, or negotiate a treaty, is the question that demands the instant attention of the veterans, who still maintain the almost revolting garrison. The terms they offer are contained in the "Literature and Religion" Act, so called. These terms will probably be rejected, as they are known to be thrown out merely to pacify, to delude, and gain time; and not with any sincere desire of peace on the only tenable basis of equal and reciprocal advantages. The daily accessions of troops to

---

[*]Since the preceding remarks were written, the following *Test* has been discovered. It applies alike to Yale College, and to its medical institution

"I, A.B. being chosen [Fellow, Professor, &c. *mutatis mutandis*] of Yale College, do hereby declare, that I believe that the Assembly's Catechism and the Confession of Faith, received and established in the churches of this colony, and in this College, contain a true and just summary of the most important doctrines of the Christian religion, and that the true sense of the sacred scriptures is justly collected and summed up in those expositions. And all expositions of scripture, pretending to deduce any doctrines or positions contrary to said doctrines laid down in those composures, I believe are wrong and erroneous. And I will take all reasonable measures, and such as Christian prudence may direct, in my place and station, to *continue* and *propagate* the doctrines contained in the summaries of religion in *this College* and *transmit* them to all future successions and generations, and use the like measures *to prevent the contrary doctrines from prevailing in this Society.*

I do also consent to the rule of *Church Discipline, established* in the *ecclesiastical constitution* of the churches of this colony."

the besieging camp, desertions from the enemy, and the voluntary rising of the people, "en masse" ensure the surrender of the citadel, when the whole force must capitulate. The victors will grant such articles as may best secure the rights and redound to the honor of *both* parties.

The "Appropriation Act for the support of literature and religion" is an expiring struggle to retain power, and to appease opposition. The effect of this state stratagem has been lost upon that very numerous and flourishing class of the community, the Methodists, who are distinguished alike for their practical republicanism and for their practical christianity. They have with a noble indignation, worthy of their profession, spurned from them the poisoned cup, and escaped the snare set to entrap them. May the other denominations view that act in the same just light of political manœvre, and equally abstain from defiling hands which religion has purified, by touching the unhallowed pelf held out to tempt them. Would any sect be so unjust, selfish and mean as even to harbor a wish for support from the taxes and labors of other persuasions? Would they convert the hard earnings of the laborious poor into a source of revenue, to indulge in indolence and pamper with luxury, one of their own number? As *Christians* they must answer, that they would not.

This perversion of civil revenue to a religious establishment, makes government a pander to the church, and contradicts every principle of legislation in a free state. In a republic, consistently with its fundamental principles, there can exist no privileged orders, no favored classes, whether civil or ecclesiastical. We are all equal, should and must be equal. Whence have our legislators derived their authority to present us with such *generous donations of our own money?* Do these gentlemen pretend to deny that all power in a republick originates with & is derived from the people? And if they do not deny it, let them point us to any time when we their constituents ever authorised them, our representatives, to establish and endow, by law, one or more modes of public worship. No such epoch is known in our history, nor in the history of any independent people. Our legislators have consequently gone beyond the warrant of their commission; they have transcended their powers; they have violated their trust. They should be recalled—their credentials cancelled—and themselves dismissed.

What plea do they offer in extenuation of their conduct? That stale apology—that exploded pretext—*the Constitution.* This self-styled constitution, a discordant mass, floating in chaos, "without form and *void,*" receives such direction, shape and pressure, as the legislature may graciously please to give it; for they created it out of nothing by the word of their power, and may destroy it by the breath of their nostrils, or turn and fashion it as they WILL.

VI. THE HARTFORD CONVENTION,* AND GENERAL CONDUCT OF THIS STATE DURING THE LATE WAR.

The reproach which our delegation suffered from the " Compensation Bill"[7] was diffused through a wider circle than themselves composed; and their responsibility was weakened by the number of actors in that drama, the catastrophe of which was so scandalous to our national morals. There is yet, however, another measure whose responsibility attaches more peculiarly to our native state. The indelible stigma which that measure stamped upon our character, years may roll their flood in vain to wash away. Time cannot obliterate it. That foulest stain on our state escutcheon is the HARTFORD CONVENTION. No heraldry blazons ensigns armorial like ours. Deeds of patriotism alone can confer a new coat of arms. This Convention was suffered to engender within our very bosom, and now sits like an *Incubus* upon the breast of every virtuous citizen, who involuntarily throws to heave it off.

That we should permit to be agitated under our eyes, within the arms of our protection, and in times of actual and *portentious war*, plans of dismemberment of the empire; that we should permit whilst foreign invasion insulted our sovereignty, and trampled with impunity upon the consecrated spot of freedom, where sleep the relics of our ancestors, a band of factionists to brood in safety and *secrecy* over civil commotions; that when the nation of Europe, which, by force of arts and arms, has finally succeeded in subjugating the most warlike power on that continent, and had subsidized the physical strength and allied the moral energy of confederated Europe in her cause; that, when thus disenthralled from other wars and unincumbered with other scenes of operations, she concentrated her exhaustless resources, and poured her congregated fleets and armies upon our shores; that at an hour like this, big with a nation's fate, and black with almost the sepulchral horrours of despair, any member of this great federal empire should fail to rally round the common standard of its country—nay, more! should attempt with impious audacity to sever by the sword of civil war the gordian knot of union, and, by a parricidal stab, to palsy the paternal arm that had just strung its nerves, and was now uplift to launch the spear and extend the buckler,

---

* The Convention sat in the State-House at Hartford, December, 1814 —All their sittings were with closed doors.

[7] The 14th Congress declined to compensate those states that had refused to place their militias under federal command for their military expenses during the war.

in defence of the liberties of mankind, against the myrmidons of tyranny—that *we*, at *such a crisis*, under *such a government*, in *such a country*, from *such motives*, and for *such a cause*, should have dared to perpetrate,—Oh, unnatural and perfidious conduct! the crimes accurst of sacrilege and treason—that *we* could have had an *heart* or *mind*, or *hand*, for *such a deed*, a deathless deed of doubly-damned iniquity,—erects to our memory an imperishable monument of infamy, and deposits in the archives of the nation a record of history, in testimony against us, which overwhelms us with astonishment and confusion, and will entail opprobrium upon our latest posterity.

The only apology ingenuity has devised and effrontery offered to the public for such unprecedented violation of the duties in which we are bound by the federal compact, is, that the commissioners of this State to that convention, were positively restrained by their instructions from engaging in any project that would militate against the integrity of the union; and that these instructions were the only effectual bar to the further prosecution and final accomplishment of such designs. This apology, it is believed, is founded in truth, and carries with it proof of the treasonable nature of those designs, and of the habitual *caution* of Connecticut. But, because our phlegmatic temperament molified the sanguine complexion of any of our co-adjutors in that plot; this accidental trait in our character would scarcely seem an adequate plea to exculpate from the offence of fostering within our bosom the machinations of a conspiracy, and of polluting the sanctuary of the laws by the councils of disloyalty, or of permitting even its footsteps to be imprinted on the land of freedom.

It has been argued that the Convention have published no evidence of their guilt, and that, therefore, the presumption is of their innocence. This may be conclusive logick in their minds who are blinded by passion, but the people, cool and impartial judges of their conduct, both see and feel its fallacy. No! a confession in open court was not to have been expected, and happily for the members, no legal proof exists, or they would be prosecuted to conviction.

They have, however, by an abundant mass of presumptive, circumstancial evidence, unfolded the plan of the piece which they fondly imagined they should be able to conduct to a brilliant *denouement. The time,* the *place,* the *occasion* and the *secrecy* of the proceedings, transacted exclusively by those States which had, by other methods and in their respective legislatures, thrown down the guantlet of defiance, and almost declared open hostilities against the federal government—the terms of their invitation for the disaffected to embody—their determination to assemble again, at Boston, in the event of the war's continuance—the political and personal character of the parties concerned, and of their advisers and advocates—and, in fine, every attending circumstance—all go in demonstration of their ulterior objects, and leave not on the mind of any American the shadow of a doubt. Would to Heaven! for the honour of our country, there were a doubt, though but the shadow of a shade!

Accordant with this policy of the HARTFORD CONVENTION was the general conduct of our State during the late war. The obstacles we raised from a forced construction of the Constitution, relative to the powers which that instrument confers on the general government over the militia of the States, were merely designed to be thrown in the way of our duty, as an excuse for not pursuing it.[8] But were the constitution really indefinite or deficient, our patriotism, at least, might have obviated the difficulty; and, by an unanimous exertion, speedy victory might have crowned the war, which, for want of such exertion, was wasted out through years and blood and treasure. If in the progress of our revolution, artificial difficulties had thus been started from the real necessities of the State, what would have been the result of that glorious struggle? *What have become of our Republic?* In the late war the same duty, if not the same necessity, existed, of a common effort in a common cause.

To a clear and impartial mind, to any eye unjaundiced by party, and free from the film of prejudice, the Constitution appears on this point lucid and harmonious. It declares in express and unequivocal terms, that the federal executive shall have command over the militia, to execute the laws of the union, to suppress insurrection, and to repel invasion: He is also invested by subsequent enactment with similar powers, even when imminent danger exists.

During our late hostilities, was there not imminent danger? Was there not actual invasion? Was there not threatened insurrection? Were not the laws of the union to be executed? And was not the President, in the language of our charter, and by his oath of office, bound to provide for the common defence and general welfare? It was his imperious duty to guard that constitution as a sacred shield, our very palladium; and to execute its provisions. To accomplish this task, means were necessary. These means were ample, and designated with technical precision. But sophistry distorts, and under its subterfuges the means are filched away. The end consequently fails. Whose is the responsibility?

---

[8] The governor and Council had refused to place Connecticut's militia under federal command.

The dire and fell hostility of faction was displayed afresh, and with equal virulence as well against the cause itself in which we were embarked, as against the measures of the federal government, by the insidious influence and open denunciations employed to discourage *loans* and *enlistments*. The emergencies of government were to cry in vain for help; whilst its defenders lay slaughtered in unequal combat. The patriot who supported the faith and the arm of his country by investing his funds in her treasury, and he who enrolled his name beneath her banners resolved to expose himself a breastwork against hostile encroachments, were decried and scouted as the base slaves of mercenary interest, by the hoarders of pelf and panders of profligacy—and as apostates from religion and order, by the veriest apostles of sedition and anarchy. We had launched forth from the haven of peace, upon the untried waters of foreign conflict, our young bark deep laden with the freight of our dearest riches; and yet, there were those—strange infatuation! who, though afloat in her with all their wealth, wished her swallowed up by the Leviathan of the ocean.

Thus has been brought up from its deep and native darkness and fully developed to your view, the plan of the CONCLAVE. They marshalled their ranks in hostile array, and waged a systematick opposition against our great federate republic: they collected all their might and poured it forth in a flood, which they fondly hoped would have no ebb. They denounced the war as "*oppressive*," when it was expressly waged for the protection of our commerce and harbours, in defence of our hearths and altars, for security of our sacred rights, and in maintenance of our common liberties. They denounced it as "*unnecessary and unjust*," when the mercantile and commercial interests had long before petitioned the government to defend them from spoliations by an appeal to arms; when the sensibilities of the nation had been stung to revenge by repeated outrage and aggression, and soothed to forbearance, only by a steady pacifick policy; when by their own confession, our national character was marked with pusilanimity, and degraded in the eyes of all Europe; and when they boldly asserted, with what truth and loyalty themselves would now blush to own, that the administration could not be "*kicked*" into a war. They denounced it as "*unconstitutional*" when it had been advised by the national councils, enacted into a law of the land by the national legislature, and duly declared by the national executive—thus sanctioned and executed by the deliberative and ministerial organs designated by the *constitution*. And, finally, they denounced it as "*ruinous*," when it was undertaken in redress of our wrongs, in vindication of our rights, in furtherance of our interests; when it has eventuated in the attainment of these objects; when it has redounded to the national honour, and established a national character, supporting it on either side by a spirit of emulation, and pouring upon its crown a stream of glory; when it has dispelled the cloud that hung with heavy, ill-boding omen on the past, and renders the opening prospect of our approaching destinies beautifully brilliant; and when it has reared up, for our defenders in future wars, many brave and skilful and veteran warriors—their arm a fortress, and their name a host.

Carrying into operation their professed principles, they not only opposed this war by invective and anathema, but meant practically to frustrate the purposes it was declared to achieve, and to force it to an untimely end. This was the motive that assembled them in *conclave*, there to concert schemes, and devise means of execution. The moment which they selected to consummate their plot, was when military and financial embarrassments clogged the wheels of government, and almost stopped their motion; when defeat and disaster trode[sic] close upon our heels and threatened the destruction of this young republick; and when the capital was wrapped in flames and threw a dismal lustre that reflected with ten-fold horror, the surrounding scene. At so critical a crisis of our political existence, Oh, burning shame! we were not found with the deliverers of our country. No! we fled her ranks. We tried to shun her fate; nor dared to mingle in the strife, on whose purple current rode the buoyant Ark of Freedom. We stood afar off and saw, unmoved, the tempest beat upon that ark, nor held out a single arm to break off the buffeting of the billows. Nay, *like the Spirit of the storm*, WE REJOICED IN IT, and hoped to rule its course and empty, where we would, the phials of its fury. Yes! even then we were sowing the seeds of discord, in hope to reap the harvest of confusion.

Whither had flown our boasted submission to the laws, when we advocated and organized rebellion, and *only not executed* it for *fear*? Where was our love of religion, when we meditated a violation of our vow of allegiance? Where was our love of order, when we scattered through society the firebrands of discord? Where was our love of country, when we were about to light the torch of civil war, whose flames could feed only on the fuel of our property, and which our mingled tears and blood alone could extinguish? Where, then, were the admonitions of Washington? Where, then, the injunctions of our fathers? Where, then, the faith we plighted to hold them sacred? Where, then, the duties we had sworn to discharge towards our children and posterity?

Thanks to the patriotism of other sections of our union, the fabric of our government is still entire. Its parts are preserved and kept together by the central attraction of our interests. To this point our affections should constantly converge. Around it every state revolves concentric, whilst it moves in its appropriate sphere, and thus produces an heavenly harmony between principle and policy; but when either diverges from the common centre of union, it must be thrown convulsive from its sphere, and send forth a direful discord between our duty and our conduct, our reason and our passions. Yet we, regardless of the course we took, and violating the laws of nature and the principles of government, with unhallowed zeal, rashly essayed to pluck our orb from so beautiful a system, and to disorder all its motions.

Praised be God! The attempt proved vain. The event has not answered to the design. The mine, which was to spring the walls and to raise the foundation of our castle has been suffered to burst in the air, unfeared, whilst it has displayed in the faction that planted it, merely the futility of their power and the malignancy of their plan.

The contest is now over; the war has ceased its roaring. We can look around us with complacency. We have gained a glorious issue to our arms, and not a patriot but rejoices in their success. We all exult that the nation has passed, unshamed, through the fiery ordeal; and that it grows with firmer strength and shines with purer lustre for the trial. The American name now stands elevated and consecrated; it is a sacred passport to respect and admiration through every country of the civilized world.

Fellow Citizens,

It has thus been attempted to hold up to your eye a mirror, in which you may behold the uncouloured lineaments of truth; in which you may see the reflection of the very measures that have passed before you, in their true hue, in their native unadorned simplicity. It was fit that your attention should be drawn to this subject, and that the subject should be presented to you fully and fairly. This arduous task, it is trusted, has now been accomplished. As polititians, as Christians and as men, we can and we ought to receive admonition without offence, and learn from experience to correct our errors.

If men whom we have crowned with power, have turned that power to the promotion of sinister objects; if those whom we have appointed to office, have perverted their official functions to purposes of venality and aggrandizement; if those whom we have invested with our confidence have abused that confidence to delude us, as to the nature of their designs; if those whom we have trusted with the guardianship of our rights and liberties and laws, have betrayed that trust, and dared, by the double crime of sacrilege and treason, to offer up, on the altar of party, the sacrifice of those high immunities; what does it become us to do? What radical remedy does the disorder demand? Shall we go on showering honours and emoluments upon the heads of men who have worse than deserted us, and continue, hoodwinked and spell-bound, the willing dupes of duplicity and corruption? Or shall we not rather dismiss from our service unfaithful servants, and receive into confidence characters supported by the fair unquestioned titles of ability and merit, of unwavering firmness, of inflexible integrity, and whose rectitude has never been warped by the heat of party politicks.

This grand problem in the system of your State Politics remains to be solved by you people, at your elections.

The important inquiry which suggests itself to the minds of us all, is—where can the man be found, who unrolled in the ranks of democracy on the one hand, and uninfected with the intrigues and factious plottings of the dominant party, on the other, is a *Federalist of the old school*, who uniting capacity with character, and possessing the rare combination of profound political science with pure and ardent love of country, stands pledged before the publick, in the event of his election, to redeem the state from the evils of its past administration? Happily for our honour and interests, such a man, long known and distinguished amongst us, a veteran of the revolution, a confident of Washington, an executive officer of the federal government, the heir of the virtues and talents, as he is of the name of two former governours, in one word a patriot and a statesman, a scholar and a Christian may be found in OLIVER WOLCOTT.

It were sufficient recommendation of this gentleman, to say nothing of his long life of eminent services, that he was selected from among a multitude of illustrious competitors, the friend of "the father of his country," of Washington, a name which no American can lisp but his lips tremble in aspiration of gratitude and love—of this man, of all whose peculiar talents, the most pre-eminent was his talent to discriminate and appreciate character.

We have it now in our power to evince our gratitude and attachment to that old and venerable family—the Wolcotts, who have twice sustained the dignity of our executive chair,[9] and upheld it with decisive energy and with unveering fidelity to the public interests, with a spotless virtue and with a

---

[9] Roger Wolcott, from 1750-1754; Oliver Wolcott Sr., from 1796-1797.

splendid intelligence. The present candidate selected for that chair, is a descendent of that family. Our suffrage may elevate him, their son and worthy successor, to the seat they so ably filled. Such an act of justice would conform to that custom which we long have cherished and loved to practice, and which indeed constitutes a just source of pride and a high trait in our public character—the custom of reverencing our ancestry, and of honoring our benefactors. The very prejudices that do credit to our nature, ally themselves, in this instance, with our duty, and urge us to pursue the policy pointed out by our interests.

Why should we halt and hesitate? The path lies open and plain before us, and the voice of conscience audibly proclaims—"Walk ye in it." A hacknied objection is always started and rung in our ears, when any improvement of an established system is proposed. *"Innovation"* cry they who batten on errour, as though there were magick *in a word* to silence argument and refute conviction! Do not these sticklers for antiquated prejudices, and for established Church and State, know that *all improvement* is "innovation"? The discovery of any principle and the progress of any science are *"innovation"* upon preceding errour and ignorance. The discovery of America was an *"innovation"* in geography. The present system of philosophy is *"innovation"* upon the old system. Luther's reformation was *"innovation"* upon Papacy and the inquisition. The revolution itself, that gave us Independence, was violent *"innovation"* upon tyranny. And the RELIGION OF THE PRINCE OF PEACE, was radical *"innovation"* upon the bloody rites of Paganism. Away then with this cant about innovation—a term that is used, like the jugglers incantation, to conjure up the ghost of danger where none really exists.

Let us press forward, heedless of censure and trampling down opposition, keeping on in the way of well doing, and holding steadily in view the goal of our career. Let us correct our past errours, and continue to improve on our principles and practice. In imitation of our divine master, we will not shrink from condemning existing abuses, nor fear to enjoin reformation. We may all have deviated from the straight line of political as well as moral rectitude. If so, our duty is not repentance only, but also amendment. With firm but cautious hand, we will probe the gangrene that festers in the body politick, and introduce into it sounder flesh and more vigorous health.

If then we value freedom, and are determined to maintain it; if we are resolved to transmit it, unimpaired, to posterity, if we design to settle on foundations deep and wide, the stable edifice of our laws, that they may neither be demolished nor impaired; if we desire to secure equal rights and common privileges, and to preserve unsullied, more especially those of *election*, of *conscience*, of *education*, of a *judiciary independent within certain limits*, and all these under the guarantee of a *Constitution*; if we would wish to assert the dignity, and to establish the rank of our State, and to reinstate her in that lofty and graceful attitude she was of old accustomed to assume; if we would cease to be a dead weight in the national scales, and are sensible to the impulse that springs from patriotic emotions, and that leads to patriotic achievements; if we are impelled by an heaven-born ambition to act a part in the theatre of our country's glory, and to exert on such a stage our moral and intellectual energies; we must step forth with a promptitude not to be abashed—with courage not to be daunted. We must change the course of our measures. We must abandon a superanuated and decript system, which later experience and better information teach us to explode. We must adopt a new and nobler line of conduct. There is no time for delay. The crisis is arrived. It portends favourable auspices, if we will but seize them. Let us be of one mind and of one heart, and we are triumphant.

Are you young? Let your first and lasting love be to the country that bore you. Cherish and support that mother with filial affection. Let not the prejudices of the nursery bind your mind, more than the bandages of childhood do your body. No! Emancipate yourselves from errour, and then burst the bonds that fetter, and break open the prison-doors that confine the Land of your Nativity. Help her to recover her former health, elasticity and vigour.—She once shone proud and brilliant in the assembly of her Sister Republicks. She now depends on the gallantry of you her sons to vindicate her honor, and on your youth to revive and again display the splendour of her beauty and her intelligence.

Are you in the meridian of life? Let your actions prove your manhood. Remember you are the channel in which the waters of the past and of the future join their current: you are the point, to and from which the tide of time ebbs and flows. You are the connecting chain between your ancestry and your posterity: your Fathers and your Children fix their eyes on you. Lead forward—you shall be well supported. The troops are numerous, disciplined and veteran. The ranks are firm, and panting for the field. Behold! Already the day is won—the victory is yours.

Are you aged? The obligation imposed on you to leave the Legacy of an example and counsel that may expand the heart and enlighten the mind, tightens its cords with the growing weight of years. You would advise a Brother or a Son to open for himself a way to public confidence and fame, the architect of his own fortunes, a skillful pioneer through difficulties, and the founder of a family. By what policy then would you close against your native State, the only avenue that conducts to wealth, to happiness and to honourable distinction? No! You would not doom your children to a never dawning darkness, but kindly point their eye to where the curtains of the night are already withdrawing. You will bequeath a wise instruction: for though the snows of many a winter may have bleached your locks with their hoary frost, they have not blasted on your cheek the bloom of your spring—they have not chilled in your veins the warm blood of your summer—nor have they extinguished those fires that burn in your bosom with a glow of devotion to the Land of your HOME.

Hamilton.

"ONE OF THE PEOPLE," *CONNECTICUT COURANT*, APRIL 1 1817

The Federalist leadership of Connecticut responded to the political challenge of Servetus, Richards, and the "Tolerationists" by portraying them as political upstarts. "One of the People," appearing in Hartford's *Connecticut Courant* a week before the April 7 elections for the governor and the Council, was not the only essay taking this approach. It echoed in succinct fashion "An Old Freeman's" more discursive dismissal of the Tolerationists that had appeared a week before in the *Courant*. The Federalist refusal to take their challengers seriously had two sources: one source was the opposition nominee, Oliver Wolcott Jr.. As a former Federalist secretary of the treasury under Washington and John Adams, he seemed like one of them. The other source was the Federalist control of the Council, which did not appear in danger because of the standing their candidates held in the nomination lists following the previous September freemen's meetings.

TO THE FREEMEN OF CONNECTICUT.

YOU are again called by a certain party to change your rulers. The attack commenced about twenty years ago, and it has been repeated in almost every succeeding year. It may be well to inquire, who it is that makes this attack, what can be the object of it, and what the people can gain by it?

The leaders of the democratic band are well known: There was something about the characters of their chiefs which did not exactly suit the correct moral notions of the people of this State. These men, therefore, were not promoted according to their own ideas of their merits. They, therefore, joined that party which had proclaimed war against the administration of Washington: They were so well known, that they met with but little success in Connecticut. But when the administration of the general government went into the hands of Mr. Jefferson, most of these persons were rewarded with lucrative offices. They have ever since, as opportunity offered, been faithfully discharging of their offices, by their abuse of the rulers of our state. And while they have received three or four thousand dollars per annum for their services, they could not forget to rail at those who were in possession of those offices in the state to which they had formerly aspired. Attached to these leaders were the numerous officers of the United States, and the more numerous expectants of office. They are the same men who, a few years ago, were declaiming against banks, loans, standing-armies[,] national debts, &c. &c.[1] They are the same men who have now become the advocates and proprietors of a great national bank—who are perfectly passive, when we have a stamp-tax, a whiskey-tax, a carriage-tax, a land-tax,[2] &c. &c., and when we have a standing-army of about ten thousand men, of which seven thousand are privates and seven hundred servants or waiters—who are no more disturbed with our national debt than with the debt of Great-Britain. These men, though their minds seem to have undergone a great revolution as to the measures of the general government, still continue their opposition to the state government,—whether administered by a [Jonathan] Trumbull [Jr.], a [John] Treadwell, a [Roger] Griswold, or a [James Cotton] Smith,[3] it is still the theme of their abuse, the object at which their artillery is aimed. They assume different names, from time to time, as seems most likely to catch the unwary; but still they are the same men, and their object is the same.—That object is none other than to change the fundamental laws and constitution of the state; to overthrow our steady habits; and, (as we have great reason to believe) they intend to destroy our religious and literary institutions.

Some of their objects have been openly avowed. We have been told we had no constitution, and a convention has been by the friends of the people called upon this subject.[4] But the people of this state manifested their total disrelish for the plan, and it has been laid aside for a more convenient season. Our steady habits have been publicly reviled, and our religious and literary institutions have been held up to scorn.

[1] Measures associated with the Quasi-War against France in 1798-1800.
[2] Measures adopted during the War of 1812.
[3] Past and the present Federalist governors of the state since 1808.
[4] Events that took place in 1804 described in the Introduction.

In addition to this, these persons intend to introduce themselves and their friends into all the important offices in the state. But what are the people to gain by all this change—what did they gain by the change in the general government? They indeed found the little finger of the *republican administration* thicker than the loins of its predecessor. Commercial restrictions, succeeded by war and taxes, have thrown a gloom over our country, which years of prosperity will scarcely remove.

What are we the people to gain by a change in this state? It was declared by a famous democratic orator, before the legislature, some ten years since, that no people on earth were happier than the people of Connecticut;—here every man sat under his own vine and fig tree. What, then, are we to get by a change?—Shall we put down a government which has made us so happy, for the sake of experiment?—Shall we be more respected, or more enlightened, by destroying those religious and literary institutions which have been the pride and ornament of this state?—Or will our taxes be lightened? It has been recently shown in the papers, that the people of this state receive from the public Treasury, for the use of schools, more money per annum than they pay in upon the tax of the State.

Did such a state of things exist in the United States, what a triumphant message would our President have sent to Congress, to be dispersed through the Union. It would have formed a theme of panegyric which would never have failed. But in this state it is passed by as a matter of course. Think you, your public offices would be better filled, or justice would be better administered? Can the democratic party bring more talents, or greater integrity, into our councils? But they tell us, they are friends of federalism. We have witnesses of their friendship for the people,

"We have heard them talk of public good,

"And mean their own,"

for a long time; and they now talk, with the same sincerity, of Toleration. Let them shew how the laws of our state are intolerant. Let them tell us whether it is intolerant that every man should contribute to the support of public worship, & whether that law is intolerant, which permits him to contribute where he pleases.—This is a mere pretence, assumed when others failed. The moment the legislature shewed a desire to evince their impartiality to the several sects of christians,[5] in this state, that moment a cry was set up from those gentlemen who very decently claim to monopolize all the toleration of the state, as they formerly did all the republicanism. But in both

---

[5] The Appropriation law that was discussed by "Servetus" and Richards.

instances they were hollow-hearted. They used names which were popular, to conceal their real designs.

One thing, however, the people will gain by change: They will introduce into office men who have been the advocates of embargoes, non-intercourse acts, non-importation acts, and finally of war; men who would have marched your sons into Canada, and who would have made their fathers garrison our forts; men who have given their countenance and approbation to a system of measures which the good people of this state have constantly and generally disapproved. By introducing such men, you libel your own principles; you tread back your own steps; you counteract your own measures. And let us remember, that "he who soweth the wind will reap the whirlwind."

One of the People

EDITORIAL, *CONNECTICUT JOURNAL*, AUGUST 12, 1817

The tone of the Federalist polemic changed after the election of a Tolerationist majority to the new House of Representatives showed a majority of Connecticut's freemen favored constitutional reform. The following essay reflects growing Federalist alarm about control of the Council which depended on the nominating votes cast in the September freemen's meetings. This writer equated the Tolerationists with the radicals of the French Revolution, whom he refers to generically as "Jacobins." Many Americans believed the Jacobins had been responsible for the Terror, the de-Christianization of France, and the excesses eventuating in the military dictatorship of Napoleon Bonaparte. Although this commentary appeared in the *Connecticut Journal* of August 12, 1817, the column heading erroneously read August 21.

Consistency of principles and conduct, is as necessary to the reputation of Parties as individuals, and when either have voluntarily published professions to the world, we naturally look for conformity of practice.

Since the Jacobins of Connecticut commenced a series of desperate exertions for the ascendancy in State Government, their great object has been to convince the people, that the federalists have not only differed from *them* in point of principle, but from all wise and good men; not content with attacking their political tenets, which in practise, have so long rendered the government of Connecticut the happiest on earth—they have professed to espy a monster in the religion of their opponents, and endeavored to clothe the pretended Bugbear in the dress of Inquisitorial Persecution. *This* indeed is *consistent*, for reasoning from analogy, and experience, all attempts to revolutionize a government are hopeless, until such principles as are accordant with the religion of the Gospel, and have long been cherished by the freemen of Connecticut can be thoroughly done away.—It is an undertaking of no small magnitude, to revolutionize a government, the spirit of whose laws, and whose administration are generally acknowledged good, when that government is virtually in the hands of a people of sober habits, enlightened understandings, and correct principles.—Bonaparte probably owed more of this success, to his Emissaries, (whose business was to corrupt the people and divide the government marked for his prey) than to his arms.—Mankind are influenced only by motives, and where the motives to be held out, are manifestly *bad*, they can of course effect nothing, until those whom they are intended to influence are rendered regardless of their moral nature.—The Jacobins of Connecticut have for a long time reasoned in this manner, and for the purpose of preparing the people to relinquish all claims to whatever is in reality *dear* to them, they have begun (in conformity with the precepts and example of their Gallic Master,)[1] at the foundation. The corner stone of those pillars which support the Temple of Liberty, must be removed—THE RELIGION OF THE GOSPEL must be brought into disrepute—The strict observance of the . Sabbath must be rendered unpopular, and those foolish notions about morality and good order, so long cherished by the people of Connecticut must be given up. This is no dream, it is no fiction, but plain matter of fact. There are many Jacobins in the State who wish for this state of things, and who are making all possible exertion to bring it about—most of the writers for the Democratic Newspapers, if we may judge from their productions are of this stamp. They have commenced their operations to be sure with some degree of caution, their first attack is not an open one, made upon religion in general, the people are not yet ripe for such an event, but it is an attack made upon what they are pleased to term "one of the Religious Sects." In this they have indeed discovered no little foresight.—That portion of the Christian community who style themselves Congregationalists embraces a much greater population than all the other sects, and so slight is the shade of difference, between their peculiar tenets and those of the other principal sects, that religion once rendered odious in *them*, is in effect rendered odious in *all*.

Those people who come out against Congregationalists, in the style which every one may witness who will look into a Democratic Newspaper, and attempt to prove that "*Platformist*"[2] is synonymous with

---

[1] In other words, "French Master" and specifically Napoleon. The allusion reflects a Federalist claim that their domestic adversaries in America operated under the controlling influence of France.

[2] A reference to the Saybrook Platform of 1708, on which the Congregationalists relied in governonmg their church.

hypocrite and persecutor, are not aiming at *Congregationalists*—this is only a pretence, to conceal the real design.—To Baptists let an appeal be made for a decision—These disciples of Bonaparte profess to hold the Baptists and their religion in high estimation. The Congregationalists and Baptists agree in every thing of any importance, relating to their religious tenets, except in the ordinance of Baptism, and even in this the difference is considered so unimportant, as to render it perfectly proper for the two sects to commune together at the same table.

Now let reason and candor decide, whether an enemy to the Religion of a Congregationalist, can be a friend to that of a Baptist, seeing both are acknowledged to be the religion of the Gospel. The same reasoning will hold, in relation to Episcopalians and Methodists.—The truth is, *religion* itself is the thing aimed at, and must be rendered *odious*. This could not be done unless by stratagem, so it was thought best to attribute designs which were manifestly odious to almost the whole world, to a part of the religious community in this State, and enlist the other part in the scheme, by representing those designs as against *them*. The policy of rendering religion itself odious by applying a term of reproach to those who profess it, is by no means new; time was when *Christian* was used as tauntingly as *Platformist*, and carried with it an idea of disgrace and degradation which it is hoped will never be attached to any term, for similar reasons in Connecticut. It is hoped also, that the policy attempted will not succeed—the Christian religion in Connecticut is the foundation of all moral considerations, and of that system of education which alone has taught the people the value of their government, and their superiority in point of privilege to other States and other nations. Now let any sober man seriously decide whether such men as resort to the means adverted to, for the accomplishment of selfish political purposes, can have the good of the State at heart.

It is worthy of notice, that while the Jacobins have done every thing in their power, to increase party spirit and excite political discord, they have been unwearied in their exhortations for peace and harmony, and constant in their professions of friendship and conciliatory feelings—the boast has been that the universal principles of Toleration will speedily unite all parties. The President's tour,[3] has brought to light the true toleration spirit—If there was ever an opportunity for laying aside party feelings since that Priest of Baal, Genet,[4] came into the United States Mr. Monroe has given one.—In the result of the war, the Democracy of the General Government found the end of her career; ruin stared her votaries

---

[3] James Monroe toured New England during the summer of 1817 in an effort to heal the wounds left over from the War of 1812.

[4] Edmund Genet briefly served as French ambassador to the United Sates in 1793 before the Washington administration had him recalled because of his efforts to compromise American neutrality.

in the face, and no alternative was left but to solicit the aid of federalism—accordingly, federal principles and federal measures became the order of the day. The Genius of discord which had so long presided over the Councils of the Nations took her flight,—harmony of views and feelings was soon manifested by members from distant States, and nominally of different parties; that course of policy was resumed which had long been abandoned for the visionary schemes of Democracy, and the Nation like the prodigal son, naked, pennyless and wretched, determined at once, to return to her Constitution and the precepts of the Father of his Country, for counsel and protection.[5]

In consideration of these circumstances the federalists of Connecticut, and of New-England throughout, were disposed to a cordial union of all parties, in shewing Mr Monroe those civilities which the nature of the case demanded—who then could have *thought*, (who does not *know* that Jacobinical professions are hollow) that the Jacobins of Connecticut, whose watchword is universal toleration, harmony of feelings, &c. would not have been willing to meet their opponents half way, and bury the hatchet forever,—Such a result would well accord with the *professions* of Toleration but far different are her real principles.

Toleration Editors say that federalist and democrat are terms no longer applicable in Connecticut, it should be, the *ins* and the *outs*—here lies the grand secret of toleration policy—put *us* in office, give *us* loaves and fishes in abundance, bend the knee to *us* and worship the God which *our* hands have made, and which it shall be commanded thee to worship, and you may show civilities to Mr. Monroe or Gov. Wolcott or any body else—only let us be *in*, until you do *this*, attempt to do away party spirit as much as you please, and we will make a noise about it.

It is true that democrat is no longer applicable to a large proportion of the disaffected party; those new fangled tolerationists are Jacobins, and have no higher object in view than to pull down the present system of State Government for the sake of getting into office, and fattening on the spoils of the people.

"TO THE FREEMEN OF CONNECTICUT," *CONNECTICUT COURANT*, AUGUST 26 AND SEPTEMBER 2, 1817

The most articulate Federalist defense of Connecticut's existing system of government came from the anonymous writer of this extensive essay.

---

[5] This standard Federalist apology for their vehement and destructive opposition to the War of 1812 was not accepted by those loyal to the national administration in Washington.

To the **FREEMEN** of **CONNECTICUT**

(August 26, 1817)

IT is hoped that you will receive an address with kindness from a Freeman of the State—a plain man, who holds no public office, and who never expects to hold one, and who yet feels a strong interest in the character of its government, and the welfare of its inhabitants. His object in doing this, is not to excite the angry passions of party spirit, nor to vent reproaches which too often disgrace our political publications, and degrade our national, and, at times, our individual character. But it is, to call the earnest attention of all the friends of the State Government, without distinction of political or ecclesiastical character, to the present situation of our public affairs, that if all is right it may be confirmed, but if much is in jeopardy, measures may be adopted in time for the salvation of our government, our institutions, our peace, security and happiness.

The present leading and essential principles of our State Government were formed and adopted, as the basis of the colonial government, very early after its first settlement, viz. in 1639.[1] They were few, plain, simple, and in the truest sense elective and republican. They were afterwards incorporated into the charter which was granted by royal authority to the colony in 1662. In that instrument will be found a catalogue of the most eminent patriots, at the head of which stands the venerable name of JOHN WINTHROP,[2] the friend, the advocate, the father, of Connecticut. These great statesmen had experienced the mild and beneficent effects of the system which THE PILGRIMS had previously adopted, and, by their great and unremitted exertions its essential principles were sanctioned and established by the parent government. Those principles, contained in that charter, have been the *Magna Charta* of Connecticut, not only in her colonial, but in her independent, condition, they have carried her through times of commotion and turbulence, through the contest for independence, and have passed unshaken through the subsequent period of revolution and distress of nations, while thrones and sovereigns, states and empires, have been subverted, and conquered, drenched in blood, and enslaved. Whilst every government in Europe, and many in this country, have been shaken or overturned,[3] the free and popular system of Connecticut has remained firm and secure; and it is, at this moment, the OLDEST GOVERNMENT IN CHRISTENDOM.

This single fact furnishes abundant evidence of its wisdom and excellence. But it stands in no need of implied or collateral proof to support this

---

[1] The Fundamental Orders of 1639 initially embraced only Wethersfield, Hartford, and Windsor. See appendix 1.

[2] John Winthrop Jr., 1606-1676, secured the charter from Charles II.

[3] The allusion is to Shays's Rebellion in Massachusetts during 1786-1787 and the Whiskey Rebellion in Pennsylvania during 1794.

all-important point. It may boldly and unequivocally appeal TO ITS EFFECTS, as testimony of the most positive and convincing character.

The leading principles of the charter, I have remarked, were few and simple. They provided for the election of rulers, by the freemen, at short intervals, for a legislative body to enact laws, for the appointment of courts to administer justice and preserve the public peace, and for the common exigencies of a body politic of that description. Under this general authority, the administration of its provisions and powers commenced. The legislature, chosen from time to time, with a degree of good sense, discernment, and public spirit, which was never surpassed in any community, ancient or modern, proceeded to establish, by law, the great principles which ought to be found in all free and well regulated societies—they provided for the literary, moral, and religious instruction of all classes of the people, by the establishment of schools, churches, and the support and maintenance of teachers in literature and religion—they introduced a system of economy and frugality, in public life by the provisions of law, and in private by their own example, the beneficial effects of which are sensibly experienced to the present day. Under their system, the great body of the people have been more universally and faithfully taught, than in any other state or nation in the world. So true is this remark, that a person, born and educated in Connecticut, who possesses the common capacities of mind, and cannot read and write, would be considered a phenomenon. The great duty of instruction & of being taught, was not left by our wise and excellent ancestors to the mere option of the people. Within a few years after the first formation of the original scheme of government, for the first settlers, viz- as early as 1650, it was provided by law—*"That all parents and masters of children should, by themselves or others, teach and instruct, or cause to be taught and instructed to read the English tongue well, and to know the laws against capital offences"*—and for the neglect of this paramount duty, they were liable to a penalty. The duty of providing for religious instruction, and the support of public worship, was also the subject of positive provision of law; and to the enforcement of these laws is it owing, that the inhabitants of all classes and stations in life, have been, from the beginning, so well instructed, and so well informed. Small compensations—too small to excite avarice and ambition, but sufficiently large to satisfy disinterested patriotism—were given to public officers—a small revenue was collected in the easiest mode, and distributed in the most judicious manner—offices were open to all, and all that was required of candidates was ability, integrity, and a fair character—the highest sense of the value of civil and religious freedom was inculcated by parents, and imbibed by their children—justice was cheaply and promptly administered—the people were free, secure, industrious, frugal, contented and happy.

The system which was thus devised and adopted by our FATHERS, has been faithfully and perseveringly pursued by their SONS.—The statute-book, as well as the state of society, will justify this remark. The laws of this State are few, plain, and mild. An octavo volume of 700 pages, would probably contain all the public acts of this state, now in force. The elementary principles of government adopted in 1639 are now in force—and there has at all times existed the same love of peace, freedom, and stability—the same regard for literature, morals, and religion, the prevalence of the same economy, frugality, and simplicity of manners, and the full enjoyment of civil and religious freedom.

Much complaint has, indeed, been made within a few years, by discontented, ambitious and designing men, within the state, and by men of similar character, out of it, that this state was hostile to the national government, and for some time past, the most unremitted exertions have been made from various quarters to change, not merely the administration, but the very nature and principle of the government, on this ground. Let it be remembered, that this charge was never made against Connecticut, whilst the national government was administered by General Washington, and his friends and followers. That great man, and most exalted patriot, held this state in the highest estimation, and he took every opportunity that was proper for the purpose, to express his feelings on that subject. Connecticut was never reviled for hostility to the national government, until the administration of that government became hostile to the constitution, and dangerous to the government of the States. And even then it was not reproached because it had changed its own character. The public affairs of Connecticut have been conducted ever since Mr. Jefferson came into power, upon precisely the same principles that they were during the presidency of General Washington and Mr. Adams. It was not the rulers of this State that changed their measures—it was the administration of the United States government. Our affairs have gone on in the good old way—we have executed our laws, distributed justice, preserved the peace, supported *our* schools and our ministers, paid our taxes, and when called upon for that purpose, have defended our territory and our people against every attempt at foreign invasion, or domestic disturbance. It is not for any defect of duty in these particulars, that we are reproached and slandered. It is, because when the character of the national administration changed, we did not change with it—it is, because we did not become subservient to the views of individual ambition, aggrandizement, and usurpation—it is, because we could not violate our duty to ourselves and our State government, and become the tools of despotism, and the slaves of power. Had the government of the State been weak or wicked enough, to have sacrificed the highest interests of their constituents, the security of their people, and the independence of the State, Connecticut might have ranked as high on the scale of merit, even as that scale has been fixed and graduated by the two last national administrations,[4] as any of the members of the confederation. But they did not consider it as a part of their duty to become the mere instruments of a man or a cabinet—they meant to perform all the constitutional duties which they owed the nation, but never to degrade themselves, or their constituents, by becoming the parasites of a dangerous cabinet, or the mean engine of towering ambition. By the aid of intrigue, cunning, and the patronage which the chief magistrate of the nation possesses in such abundance, such a cabinet found means to raise up a party of men here, in whose character or talents the freemen of the State had never placed any confidence, and through their instrumentality, our statesmen, our clergy, our constitution, laws, morals, religion, manners, and republicanism,—all that was respectable, useful, venerable and sacred, have been stigmatised, reviled, and libelled. The objects which these men have had in view, could not be mistakes. The friends of the State, clearly discerned the tendency of their conduct and the objects which their measures disclosed; and they steadily maintained a firm, dignified, and patriotic course, resolved, at all hazards, to save the government and its institutions, from the attacks of all their enemies without and within. The measures they pursued were wise, prudent and efficacious. They followed the footsteps of their ancestors, and guarded the edifice which their hands had erected. CONNECTICUT HAS BEEN GOVERNED, FOR THE LAST SIXTEEN YEARS, UPON THE SAME PLAN AND COURSE OF POLICY THAT IT WAS DURING THE ADMINISTRATION OF GENERAL WASHINGTON, WHEN IT MET WITH HIS APPROBATION AND APPLAUSE, AND WITH THE ADMIRATION OF ALL GOOD MEN THROUGHOUT THE COUNTRY. In support of this remark, the statute book, and the experience of the freemen, are appealed to with confidence. The fundamental laws of the State remain essentially the same they have been for one hundred and fifty years. The laws for the support of schools and public worship, and the abstract of rights, are still in force.

---

[4] The administrations of Thomas Jefferson, 1801-1809, and James Madison, 1809-1817.

The penal code is still distinguished for its mildness and mercy, justice is cheaply and promptly administered, compensations are still low, elections are frequent, the freemen all partake in the rights of suffrage, offices are open to the whole community, taxes are light, the treasury is well regulated, the State free from debt, and the people are protected by the laws. These remarks are sufficient to shew, that it is not the character of the State, or the administration of its government, that has altered. No, it is the administration of the United States that has changed, and it is they, and their pensioners and place-men in the State, that are desirous of binding the State and its government to their own purposes; and it is because the freemen have not hitherto been disposed to resign themselves into their care and management, that they are so much slandered, and persecuted.

A new state of things has, however, occurred, and the State of Connecticut, so long the admiration of the statesman and the patriot for the wisdom of its policy, the mildness and freedom of its laws and government, the disinterestedness of its rulers, the purity of its morals, the intelligence of its inhabitants, the stability and firmness which it has manifested through the dark and tempestuous period of modern revolution, is, after the storm that desolated the nations has passed by, and the rest of the world has learned by bitter experience to shun and abhor its approach, and its effects, threatened with its tremendous visitation. Yes—to the astonishment of its foes as well as its friends, at this late period, when the administration of the national government, from the vain and pernicious character of their own measures, have been driven, with disgrace, to abandon their favourite schemes of policy, and to return to the plans of the federalists whom they have so often, and for so many years, ridiculed and reviled, and thus impliedly to acknowledge their own folly and wickedness, and to subscribe with their own hands to the wisdom and integrity of the men whom they have calumniated, this State is invited to the same destructive course. It is now claimed by the parasites and office-holders of the national government, within this State, that Connecticut is at last revolutionized, has renounced her former errors, and returned to the bosom of the national administration. If this boasting be well founded, it would be well for the freemen of the state to pause for a moment and consider where they are, and where they will shortly be, by this so important a change in her condition. Connecticut never departed from the national administration. While they pursued the policy of Washington, and kept within the letter and spirit of the constitution, there was no want of harmony between them. The administration departed from their duty, and the great interests of the country, and that created the division which existed. Now the Administration have returned from their wanderings to the Washingtonian policy—now they appear disposed to execute the government according to the spirit and letter of the constitution. Connecticut does not stand aloof from the national government. They have returned to their duty, and they have found Connecticut where they left her—administering her own government according to its primitive principles, and maintaining the rights, and freedom, and supporting the measures, the laws, and the institutions, which have descended unimpaired from the days of the illustrious WINTHROP, and which are still in force.

Still, a change in our affairs has taken place—a new era has occurred—the last General Assembly shewed a state of things never before realized—and the state is threatened not only with a change of character, but, what is of inconceivably more importance, with the loss of its ancient and venerable government. It therefore becomes necessary to enquire,

1. *By whom this change has been effected?*
2. *What means have been used for the purpose?*
3. *What will be its effects if suffered to be completed.*

1. *By whom has this change, so far as it has taken place, been affected?* On this subject it is not expedient to be squeamish. The cause is of too much importance to be sacrificed by the exercise of such a spirit. Men in the pay of the United States, Collectors of Revenue, Marshals, Clerks, and Attornies of the general government, and others of the same general character, are the men who have brought it to pass. Who are these men? We all know *who they are not*. They are not the friends of the liberty, independence, prosperity, and happiness, of the state. They are not the men who support the laws, government, and institutions of the state. They are not the men who have maintained the rights and privileges of the state, or of its freemen, in the hour of danger and trial——they are not men whom an honest discerning man would make executors of his estate, or guardians of the education and morals of his children. But who are they? They are jointly and severally officers of the national government, and, of course, the place-men of the national executive; they enjoy large incomes from the national revenue, and have grown rich, haughty, and luxurious, under the wealth which they have drawn in the worst of times, from the labour and property of the farmers, mechanics, and people at large of the country. When these men were appointed to the offices which they now hold, they were in poor and strait-

ened circumstances—not one of them had talents or character enough to gain more than a scanty living by his profession. Not one of them, by the force of his own merit, or abilities, could have gained the confidence of the freemen of the state, so far as to have received from their gift any important office of honour or profit. Now, nearly all of them are wallowing in wealth, and are able to live at an expense, which, a few short years ago, they could not have supported by any honest means in their power. These men have been the friends of the national administration, while that was the adversary of the state of Connecticut. But is this any good reason why the freemen of this state, out of whose hard earnings a proportion of this wealth and prodigality have been obtained, should go on still further, and enable them, as an additional gratification, to overturn their government? Can any of these men, or of the long list of postmasters, assessors, collectors, &c. &c. who are confederate with them, in their attempts to destroy our government, mention a single act or deed which they or either of them have done or performed for the benefit of the state, or its inhabitants? They are one and all challenged to the task. On the contrary, have not all their speeches and all their writings, for many years past, been filled with the foulest reproaches, slanders, and falsehoods, against the character of the state, its government, laws, morals and religion, and of its best, wisest, and most virtuous and public spirited citizens? Is the government of the state to be given up to ruin at the call of men of such a description as these?

(September 2, 1817)

2. *What are the means that have been used for the purpose?* It cannot be expected that in the compass of such an address as this, a thorough detail can be given. The answer to the enquiry must necessarily be general and confined to few subjects.

One ground of complaint has been, the course pursued by the State government in the late war, relative to the militia. As that course was, for several successive years, a subject of examination by the people of the state, and as it received from several successive legislatures their strong and unequivocal approbation, it would seem as if it could not be necessary, at this late period, to go into a vindication of it. Let it be borne in mind, that the State never refused to order out their militia to defend the state when it was in danger. But the state did refuse to yield up their militia to the president of the U. States, to be placed under the command of U. States officers, and turned into, and subjected to all the hardships, and severe sufferings of regular soldiers—they never refused to answer a constitutional call, but they did refuse to submit to an arbitrary and unconstitutional one. The state never prohibited any one of its citizens, who was disposed to join the forces of the nation, from entering their service. The friends of the war in the state were perfectly at liberty, if they had been so disposed, to have volunteered in the service of their country, to have fought her battles, and exposed themselves to as much danger, and gained as much glory, as their hearts desired. If they did not go into that service, encounter that danger, and acquire that glory, it could not have been owing to the state authority—it must have been the object of their own unbiased choice. But, surely, this ground for revolutionizing the state, cannot be admitted by the great body of the militia. Those free and independent inhabitants of the State, and owners of its soil, can never reproach their rulers with that firm and noble act, by which they were saved from hardships, and from degradation, from being dragged from their families and their homes, to carry on a war of invasion amidst the frosts of Canada, or the swamps of the south and the west. Do our militia regret that they were preserved from the fate of [William] Hull and [James]Winchester, of [John] Chandler, [William H.] Winder, and [C. G.] Boerstler; that they were held back from the command of [Henry] Dearborn, [Morgan] Lewis, and [James]Wilkinson, or that they were protected from the sanguinary code of the regular army?[5]

But a different cause of complaint, and of resolution, has been discovered within a couple of years, which seems to have been urged with an unexpected degree of force and success, in this extraordinary attempt to destroy the state—I allude to the magic word "*TOLERATION.*" Yes, without one single legal obstacle in the way of any class or denomination of christians, either in the acquisition of wealth, the attainment of office, or the gratification of ambition—without one shackle upon the mind, or one ligature upon the conscience, it has been discovered, by some profound searcher after political mischief, that somewhere in our system there exists a rigid and unfeeling intolerance. Let the enquiry be put to any one of these reformers of government. Pray Mr. Alexander Wolcott, or Mr. Abraham Bishop, are you not at liberty to worship God in the way which your judgment dictates, or your conscience approves?[6]

If either of you should prefer the episcopal, the baptist, the methodist, or the universal mode of worship & confession of faith, to the congregational, do not the laws make abundant provision for you to pursue your wish-

[5] U.S. Army officers who were involved in the most notable military failures of the War of 1812.
[6] Republican leaders and federal office holders in Connecticut

es, and obtain the object of your choice? Is there any legal disqualification to your holding any office in the state government, to which the freemen might, if they were disposed, elect you, except, indeed, that you hold offices under the United States, and even that might be removed by resignation? If either of you should be desirous of changing from the denomination of christians to which you now nominally belong, & to join another more consonant to your wishes, are you not at perfect liberty to do it? Where then is there to be found either civil or religious intolerance? Surely it will be difficult to say, so long as the laws equally protect all classes, while the avenues to office are equally open to all, and every man may worship in the mode most agreeable to his conscience, or even his whims.

But it seems to be supposed, that one particular class of christians, and that a very respectable one, labour under some hardships of this sort, and on that supposition a perfect phenomenon exists, viz. that of professed presbyterians, baptists, and methodists, and above all, democrats, are full of anxiety, and full of sympathy, for the hardship of the episcopalians. Let the eldest, most intelligent, and pious episcopalians be enquired of on this subject, and see if they will complain of intolerance? Let the aged and venerable [William Samuel] JOHNSON, over whose sacred head the last half score years of a century are now fleeting, whose eyes almost see without the veil which separated him from, and whose ears almost hear the songs which are chaunted in, the celestial regions, whether through his long life he has endured the pangs of intolerance from the government of his native state? Ask the present Lieut. Governour, the Speaker of the House of Representatives, two or three members of the Council, and others to whom offices have been recently offered, and rejected, whether they are conscious of any intolerance? And if they, one and all, answer as they must, and as they will cheerfully, in the negative, let the enigma of the extreme solicitude of the various descriptions of persons above-mentioned be solved by whom it may. It is an insult to common sense to pretend that there is any want of toleration in this state, unless it may be the *toleration of vice and immorality.* Yet, strange as it may seem, *"Toleration"* has had seemingly more agency in throwing the state into confusion, and endangering its government, than all other causes put together. Yes, Abraham Bishop, and Alexander Wolcott, and men like these, have discovered that, which has escaped the searching eye of the great *Johnson* for almost a hundred years. And can it be thought the firm, enlightened, and high minded freemen of this state will yield up all that is valuable and venerable in their government, at such an undefined, unfounded, and ridiculous pretence, as this? Will they leave the rich inheritance derived from their ancestors, for such a jack-a-lanthorn as these restless, designing, and vindictive men have set up? Before they come to so pernicious a conclusion, let us, for a moment, attend—

3. *To the consequences that will inevitably follow a revolution in the State Government.*

It may, however, be necessary, for a moment, to make a preliminary enquiry viz. *What reasons have we for believing that the democratic party, should they gain the ascendency in the State, will go the length of producing a revolution?* This is an important point in the case—because, if there is no probability that a revolution will take place when they are able to command all branches of the legislature, it would be wasting time to discuss the question— *what will be its probable consequences?*

For twenty years past, there has been a constant effort, sometimes more secret and concealed, but generally open and avowed, to obtain the supremacy in the state, for the purpose of changing the form, as well as the character, of the government. In pursuing this object, all the arts of intrigue, falsehood, fraud, calumny, and misrepresentation, have been resorted to from year to year, and from day to day. Their newspaper publications, their pamphlets, and orations, their conversations and speeches, have all held the language, that the state was without a constitution, and a number of years since,[7] a formal meeting was held at New-Haven, composed of delegates from the different towns in the state, by the adherents of the party whose open and avowed object was, to take measures to procure a new constitution for the state, and the result of whose proceedings was, the drawing up the form of such an instrument, which they published for the consideration of the freemen. This event cannot be forgotten by any person who was then of a sufficient age to have noticed the passing occurrences of the times; and it affords the most unequivocal and decisive evidence of the fact, that nothing short of a revolution has ever been in view by these men, who have so long disturbed the peace and harmony of the state. And it should be remembered, that the same men who now cry out aloud for "*Toleration*" are the same men who then clamoured with equal noise *for a constitution.* The office-holders under the U. States, who are so deeply oppressed by *Intolerance*, were then just as much so for the want of a constitution. Again, let resort be had to the general and undeviating course of their news-paper publications, from the days of the renowned "Cassius," to the present time, and it will appear,

[7] In 1804.

that the character of the State Government has been the theme of their uninterrupted abuse. Sometimes the Governour, but more frequently the Council, have been loaded with every vile term of reproach. This has been the course pursued for so many years by men, calling themselves exclusive republicans, relative to a government more emphatically republican, than any other on the globe. If a free and popular government is what these restless demagogues are after, can they not be satisfied with one in which the chief magistrates, and one legislative house, are chose annually by the whole body of freemen, and the other legislative house is elected half-yearly, in the several towns—where every judicial officer in the government is elected annually by the concurring votes of both houses of assembly, and where the governor has no negative, except the vote he can give upon an equal division of the council, as a member, *ex officio*, of that body?

Once more—their conduct at the last session of the general assembly proves, most conclusively, that it is *revolution*, not '*Toleration*' that they are in pursuit of. For the first time, at the last May session, they claimed a majority in the house of representatives, and were able to carry such measures as they might choose through that body. As might have been naturally expected, they would excite great attention to their proceedings, especially on the great subject of "*Toleration*," by virtue of which they had gone such lengths towards overturning the government of the state. The Governour, who had been elevated to his office by their exertions, for the great purpose of aiding them in their efforts towards the accomplishment of so important an object as the overthrow of ecclesiastical tyranny, and the establishment of religious freedom, and "*Toleration*," alluded so directly to the subject in his speech, as to give them a fair opportunity to refer the matter to a committee, and in that way to obtain a *report* which should thoroughly expose the existing evils, and prepare for them an efficacious remedy. Accordingly a committee from both houses was appointed, and that part of the speech which related to ecclesiastical affairs was referred to their consideration. The chairman of that committee was an episcopal member of the council, and as the grievances which were claimed to exist have been all along stated to have a more immediate relation to that class of christians than any other, it was certain that if such grievances did exist, they could not possibly have escaped the attention of a gentleman of his accuteness and observation. There were also several thorough-going members of the '*Toleration party*' on the committee, on whom the task would naturally devolve of bringing before the assembly, and the world, the hardships experienced from the severity of our laws on the subject of ecclesiastical affairs, especially as they had themselves made that severity the prime cause of an attempt to change the whole character of the government. But, strange to tell, all their researches and investigation ended *in smoke*. The bill reported by that committee, which was afterwards passed by both houses, and has become a law of the state, contained nothing of any importance on this *great* subject, except a provision THAT CERTIFICATES OF PERSONS GOING FROM ONE DENOMINATION OF CHRISTIANS TO ANOTHER, INSTEAD OF BEING LODGED WITH THE CLERKS OF THE SOCIETIES, AS THE LAW FORMERLY REQUIRED, SHOULD HEREAFTER BE LEFT WITH THE TOWN CLERKS!!! On this ground, then, it thus appears, has rested all the uproar that has been made in this state on the subject of *"Toleration"* and for the purpose, it would seem, of changing these certificates from the office of society clerk where they could with far greater ease have been left, to that of town clerk, which is much more inconvenient to the parties, has the very government of this state, now almost two hundred years old, been put in jeopardy?

Can any rational man believe that this has been the real object in view with these designing & bad men, in all their clamours for *"Toleration?"* It is impossible—and their conduct at the assembly, in other particulars, shews that it was not. No—the *"Toleration"* that they were after was *to turn the old tried and approved magistrates and public officers out of their places, and to get themselves in their room.* How often have we been told by them of the enormous increase of offices, particularly Justices of the Peace, *and yet these very men,* who bro't the charge of multiplying them so enormously against the men who have heretofore administered the government, *made nearly one hundred new Justices during the last session.* It is *office,* and not *"Toleration,"* that these men are in pursuit of, and despairing of obtaining their ends, while the old government, and its faithful and upright administrators remain, they would sacrifice the former, to get rid of the latter, expecting in that way to obtain their end. This is not clearly avowed—*"Toleration"* is still impudently called for—but, in private conversation, individuals or the confederated band, are less reserved, and more frankly avow their real object.

What then, to resume the 3d subject of enquiry, will be the effects of a revolution in this State?

We have been so much accustomed, in the last twenty years, to hear and to talk of revolutions in states, nations, and empires, we have been so familiarized to the overthrow of republics, the destruction of kingdoms, and the pulling down and setting up of governments, that we have not only ceased to wonder at such events, but, for a long time, we looked for them almost as a matter of course. God be praised! that period has passed by—the great spirit of revolution is crushed, and the world is settled down in peace and security, with abundant leisure to reflect on its folly and its sufferings, and to form future plans of prosperity and happiness. But, with whatever feelings we may regard revolutions abroad, we can never be indifferent to one at home. Here is all that we regard in this world—here are our fathers and mothers, our wives and children, our brothers and sisters, our neighbors and friends—and here is that happy, that unexampled state of domestic peace and virtue, of civil and religious freedom, of equal rights and enjoyments, which has been so long and so justly admired by all good men. A REVOLUTION WILL, IN THE FIRST PLACE, DESTROY OUR PRESENT TRULY EXCELLENT AND VENERABLE GOVERNMENT. This government possesses all the essential qualities that are requisite for the security and happiness of the people. It has been tried and proved. A new constitution will put all things afloat on the ocean of visionary experiment. Remember that the object is not to obtain a better government for the people at large than the present, but it is, to obtain one that will better answer the sinister purposes of those persons to whom I have so frequently alluded. Instead, then, of our present truly popular and republican system, we must expect one more aristocratic, and more nearly conformed to the monarchical plan—that is, a governour to form a distinct independent branch of the legislature, a senate, probably like many of the professed republican states, for three or four years—the state divided into districts, and each district to become, of course, the theatre for demagogues to display their talents, and to carry on their frauds and intrigues—judges and justices appointed, instead of [by] the General Assembly, by the Executive according to his whims, passions or resentments, or perhaps, like those of a neighboring state, by a council of appointment.[8] With this, we must look for the abrogation of all laws for the promotion and support of schools for public instruction, and for public worship, and for the suppression of vice and immorality—for it must be borne in mind, that it does not comport with the notions of modern "*Tolerationists*" to discourage vice, or cherish virtue and piety. The funds of the state will be exposed to similar evils—and it is to be expected to form a material part of the new system, that the GREAT FUND established with so much wisdom and liberality, by the freemen, and cherished with so much care and anxiety by

[8] New York.

the legislature, for the support of common schools, shall be dissipated, *or turned to objects, in their view, of more importance.*

Besides, what is, if possible, of as much importance as all of them put together, the habits of peace, freedom, reverence for the laws, morals, and religion, and the state of peaceful equality, frugality, and virtue, will be necessarily broken up and destroyed, and all that good and great men have taught, and the people have learned and experienced, for nearly two centuries, will be annihilated, and their places supplied by turbulence, intrigue, disquiet, discontent, and profligacy. This is no imaginary picture. The experience of ages will verify it. Nothing is more fatal to the peace, prosperity and happiness of a people, than to change, by violence, all their regular well-formed habits and manners.

My fellow citizens, when we look back upon the long line of the fathers of this State and Colony—when we call to remembrance the names, the deeds, and the virtues, of the Winthropes, the Wolcotts, the Trumbulls, of Ellsworth, Griswold, and [Chauncey] Goodrich, and a numerous of band others who have contributed so much to the welfare, the prosperity, the happiness, and the dignity of the people—when we place before our eyes the monuments of their wisdom, integrity and patriotism, manifested in our statutes, our schools, our college, our churches, our manners, morals, and general state of society, and place in contrast with them almost all else that exists in established society; and above all when we compare these names of renown, of respect, of national gratitude and reverence, with those of the men who are now threatening all the blessings which we enjoy, and have good reason, under the smiles of Providence, to anticipate for the future, if we preserve our government, can we be indifferent to the present state of our affairs? The administration of our State Government has hitherto been conducted upon the same general principles, which governed the great men who have preceded those now in power, and has only been changed in such degrees, as the lapse of time, and the changes of manners, has rendered expedient from time to time. Is all this to be bartered, or thrown away, and a state of things to be created by us, which will prove as fruitful in unhappiness and mischief, as the present is of comfort and advantage: Ponder, seriously ponder, this subject. It is worthy of all your attention, and of all your exertions. On the fate of the approaching freemen's meeting depends, under God, the fate of the State and its government. If the present federal nomination shall be chosen, the revolution cannot be effected. If it is lost, if the State shall be lamely surrendered to the management of men, destitute of talents, and of patriotism, foes to their own state, and pensioners of another government, all the goodly fabric of our political system, planned by the most profound wisdom, built by the most consummate skill and integrity, and protected and defended by the most resolute and invincible courage and fortitude, will be overthrown and destroyed, and this once happy, and delightful State, will become the theatre of intrigue, corruption, and political discord and misery.

REFLECT ON THIS SUBJECT—AND BY THE CONSIDERATION OF YOUR COUNTRY, YOUR FAMILIES, YOUR CONSCIENCES, AND YOUR AWFUL FUTURE RESPONSIBILITY TO YOUR GOD, ACT WITH VIGOUR, WITH RESOLUTION, AND WITH UNANIMITY.

"SOBER SENSE," *CONNECTICUT COURANT,* AUGUST 26, 1817

In contrast to "One of the People" on April 1, this panegyric to the state's traditions by "Sober Sense" invoked nostalgia to resist change.

STEADY HABITS.

THE steady habits of New-England, and particularly of Connecticut, have been, and still are, a subject of eulogy, with many, and with other many, a theme of perpetual ridicule, sneer, and reproach.—Hence, it is well worth while, especially at the present momentous crisis, to review their origin and their nature.

The peculiar habits by which New-England, or a great part of it, has, for almost two centuries, been distinguished, originated in her literary, moral, and religious institutions.

Within ten years from the first settlement of Massachusetts, the colonists founded a college at Cambridge. In the result of a synod, 1679, are these words. "When New-England was poor, and we were but few by number, there was a spirit to encourage learning, *and the college was full of students.*"

Shortly after Cambridge College[1] was founded, companies of adventurers, emigrating from Massachusetts, laid the foundations of New-Haven and Hartford.

New-Haven, and the Hartford district that took the name of Connecticut, not being able to erect a college, contributed to the support of that at Cambridge, and educated their sons there. Frequent contributions were made for that purpose, and money sometimes was paid from the public treasuries.

---

[1] Now Harvard University.

In 1644, by order of the General Court, and for the encouragement of literature, a contribution was made, and thereafter yearly made, for the support of such scholars at Cambridge college, whose parents were needy.

Very early in the New-Haven and Connecticut settlement, every town, consisting of 50 families, was obliged by the laws to maintain a good school, in which reading and writing should be well taught: and in every county town, a grammar school was instituted. Large tracts of land were given and appropriated by the legislature, to afford them a permanent support.

In 1659, the legislature instituted a grammar school at New-Haven, which grew up into the present university. The sum of forty pounds annually was ordered to be paid out of the public treasury for its support; and the sum of one hundred more was also appropriated for the purchasing of books for the school.

By all these means, knowledge was early diffused among the people of all ranks. There were very few comparatively, even of the first rising generations, but were learnt to read at least. For the select-men of every town were obliged by law, to keep a vigilant eye upon all the inhabitants and to take care that all the heads of families should instruct their children and *servants* to read the English tongue well.*

Turn we now to certain early institutions and enactments in this section of the country with respect to morality and religion.

The late governor Sullivan,[2] in his history of the Province of Maine, has the excellent observations following:—"From the histories of all countries and governments, this great truth is firmly established, that the political happiness of a people will be always commensurate with their virtue and morality; and that public schools, academies and colleges, aided by teachers of piety, religion and morality, are necessary, to give efficacy to the civil institutions of a free country."

Such sentiments as these, animated the first settlers of New England, and have continued more or less to animate their descendants, all along throughout so many ages and generations.

By one of the primitive enactments of the government of Connecticut, the select-men of every town were authorised and enjoined to take care that every family should be furnished with the bible, and that the parents, or heads of families, should, once every week instruct their children and servants in the principles of religion.

In New England, the employment of teaching children and youth has ever been held in honour; and some of its most distinguished statesmen,

---

*The foregoing facts are gathered from Dr. Belknap's history of New-Hampshire, and Dr. Trumbull's history of Connecticut—mostly from the latter.

[2] James Sullivan, subsequently governor of Massachusetts between 1807 and 1808.

after finishing their public education were first employed as village schoolmasters.

Throughout most of New England, and particularly in Connecticut from its primitive settlement, the school house, or academy, has been found in close neighbourhood and affinity with the house of worship. The ministers of our holy religion, generally and with very few exceptions, have regarded it as a part of their parochial duties, to promote literature as well as christian morals in their respective parishes. Between them and respectable teachers of schools, there has been commonly an intercourse of familiar friendship. They visit the schools; advise with the instructors; inspect the manners and morals, and the proficiency of the pupils; bestow encouragement on dawning genius; and by their aids, many a poor and obscure child, of promising parts, has been enabled to obtain an education, and to become of eminent usefulness to the public.

The eye of the passing stranger is presented with a singular aspect of country. Every few miles, he beholds a school house here, a meeting house there, and near by the mansion of the minister, where, if he alight, and enter in, he meets with a hearty welcome, is hospitably regaled, sees around him the marks of competence and of considerable elegance—and all from an income of four or five hundred dollars a year, or perhaps less!

Out of the state of things, of which I have given but an imperfect sketch, there have risen certain peculiarities of feeling, of sentiment, and of habit. Particularly,

1. An inquisitiveness of disposition after information; which, when it meets with the way-faring stranger, is apt, with some honest-meaning men and women, to be carried to improper lengths.

2. A more prevailing taste for reading, and especially for religious reading, than is found in the other sections of this country, or perhaps in any other part of the world except Scotland.

3. A general acquaintance, among the people of all classes, with the contents of the Holy Bible.

4. A great reckoning of the higher branches of scholastic learning, and peradventure, in parents in but small circumstances, a desire too general and too ardent, to bestow upon their sons a collegiate, and upon their daughters an academical education.

5. A high respect to the christian ministers as such, and a great respect to the able and faithful instructors of youth.

6. A decorous observance of the Sabbath, not only in the time of public worship, but throughout the day.

7. A love of order, and submission to the laws.

8. An utter and universal abhorrence of deciding private quarrels by the *Duel*; insomuch that it would disgrace and ruin, with the people, even the greatest or the most popular character, to be known to have given or accepted a challenge.

Now if these, and other similar peculiarities of character, are all or any of them, worth preserving, it is a clear point, that the only way of preserving them, is by supporting the institutions from which they originated, and with which they are intimately connected.

Most people are very little aware, how delicate is the task of altering for the better political establishments which long experience has tested to be good in the main. If it require talent to frame a good government for a free people, it requires, perhaps, greater talent *judiciously* to alter one that has had a very long trial and been found, excellent as to generals, though deemed defective in certain particulars. Because "the several provisions of which it is composed are so intimately connected with each other, that it is always difficult to determine what effect would be produced in the operation of the whole structure by an alteration of some of its parts." Never be this arduous work committed to the men, who for a long series of years have scoffed, as well at the institutions as the steady habits of Old Connecticut! *No never.* Against that profanation rise up, ye hoary heads, ye flowering youth, ye freemen of all ages and descriptions, in whose patriotic bosoms is a glowing desire to perpetuate the prosperity, the virtues, and the true honour of your native state.
Sober Sense.

"STATE CONSTITUTION AGAIN," HARTFORD *TIMES*, FEBRUARY 3, 1818

The Federalist dominated Council had agreed to the repeal of the Stand-up law during the October, 1817 legislative session because they recognized it was doing them more harm than good. The Tolerationists were heartened by the development and on February 3, 1818, an editorial in the Hartford *Times* urged the town of Hartford to take the lead in mobilizing the people to draft a new constitution. Eventually more than thirty Connecticut towns passed resolutions urging that a constitutional convention be called. This editorial argues that a constitution was

essential to provide against the abuses Federalist critics alleged would accompany any change in the state's political system. By doing so it blunted some Federalist objections to reform.

State Constitution—again.—Whilst this important subject, which is the principal, and ought to be the first object of reformation in the State, as it is the basis upon which all others must depend, seems to be justly appreciated, and to have excited a prompt attention, in almost every section, it is observed with regret, that in this county, which ought to be behind no other in a devotion to principle, and the best interests of the State, it has been attended to, as yet, in one town only. When we consider the high character for republicanism, which many towns have so long and so justly sustained, we are at a loss to account for this seeming apathy and indifference of the republicans of this country, upon a subject so important in itself, and which has so long been regarded, politically speaking, as the final goal and consummation of their plans and their wishes.

Perhaps the other towns are waiting for Hartford to set them an example. Whether this is or is not the case, we would, with much deference, beg leave to suggest to our citizens the expediency of a public meeting being held to take this subject into consideration. This is no party question; neither is it a question involving only views of a temporary policy. It is not confined in its effects to the present time, nor to the present age. Should it be supposed by any one, that now it might be for the interests of the republicans, as a *party*, to suffer the government to remain as it is, would it be wise, to say nothing of the inconsistency of such a course, for so unworthy a consideration, to neglect so favourable an opportunity—one which has never before, and which, perhaps, may never again occur, to provide for ourselves and posterity the only efficient security of our civil and religious rights? It is or it is not expedient to act upon this subject. If it is, then we think there can be no reasons why *this town* should remain silent, or affect a fastidious scrupulosity. Or will it be said that the capital of the State ought to *receive*, rather than to *give* a tone to the public mind?

The principal question, "the expediency of forming a written constitution of civil government for the State of Connecticut," is to be considered either in the abstract, or with reference to time and circumstances.

There are, we believe, no class of republicans, who consider that it is not necessary and proper for the State of Connecticut to adopt a written constitution. This is not only necessary to prescribe a rule, and define the character of the government of the State, whereby the rights of *individuals* may be recognized and secured, but it is also necessary, from federal principles, or considerations growing out of the constitution of the United States, to provide for enforcing the obligations, and guarding the rights of the *State*. The constitution of the U. States defines and recognizes certain rights, as belonging to the States, considered as corporations, and at the same time subjects them, in their corporate capacity, to certain obligations.

From this consideration it was perceived necessary, that each State should have a fit and proper constitution of government; and from hence, that article which provides that congress *"shall guarantee unto each State a Republican Constitution of Civil Government."*

But not to pursue this enquiry, as that would extend our views to a limit not intended; it may be supposed that there is not much diversity of opinion upon this question. All republicans, we believe, must be sensible, from the unique and strange spectacle which this State exhibited during the war, of the necessity of a written constitution, which may tend to check the unhallowed and mischievous views of faction, and to keep our rulers, to whatever party they may belong, within the pale of their duty.

The principle question, therefore, being disposed of; the only remaining enquiry is, whether the present is a *fit time* to act upon this subject. There is, probably, considerable diversity of opinion upon this point. We will, therefore, notice cursorily, some considerations, why we deem the present not only a proper time, but probably the *most favorable* time which will ever be presented.

Recent events have produced in this state a sort of political *chasm* in the government. It is now universally admitted, that the republican party comprise a large and decided majority in the State. Yet the government is still essentially in the hands of the federalists. This state of things cannot continue. The Republicans must & will go into power. Under these circumstances, then, it behoves the *people* to consider whether there will not be likely to be difficulty after a new set of men have taken possession of government, and entered into the enjoyment of the *"loaves"* of office.

It would be folly and weakness to suppose that there is essential difference in men. If there is no difference in principle, between the two parties in the State, then it is of little consequence to the people which is in power. The same condition and circumstances will generally produce the same effects upon all men.—This may be considered not only as an axiom in politics, but a rule which will hold good in most concerns in life. Now it is well known, that from the peculiar character and policy of our government hitherto, whilst in the hands of federalists, the subject of a constitution has met with a uniform and zealous opposition from the men in power, and all the office holders in the State. It has always happened heretofore, that there has been in the Legislature such a number of Judges and Justices of the Peace, as to give a decided tone to the House.

These men, and all other office holders in the State, have always been opposed to any change; and for very obvious reasons. Now the adoption of a constitution would be the greatest change, as it respects men in office, that could ever occur. It will be a revolution with respect to them, however tranquil the public mind may be. We all know very well, the sensibility which the federalists in place have felt upon this subject; they have even interdicted its discussion. They have laboured with a zeal and industry worthy of a better cause, to excite alarm; which they succeeded in doing to such an extent, as to distort every feature of society.

When we consider these things, and the known character of human nature, does it not appear that when a new class of men come in to power, that they will be likely to become subject to the same feelings as their predecessors? Is there not reason to fear that the men in place will be opposed to so great a revolution as will vacate all existing offices? Is there no reason to fear that the influence of the Judges of the Courts, and of Probate, Justices of the Peace, and other officers of the government, all of whom are eligible as members of the Legislature, will, as it has heretofore, give a decided tone to legislation?

If there is any weight in these considerations, then there is a necessity of forming a Constitution, before we form an Administration of Government. Let us not place our friends in the awkward and exposed situation in which our opponents have been; commissioned to perform official duties without knowing what those duties were; without any rule to regulate their conduct; exposed to the veering gales of party feeling; the unsteadiness of passion, the allurements of interest, and the abberrations of their own will.

"Constitution," I-IV, *Columbian Register*
February 28- March 21, 1818

These four short essays on the importance of a properly framed and ratified constitution appeared in the *Columbian Register* between February 28 and March 21, 1818 under the penname "One of the People." They followed another five-part

series with the same title, but using the penname "Reform," that appeared in the *American Mercury* between January 6 and March 10, 1818 and deployed similar arguments, though not as succinctly.

CONSTITUTION No. I. (FEBRUARY 28)

This important subject seems to engage the general attention of the public, divested of party feelings, and party prejudices.—It claims the deliberate attention of the understanding;—its vast importance forbids the mixture of passion in its investigation.—It is the grand foundation of civil society.—No nation or state can attain any degree of perfection or happiness, or fulfil the design of their association without a Constitution. Man is by nature free and independent, and all men possess equal rights; but in the progress of civilized society, it becomes necessary to give up or surrender some of our natural rights, in order to secure the quiet and peaceable possession of others—But these rights will not, and ought not to be surrendered for the benefit of the community, without receiving an equivalent. The formation of society, and the establishment of government, becomes then of necessity a matter of contract—for it will not be claimed, that any man or body of men have by nature a right to govern, or control others. This right can only be acquired by force, or the consent of the governed. Usurpation of power is abhorrent to our natures, and particularly to our feelings and habits. No other legitimate source of the power of governing is recognized in this country, but by express delegation. If this position be true, rulers can have no power except what is entrusted to them by the people—who certainly in their individual and corporate capacity, possess the power of self government.

It follows then conclusively, that the power of rulers must be in some degree limited—and it is of vital importance to the community, that these powers be clearly defined, that both rulers and ruled should distinctly understand their privileges, and their duties.

It must be recollected that rulers are the creatures, the legitimate off-spring of a constitution—not the creators or fathers. The framing of a Constitution belongs to the people, because by this instrument (which of all others ought to be considered sacred,) they are invested with all their powers, as rulers; and it would be indeed a solicism, to suppose that rulers can create themselves. A Constitution must of course be a fundamental law, and paramount to all legislative power—It is the charter of the rulers rights, and to be perfect, must also be the charter of the rights of the people—limiting the powers of rulers, and clearly defining, or reserving and securing the unalienable rights of the people.

An important question arises here—Has Connecticut such a Constitution?

CONSTITUTION No. II. (March 7)

Has Connecticut a Constitution which defines the powers of Rulers, and secures the rights of the People?

Vattel[1] defines a Constitution to be, "the fundamental regulation that determines the manner in which the public authority is to be executed."

This subject deserves a serious and candid investigation—and happily *at this time*, it may be considered without fear, or molestation from persecution:—it is no longer considered as but a "step from treason," to enquire whether Connecticut has a Constitution which deserves the name.[2]

The Legislature, by a public act, has declared that the Charter of Charles the 2d, shall be the Constitution of this State.—Here let me ask, by what authority the Legislature have so declared? If in their legislative capacity, they certainly have no such power—because if it be admitted that the Legislature have the power of making a Constitution or form of government by which they themselves are made rulers, they must have the power of self-creation—which belongs to nothing short, even if it does not exceed omnipotence. Have the people in their corporate, or individual capacity, ever adopted that charter as their Constitution? This was never claimed. The most strenuous advocates for an old Constitution in Connecticut, have never relied on this instrument as a legitimate Constitution, but they have claimed that the Constitution of this state, is to be found in long usage and habits. Let us fairly examine both these claims—Give king Charles's Charter, full credit for what it is worth—and examine the long usages and habits, and see if even the skeleton of a Constitution can be found in either, or both combined.

If a Constitution is a fundamental law, and above the reach of legislative power, it must be acknowledged that it cannot be altered in any respect by the Legislature.—Of course Connecticut is now to be called and known by the name of, "Governor and Company of the English Colony of Connecticut"— And "the General Assembly shall nominate and appoint such as they shall think fit to be Freemen"—"And the General Assembly may ordain and make all Laws, not contrary to the laws of England"—and put the "inhabitants in

---

[1] Emerich de Vattel (1714-1767), a Swiss philosopher and jurist, whose *Law of Nations* (1758, trans. 1760) had acquired considerable authority in America.

[2] An allusion to the manner in which those pressing for a constitution in 1804 had been treated.

warlike posture to repel any enemy by the sea or land, and invade and destroy the enemies of said colony."

If this is the Constitution of Connecticut, why is not Connecticut still an English colony? Why do not the General Assembly nominate and appoint the Freemen? Why are not our Laws subject to the revision of the British Parliament, and the decisions of British Courts? why has not Connecticut the power to make war and peace? It is not pretended that king Charles ever altered or amended the Ch[ar]ter—or that the good people of this state have ever altered it—or even that the Legislature have attempted to alter it—for it still remains entire in our statute book. But who will say it is the supreme law of the land, and its provisions are still in full force, power and virtue? What rights or privileges are reserved in this instrument to the people?

It certainly will not be claimed, that this is our Constitution.

CONSTITUTION No. III. (MARCH 14)

We come now to consider that invisible, intangible, unintelligible, pretended, boasted instrument, called the Constitution of Connecticut; which *consists* and *exists* in *long usages* and *steady habits*: and here if my readers do not find clear and lucid explanations, and expositions of all the latent valuable qualities which our "excellent Constitution" is said to possess, I trust they will be willing to lay the blame where it ought to rest, viz. on the instrument, called Constitution, and not on the writer. Can a constitution, or even the raw materials of a constitution be found in the long usages and habits of the Legislature of this State? Let it be remembered that "a constitution is a fundamental regulation, which determines the manner in which the public authority is to be executed." Where can such fundamental regulations be found in any ancient usage? What are fundamental regulations? The manner of making freemen, and the qualifications of freemen—the election of rulers, with a delegation of their powers—and definite fixed bounds set to the powers of rulers—and a reservation of those unalienable rights and privileges which the people have never delegated—These are fundamental rules which every good Constitution must possess. Have these been fixed and permanent by long usage and habit? This is the question, and it is an important one—it is absolutely essential to form this sacred instrument called a Constitution, *that these should be permanent.* Has not the mode of making and admitting freemen been altered? this will not be denied.—Have not the qualifications of freemen been varied by the Legislature? this must be acknowledged. Has the mode of electing our rulers never been changed by legislative acts? A satisfactory answer to this question may be found in fourteen acts in our Statute book on the subject of Elections.

Where can be found any act, law-usage or habit, which sets bounds to Legislative power? If such can be found, diligent search ought to be made, and no pains spared in the pursuit—for it is evident the Legislature themselves have never found it, and I challenge all the Lawyers in Connecticut to find it.

Where can be found any usage or habit or legislative act, or act of the people, which secures to them rights and privileges not delegated to their rulers? If no power has been expressly delegated by the act of the people, it cannot be expected that any rights have been expressly reserved.—If the rulers claim their powers from the people by tacit or implied consent, they may with the same implied consent claim absolute power, until the extent of their power be clearly defined—and from this arises the necessity of framing and adopting a Constitution, clearly defining the powers of rulers, and securing the rights of the people.

CONSTITUTION No. IV (MARCH 21)

After examining the Charter of King Charles, and the Usages and Habits of Connecticut, in search of what may properly be called a Constitution, without success, it may fairly be presumed that the good people of the state, without distinction of party, will unite in any proper measures to secure to themselves and their posterity the blessings of a good constitution of civil government, which can alone guard their rights from legislative encroachments, and give stability to our government.

The present crisis in Connecticut affords the most favorable opportunity, that ever has and perhaps ever will offer.—Peace, plenty, health, and general prosperity, are seasons peculiarly favorable, for examining the real situation, and comparative excellence or defects of a system of Government by its citizens—in addition to these, the violence of party spirit in our country is much abated—the present period is peculiarly suited to calm and sober investigation, and ought certainly to be improved by us in perfecting the system of our government, by ascertaining its defects and applying a remedy: no human government is perfect, but almost all are capable of progressive improvement. No one doubts but that many defects in our own do exist, and may easily be remedied—and it is believed the importance of a written Constitution is

universally felt, and by the united and patriotic exertions of our citizens, many and valuable improvements may be made in our system of State Goverement[sic], which will amply repay all our united labors, and be a lasting blessing to our posterity.
One of the People

PRE-CONVENTION COMMENTARIES

"A FREEMAN," *CONNECTICUT JOURNAL*, JUNE 16, 1818

The May 1818 meeting of the legislature passed several reform measures including one that reduced the size of the county courts. The Federalists claimed this was a device for dismissing Federalist judges. A more significant reform allowed all white males over 21 to qualify as a freeman after four months residence in one place. But the most important action taken by the legislature was a summons to the towns to elect delegates on July 4th to a convention that would meet at the end of August.

The response of "A Freeman" to that summons appeared first in New Haven's *Connecticut Journal* on June 16, 1818 and was reprinted in the *Connecticut Courant* on June 30. The piece could be construed as reflecting either a new willingness on the part of Federalists to participate constructively in drafting a constitution or as a manifestation of an old Federalist strategy for discouraging popular involvement in politics by pretending parties should not exist.

NEW CONSTITUTION.

ON the 4th of July next, by the appointment of our Legislature, the freemen of Connecticut are to meet for the purpose of electing delegates, to meet in Convention, at Hartford, on the 4th Wednesday of August, for the purpose of forming a Constitution.

Never, it is believed, has there been a more interesting period in our history. It is now to be decided whether we are to live in a condition of happiness and freedom, and to transmit the same blessings to our posterity; or whether we and our children are to be subject to a bad government, which either cannot protect our rights, or in the hands of bad men, may be made the instrument of their invasion, and the rod of our oppression. By the blessing of God, we have hitherto reposed with security under the shade of a government which our present governor has been pleased to entitle "the most precious monument of republican government existing among men." The Convention to be formed in August, are to determine whether the principles of the present government shall be embraced in the new one, either in the whole or in part; or whether the form and the substance are both to be abolished, and the citizens of Connecticut be committed to the protection of a new and untried system. In this case it will be admitted by all, that the interest of every man in Connecticut is in the line of his duty. Whatever party may predominate in the state, it is for the interest of all parties, and all men in it, that the government should afford the best protection to the lives, the property and the happiness of its citizens. On such an occasion then, how desirable would it be that every feeling hostile to social harmony should be sacrificed and forgotten; that the general good alone should be regarded, and that the freemen on the 4th of July should meet like brethren in the promotion of the common cause. United with such views and such feelings, we may look with certainty for the most successful and happy consequences. It cannot be doubted that there is wisdom and intelligence enough in the state to form a constitution as free and as happy, and as well adapted to our circumstances as any freeman can rationally expect, or even entertain a hope. It is then pre-eminently the interest and duty of the freemen to elect delegates of the greatest wisdom and intelligence. And how is such an election to be made? The wall of partition between parties must be prostrated; the scales of prejudice, which have heretofore blinded the eyes of political opponents to each other's merits must be magnanimously removed. When this is done, we may confidently expect that the freemen will discover and elect the wisest, and the best men, for this most interesting and important purpose. In this event the people will act as brethren, and the turbulence and rage of party will subside and languish in the desire to promote the public good. But should the freemen attend the election, and act under the influence of party prejudice and animosity, is there not danger that the delegates to be made, will be elected with a view to party purposes? And should this be the case, how great must be the alarm and anxiety of every honest well wisher to the state? The government will be made for a party, designed for their particular interest and benefit. And, fellow citizens, what are the interests of a party, but the interests of its leaders? The leaders, or rather those alone who partake of the loaves and fishes of office, receive any benefit from party ascendancy. And shall a constitution be formed and adopted with a view to promote the interests of factious leaders and designing demagogues? or shall it be made only for a portion of the people; a political party? If so, then no portion of the citizens will be safe. For who can depend upon the ever changing tide of popular opinion? That political party which is at the top of the revolutionary wheel to-day, may be at the bottom to-morrow. The revolutionary leaders of France, in their turn, were overwhelmed in the commotion they had excited, and bled on the scaffolds they had erected. Besides, if we engage in this great work with party feelings; it is most probable, that, should a constitution be formed and adopted by a party only, that it will continue to be a bone of never ceasing contention, jealousy and discontent, until, perhaps, at some future period, the opposite party shall become predominant, and put it down, and erect another suited to their own views and purposes. We are surrounded with examples of all such things. At the expense of much blood and treasure, the revolutionary wheel has been rolled over private peace, and public happiness in other states and nations. The disastrous consequence with which an offended God has marked the path of revolutions all around the globe, should be an awful warning to us of the danger of being blinded by the influence of party feelings. Let us then my fellow citizens on the next 4th of July, voluntarily surrender all our political jealousies and animosities. As it was the birth day of our independence, may it hereafter be celebrated as the birth day of political peace and quiet in the state. Then shall we have confidence in our delegates, confidence in our new Constitution, and be confident of the possession and long continuance of happiness and freedom.

A Freeman

"HAMILTON," *CONNECTICUT COURANT*, JUNE 30, 1818

Following the recommendation of "A Freeman" to abandon partisanship, "Hamilton" weighs the pros and cons of a large versus a small legislature, of frequent versus infrequent meetings, and of a restricted versus universal suffrage. For comparison he consults the practices of other states. His apparent open-mindedness reassured the Tolerationists that at least some of their former adversaries would join in the task of framing the best constitution possible.

AT the present time, it is very important that the people of this state should have correct opinions on several very essential points in politics. They are soon to decide on measures which will affect not only themselves, but their posterity. They are measures too, which are not so obvious to the view as to require only a superficial examination. Some of them involve questions which have perplexed many a statesman and political philosopher. They call for close and leisure examination, for much political information, and for a great deal of candor. I propose to exhibit some arguments on both sides of some of the questions which are to engage the public attention, leaving it with others to form their own conclusions. The great reason why, we differ in opinion on most subjects which we attempt to examine, is that we look on opposite sides of the *canvas*. Were we carefully to survey one side and suspend our decision until we have as carefully and candidly surveyed the other, we should then be prepared to form a fixed opinion.

In the first place then what should be the *number* of our representatives and how *often* should they meet?

The principal *advantages* of a large *house* appear to me to be,

1. The *larger* the house the more local *information* it will possess of the circumstances of the people.
2. The *larger* the house the *less danger* is to be apprehended from *combinations* to consult their own interests and trample on the rights of the people. Were all the people to assemble, there would not be much danger to be apprehended from this source, and the larger the house, the more does it partake of the nature of a popular assembly. The interests of members in a large house are more nearly identified with those of the people; they have also a stronger partiality in favour of the people and a stronger sympathy with them.

The principle *objections* to a large house appear to me to be,

1. The *expense*. It should be observed, however, that as the number of representatives *diminishes*, their wages will probably *increase*, because their individual labor and responsibility would be greater.
2. The larger the house, the *slower the progress* of business.
3. The larger the house, the less the *responsibility* of individuals. It should be observed, however, that the smaller the number of constituents, the more will the representative be made accountable for his conduct, I think.
4. The larger the house, the greater will be the influence of *passion*, and *prejudice*, because there will be more ignorance and weakness of intellect in the house, and because in a large assembly, sympathy is more easily communicated. When the feelings of a multitude are excited to a high pitch, "he must be either more or less than a man," says Mr. Hume, "who kindles not in the common blaze."

From the two last heads perhaps the paradoxical conclusion may be drawn, that the *greater* the number of representatives, the smaller will be the number of those who will direct most of its concerns.

As to the number of representatives in other states, it is smaller I believe in proportion to the population than it is in this. Massachusetts, however, has one representative for 150 polls, and another for an addition of 225 and so on, while Connecticut has I believe about one representative for 200 freemen. In Delaware there are 7 from a county. In New-Jersey 3. In N. Carolina 2. In Maryland 4. In Virginia 2. In S. Carolina the number is limited I believe to 124. In Pennsylvania to 100 (according to its constitution framed in 1790). Kentucky to 100 (according to its constitution of 1792) &c. &c. Vermont has one from a town. Great-Britain has about 580 members in her house of commons, which makes 1 to about 29,000 tho' the population is denser. It should also be observed that the population of Connecticut is denser than that of the southern states.

How often shall they meet?

The principle advantage of frequent elections is they give the people a stronger hold on the representative. It is also a satisfaction to the people to have frequent elections. The principal advantage of unfrequent elections appears to me to be, the representative has *less opportunity* to become *experienced*. The *expense* too is less. People will be more careful too in choosing proper persons. The other states have *annual* elections I believe, excepting Massachusetts, R. Island and S. Carolina. The two first have semi-annual and S. Carolina biennial.

In the next place, *What shall constitute a voter?* All agree that a *good moral* character and a *proper age* should be requisite. The only question is, *Shall any amount of property* be required? The principal advantages of requiring property to some amount appear to me to be,

1. It gives a *greater security* to property by making those more interested in it who make the laws. The great body of laws some way or other respect property. It is important therefore that those who make laws should have an individual interest in providing well for the security and increase of national wealth. How very willing for instance would the pauper be, to raise a heavy tax for the support of the poor.

2. *Extreme poverty* is generally connected with *incapacity* and *bad character*. The dregs of society—the floating population of every nation are, as a general thing, sunk into the depths of poverty. The number of such in this state is not comparatively great, but it is great enough to turn the scale of many an important question, especially when corrupted by the gold of an office-seeker.

3. It encourages *industry*, and holds out an inducement to rise to *respectability*.

The principal disadvantages of requiring any amount of property appear to me to be

1. The *poor* as well as others have important *rights* and *interests* to be consulted, and so far as government has any thing to do with these rights and interests, it is important that they should have a share in it.
2. It holds out a temptation to the dishonesty of receiving *temporary transfers of property*, and swearing it belongs to the persons to whom in reality it does not belong.
3. If much property is required, it tends to *discourage* industry, and to *depress* the hopes of rising to respectability.

In conclusion, it ought to be remarked that the *right of suffrage* is an *adventitious*, not a *natural* right, so that no one who is excluded has reason to complain of any thing but the *impolicy* of the law which excludes him.

A voter must have in Massachusetts, an estate of the value of £60, or an annual income of £5.—In New-York a freehold worth £20, or rented tenement at 40s.—In Maryland, £30 and one year residence.—In S. Carolina, 50 acres of land, or he must have paid a tax of 5s the preceding year.—Pennsylvania, no property, but only he must have paid taxes or had them assessed 6 months previous to the election and a two years residence.—N. Carolina, one years residence and taxes.—Georgia, six months residence and taxes.—Tennessee, six months residence.—Vermont, one year residence.—Ohio, one year residence.

Hamilton

"Judd," I-VI, Hartford *Times*, July 21-August 25, 1818

William Judd was the nearest thing the Tolerationists had to a martyr. In October, 1804 he along with four other Republican justices of the peace had been summoned before the legislature and dismissed from their offices after a quasi-judicial hearing in which they were accused of sedition. All five had been delegates to a state-wide convention held the preceding August at New Haven that had unanimously resolved the state lacked a constitution. Judd had been chair of the meeting, which adopted an address to the people urging them to replace the existing government with a new, constitutional one. He had been gravely ill at the time he appeared before the legislature, but nonetheless assisted in drafting a pamphlet that defended both the convention and the five dismissed magistrates. Shortly before it was published as *William Judd's Address to the People of the State of Connecticut*(1804), Judd died. For that reason his surname provided a good pseudonym for anyone advocating constitutional reform. The author of another piece that appeared in the *Columbian Register* on July 4, 1818 used the same pseudonym.

The author of this series, which ran in the Hartford *Times* in six installments from July 21 to August 25, 1818, was conciliatory enough to acknowledge the state's "steady habits." But the author did so without compromising the call for change. He was also wise enough to avoid arguing that any constitution was better than none at all. This attempt by a Tolerationist to canvass the major issues requiring consideration by a constitutional convention must have struck some Federalists as reasonable. "Judd" also wrote a seventh installment that appeared on September 15, 1818. It is omitted here because it did not address constitutional issues.

THE CONSTITUTION—NO. I. (JULY 21)

THE people having proceeded so far, that it may now, perhaps, be considered as certain that a Constitution is to be framed, it becomes important that the public mind should be so enlightened and directed as to secure a *good one;* for it must be admitted that we had better have no Constitution than to have one that is worse than none. However vague and indefinite the features of our present government may be considered, and notwithstanding the advantages of a written Constitution; from the situation of the state, it being but a fractional part of a larger community, and from the enlightened and orderly character of our citizens, and the wonderful influence of our "Steady Habits," we can, undoubtedly, as we have for a length of time, maintain authority under our present system, adequate, perhaps, to all the purposes of civil government. As emphatically and as strongly as we have urged the necessity of forming a *written Constitution*, we would not be understood as recommending the adoption of *any* written Constitution, in preference to remaining in our present situation. It is certainly desirable to have the rights of the people *defined*, but it is better that they should remain undefined than to be *compromitted*. It is important that the limits of authority should be bounded by fixed and known landmarks, but it is better that they should remain unsettled, than to sanction an encroachment upon the rights of the people. It would be important to secure the rights of conscience by interposing a barrier which would forever separate the civil and religious interests of the community; but it is better to endure the evils which exist at present, than by an ill-advised spirit of accommodation, attempt to procure a *partial* relief at the expense of a *recognition* of the erroneous principles which are the source of these evils.

In the formation of the Constitution of the United States, which necessarily involved the important principles of State Sovereignty, and State rights, and various other local interests—a spirit of compromise and concession became a *sine qua non* to the success of the undertaking; and the imperious necessity which existed for "a more perfect union," urged most powerfully the expediency of such mutual concessions as were necessary to ensure success to the wishes of the friends of a federative government. But in forming a Constitution for this state, the case is entirely different. Here there are no state rights, nor local rights or interests which require a spirit of compromise.—If any thing is to be compromitted, it will be abstract principles—if any rights are to be conceded, they must be the "rights of man."

From what has been observed, it is scarcely necessary to add, that it will be a principle with us, in relation to the subject under consideration, that if the Constitution which may be made and submitted to the people, shall be defective or erroneous in any of its fundamental principles, we shall feel it a duty to oppose it.

But although we believe it to be neither justifiable nor expedient to support a Constitution which is defective or false in its primary principles, yet we would by no means withhold our support from it, because it was not in all respects in conformity to our wishes—We would cheerfully sacrifice our opinion upon all subordinate and minor points.

The necessity of having the public mind enlightened, and made acquainted with the first principles of a Constitution of civil government, founded upon a republican basis, so that the people may act understandingly upon the subject, is most apparent. And when it is considered that from the terms of the "Resolution," it is to be submitted to the people and acted upon by them; either ratified or rejected in the short space of three weeks from the rising of the Convention, it is evident that the subject must be discussed, if at all *before* that period.

We shall therefore offer some views upon the subject in several numbers which will succeed this; but from the pressure of other avocations they must be written in great haste, and without that examination and reflection which the subject requires.

In the mean time we would invite the attention of our friends to this subject—May we not hope that the advocates of a Constitution, and the friends of civil and religious liberty, and the sacred rights of conscience, will not neglect this, the first, and probably the only opportunity which will ever occur, of affording their aid towards an improvement of the political condition of their fellow citizens, by breaking the chains of prejudice, dis[s]ipating the clouds of ignorance, strengthening the weak, encouraging the timid, removing groundless fears, conciliating asperities of feeling, and exhibiting in the sacred vestments of truth the loveliness of the divine principles of *equality, liberty,* and *justice?*

THE CONSTITUTION—NO. II. (JULY 28)

IN the consideration which we propose to bestow upon this subject, we do not intend to go into a disqu[i]sition upon the abstract principles of civil government, but merely to examine certain distinct propositions or principles which are necessarily comprised in every free Constitution; considering them not so much in the abstract, as with reference to the political situation of this state, and the moral habits and modes of thinking of its citizens at the present time.

Most of the propositions which we propose to consider, are those which it is believed involve the most difficulty, and with respect to which, there exists a diversity, or contrariety of opinion—of these, the following are most conspicuous.

1st. Of a preamble and declaration of rights.

2d. The character, or nominal designation of sovereignty.

3d. The Executive.

4th. Appointments.

5th. The principle or ratio of representation, and the qualification of Electors.

6th. The Senatorial branch of the legislature.

7th. The Judiciary

8th. Rights of conscience, or religion considered with reference to civil government.

Several of these propositions are of minor importance, and we notice them merely from an apprehension that from this very consideration, they may be passed over as not deserving *any* attention.

In Massachusetts, Vermont, and some of the other states, they have a bill, or declaration of rights, which forms a part of their Constitution. The object of this is to guard against an abuse of power by the constituted authorities—but this object can be better secured, so far as there is any security in mere declarations, in a different way; and there seems to be an impropriety if not an absurdity in a declaration of the *rights of the people,* in a Constitution made by *themselves.* The very act of instituting a government, suppose that they possess all civil rights. A declaration of rights is of the nature of a *grant*, and indeed this is the original character of an instrument of this description. In England they have a bill of rights, a declaration or petition of rights—a Magna Charta, and various other charters, all of which are of the same character, being *grants* from the crown, whereby the people claim or hold the rights guaranteed in them. Upon these various grants and certain important acts of Parliament, of which the *Habeas Corpus* is the most conspicuous, depend what are called the "liberties of Englishmen."

It is apparent how fallacious and degrading a foundation the "rights of man" are placed upon when derived from such a source, and having such a character as this. 'Chartered rights,' for this is their appropriate appellation, or rights claimed from the authority of grants, suppose, and indeed recognize two ideas; both of which are fallacious and preposterous, (viz.) that the party, making such grant, possessed the right and power to convey, constitute, or *create* the rights and priviliges which are claimed as being derived therefrom; and secondly, that *without* such grant or charter, the people *would not possess* such rights and privileges—According to the doctrine in Great Britain, of the "liberties of Englishmen," these boasted liberties are all derived from the King, and consequently agreeably to the theory of their government, *all the civil rights and liberties of fifteen millions of people, were originally united in one man, who has been graciously pleased to make so liberal a distribution of them, taking care however to reserve to himself the right of doing as he pleases, and the additional privilege that let him do as he may, he can do no* WRONG. Such is the boasted theory of the English government, and of the doctrine of chartered rights.

It is not contended that a "declaration of rights," as a part of the Constitution of a free people, is precisely of this nature; but it is allied to the same doctrine, and originated from the same source. What can be the use or propriety of a people who acknowledge no authority on earth by their own *will*, when exercising the right of self government, to make a formal declaration that they possess the rights of "life, liberty, and the pursuit of happiness"—that they were born free, that all are by nature equal, &c. "We hold these truths to be self evident," and if so, can any "form of words" render them more evident.

A declaration of the "rights of man," must be regarded with respect to those rights, either as wholly nugatory, or as having some authority—and can these rights receive any confirmation from any earthly power whatsoever? Will posterity wish to claim from a written declaration of their ancestors, those rights which they receive as a free gift from the God of nature? Let us not, in imitation of the slavish doctrines, of English theory, neither change nor pervert the *tenure* of our rights. Let us not say that here is the charter of our liberties; but let us rather say that we were born free! But although a declaration of rights, as such is inconsistent with our ideas of a Constitution, yet certain negative provisions, contained within the instrument itself, limiting more specifically the powers of the constituted authorities, and to secure more effectually, the rights of the people may be very proper; as a provision that the legislative authority shall not abolish the trial by jury—suspend the habeas corpus act, make *ex post facto* laws, establish a religious test, or provide for a religious establishment, &c.

The preamble to the Constitution of the U. States, is unparalleled for its conciseness, clearness, simplicity, and just principles. "We the PEOPLE of the U. States, in order to form a more perfect union, establish justice, ensure domestic tranquility, provide for the common defence, promote the general welfare, and secure the blessings of liberty to ourselves and our posterity do ordain," &c. Here in the small compass of a few lines, are comprised all the proper objects of civil government.

Next to the declaration of Independence, this caption to the only free national Constitution in the world deserves to be engraved upon the heart of every American Citizen. What real dignity there is in the expression, "we the people"—how unlike the puerile degrading courtly style of monarchy. His majesty is graciously pleased—his royal highness—the king, my master, &c. On a comparison, it is not difficult to determine, where the attributes of *majesty* and sovereignty, are in reality to be found. But there is one defect upon this point in the national Constitution; the *nature* of its sovereignty ought to have been preserved in its *name,* and its acts of authority— Its style is the United States of America—by the authority of the United States, &c. It ought to have been the *people* of the U. States of America, and by the authority of the people of the U. States—The *sovereignty* rests in the people, and it ought so to appear in its appellation—In New-York and Vermont, they have adopted this style—all acts of power are "by the authority of the people of the state of New-York." These distinctions may be thought by many as trival [sic], being mere matter of form. But what is government itself but a system of established forms. And as the people are the only legitimate sovereigns, it is unjust and extremely improper that *they* should be defrauded of the *name,* when all mimic sovereigns maintain it—

and it is even dangerous, for the loss of the name may lead to the loss of the reality.

THE CONSTITUTION—NO. III. (August 4)

In pursuance of the arrangement which we have adopted in examining this subject, we will proceed to make a few observations upon the *Executive power* and *Appointments*. The duty of the Executive consists in *action*—those of the Legislature in *deliberation;* and hence it has long been an axiom in politics that the supreme Executive power should be invested in a single person, and the Legislative power in a numerous body. But as there are few political principles so established as to have a universal application, this cannot be considered as one. From the nature of the government of the United States, the Executive authority of the Chief Magistrate of the states, has but a small portion of that power which consists in *action;* and if this authority was invested in an Executive council, consisting of several members, with power to choose a President, who should convene them, preside at their sittings, and be the organ of their will, it would probably be quite as consistent with the genius of our government. But as the Governors of few, if any of the states, possess powers which might become dangerous, even if they should fall into the hands of unprincipled and ambitious men, there is nothing to be apprehended from this source. It is therefore hardly worth awhile to make innovations, where the subject to be gained is of inconsiderable importance.

In several of the states the Supreme Executive power is vested in a Governour; in others in a Governour and Lt. Governour, and in some of them it is vested in a Governour, Lt. Governour, and Executive Council. From deference to our steady habits, the Executive authority had better be continued in a Governour and Lt. Governour.

But the Governour ought not, as heretofore, to be a member of one branch of the legislature, which has produced a confusion of the Executive and the Legislative powers, or wholly *merged* the former in the latter.

The Executive, the Legislature, and the Judicial authority, being co-ordinate; each ought to be in the same measure independent of the other two.

By whom shall the Governour be chosen, and for how long? He ought by all means to be elected by the *people*, and annually. The practice which prevails in some of the States, of electing the Governour by the two houses of the Legislature, is incorrect in *principle*—it destroys his independence, and derogates from the dignity of the office.

The advantages of an annual appointment are not very important, but it is most correct in theory, especially in a state of so small a territory as this. But if the Governour is appointed annually, let him not be eligible for more than six years in succession. The principle of rotation in office, ought to be incorporated into the Constitution of every free people.

If the Governour is separated from the Legislature, what authority shall he possess over that body, and what portion of Legislative power? Shall he have a qualified *veto* or negative upon their proceedings? With respect to Legislation, the Executive should possess the power of *proposing*, not of *enacting*. It being his province to execute the laws, he must be supposed to be best acquainted with their defects, and to possess the most information as to what new subjects require legislative interposition; yet, if after having submitted to the Legislature such subjects as may appear to him to deserve attention, if that body, after *deliberation*, shall entertain a different opinion in any respect, it is questionable whether such opinion ought to be controled or even checked by the will of the Executive.

If there is to be a qualified negative, upon the proceedings of the Legislature, this power ought to be vested in a council of revision, consisting of the Governour, and all, or a part of the Judges of the Supreme Court; this is the case in the state of New-York. But if this principle is not adopted, let the Governour have the same power over the opinions of the Legislature, as a judge has over those of a jury. If he disapproves of a bill, let him send it back with his objections in *writing*, and if upon a second consideration with his objections before them, both houses of the Legislature remain of the same opinion as at first, let it become a law.

What power shall the Executive possess with relation to *Appointments?* This part of the power of the Executive, is the most difficult to be settled satisfactorily, and being so intimately connected with the subject of Appointments generally, that they can best be considered together.

How shall the magistrates, the officers of the militia, and all public officers which are not elected by the people, be appointed? Shall these Appointments be made by the Governor, the Senate, the House of Representatives, or any two of them, or by a distinct authority created for the purpose?

In the government of the United States, the President has the power of *nominating*, with respect to which the Senate have a negative authority. In the state of New-York, they have a council of Appointment, possessing an immense power, which if it should fall into the hands of violent partizans and unprincipled and ambitious men, would become a tremendous political engine, and scarcely compatible with the public tranquility. In Massachusetts and New-Hampshire, the Governor and Executive Council, constitute a kind of Council of appointment, but with much less extensive powers. In Pennsylvania almost all appointments, not made by the people, are entrusted to the Governor, who has a most extensive patronage—hence the unparalleled violence of their gubernatorial elections. Appointments by the two branches of the Legislature, by bills according to the ordinary principles of legislation, as has been the practice in this state, and Rhode Island, is absurd in principle and extremely inconvenient. The qualifications of candidates even for the most paltry office, such as Justices of the Peace, becomes a subject of public enquiry and debate; thereby exposing individuals to severe and unjust animadversion, from the influence of party spirit, or personal animosities, without any opportunity of defending themselves, and occupying in this business a considerable portion of the time of the legislature.

It would be useless to notice the objections to this mode of making Appointments, when there is nothing that can be advanced in favor of it.

THE CONSTITUTION—NO. IV. (August 11)

Having noticed in the last number, the different modes which prevail in several of the states, of making appointments, and pointed out some of the objections to which they all seem to be exposed, we will proceed to suggest a plan formed by a modification of the principles adopted in several of the other states, which appears to be more correct in theory, and better calculated to give satisfaction in practice.

Instead of a Council of Appointment, let there be a Council of *Nomination*, consisting of six members; the Governour and Lt. Governour, to be members, *ex. officio*, and the other four to be elected by the House of Representatives[,] members of the Senate to be ineligible. Let this board have the authority to *nominate* magistrates and all civil officers, their nominations being presented to the Senate for their concurrence and approbation, and when approved by them to become appointments. The council of nomination, to convene regularly at each session of the legislature, and to meet at other times if thought necessary by the governour, to fill vacancies, which may have been occasioned by death or resignation, during the recess; which nominations to have the effect of appointments until the next session of the legislature, when they must be submitted to the Senate.

A council of Nomination of this description, would have little of the power or influence of a council of appointment. The greatest objections to a council of appointment, are that such an extensive patronage, entrusted to a few individuals is a powerful temptation to make use of it for *their own* advantage, by attempting to acquire popularity—that they are liable to be influenced by *personal* considerations and favouritism, rather than a regard to the public interest—that if they should be above these and all other impure motives, they are liable to make improper appointments from a want of *local information*, or a knowledge of the local interests and wishes of the people. But where the same number of men have merely the power of nomination to office, and their acts are to be canvassed by another body, no way connected with themselves, they will be cautious how they bring forward candidates who have no other recommendation than the personal friendship of some of the board who nominate them; and if the influence of favoritism should operate upon the Board of Nominations, it could be resisted in the Senate. If improper nominations should be made from a want of local information, the Senate, composed of members from every part of the state, bringing with them the wishes and feelings of their constituents, would be enabled to perceive and correct the evil.

This mode of making appointments would give to each branch of the government its proper influence; the governour would be a member of the Council of Nomination; the House of Representatives would possess the power of appointing a *majority* of the members, and the Senate would possess a negative authority upon all their official acts, but not the power to *originate* any appointment.

The system of military appointments, adopted in Massachusetts, appears to be a just one. Company officers are appointed by the members of the company, regimental officers by the company officers of the regiment, brigadier officers, by the regimental officers of the brigade. These appointments or nominations, ought to be submitted to the Senate, for their approbation, and to be commissioned by the Governor. The major generals in Massachusetts, are appointed by the General Assembly; but there can be no objection to there [sic] being nominated and submitted to the Senate in the same manner as civil officers.

The principle of representation, and the qualification of electors, are next in order. It is evident that our representation at present is extremely unequal and unjust. There is no *principle* of representation—it is neither population nor property; or if there is any principle, it is that of the

"Borough system" of England. Union and Durham, have each two representatives; the former contains 752 inhabitants, and the latter 1100; and Hartford and New Haven, with the same representation, contain the one more than 6000 and the other 6967, at the last census, both of which have increased considerable since. Waterford contains 2185, and Montville 2887 inhabitants, which have but one representative each, being nearly *three times* the population of Union, and having but *half* the number of representatives, and New-Haven has more than *ten times* the population of one of the towns here noticed, having the same representation.

If we consider *population* as the only correct principle of representation, (a position which it is believed few will attempt to deny,) a more equitable ratio ought to be adopted. If every town was allowed one representative, every one having a population of 2000 or more, two representatives, those having 4000, three representatives—those having 6000, four representatives, it would perhaps be as just a principle as can be adopted under our present situation; as it would not do to deprive any town of its representation, on the one hand, nor will it answer on the other, to increase the whole number of representatives. This principle would make little or no variation in the whole number, and it would distribute them more justly with reference to population.

THE CONSTITUTION—NO. V. (August 18)

HAVING, in the preceding number, noticed the injustice and inequality of the representative principle, under our present system, and suggested a more just and equitable ratio of representation, we will proceed to make a few observations upon the *qualification of electors.*

It cannot, we think, be made a question, whether the *principle* of the "right of suffrage" ought to be established by the Constitution? This right in a representative government, involves the "vital spirit" of sovereignty. In a democracy, not possessing the representative character, and in which the people make the laws *themselves*, the fundamental principle, both as it respects the political rights of individuals, and the sovereign power of the state, would depend upon the question: *Who shall participate, and take a part in public affairs?* But in a *representative* democracy, where the people do not exercise the power of government themselves, but delegate it to others to be exercised for their benefit, the fundamental principle of sovereignty and the primary political rights of individuals depend upon the consideration, *Who shall possess and exercise the right of constituting the authorities of government?*

If it is left with constituted authorities, without any limitation or restraint, to say *who* should create or appoint them; they would have the power to deprive a portion of the people of their political rights, and of all participation in the concerns of government, by annexing such qualifications to the right of suffrage as few only would possess, and thereby establish an aristocracy and perpetuate their own authority—for wherever a considerable proportion of the people are *deprived* of all participation in the government, and consequently of all political rights, the principle of democracy is destroyed or corrupted to an aristocracy. However dissimilar these too [sic] systems of government may be, in their practical character and operations, their features and principles are often more nearly allied than we are apt to suppose—

And oft the shades of difference are so nice,

Where ends the virtue—Where begins the vice,

are points not easily determined.

If the *principle* of the qualification of electors is to be settled by the Constitution, it becomes an enquiry of no small importance to be determined, what principle ought to be adopted?

Shall the "right of suffrage" depend upon *personal* considerations, or shall it depend upon *property*, or a modification of both?

We have no hesitation in saying, that the only correct principle of the right of suffrage is founded upon *personal considerations*. What, it may be asked, would you have universal suffrage? Literally, universal suffrage cannot exist; the expression, therefore, is vague and deceptive. All men being by nature *equal*, no one man on entering into a state of society, ought to relinquish or be deprived of more of his *natural rights* than another, without strong and special reasons therefor; and there can be no such reasons unless it is the *security of society*. Hence then, no individual who can be admitted to a participation in the government with *safety to the public*, can be deprived of such right without oppression and injustice. This, then, is the correct principle of suffrage, call it universal or partial. *All*, who can have a voice in the concerns of government, without endangering the security of society, ought to enjoy this right. The question then is simply this, what individuals in society are most dangerous to the rest? Is it the simple, the ignorant, the weak, and the poor, or is it the cunning, the artful, the learned, the wealty [sic], and the powerful? To assert that the ignorant are more dangerous to society than the cunning, is ridiculous. But of all the absurdities which have obtained currency in the world, and been support-

ed by authority, and consecrated by time, there is none that exceeds the pre-
tention that a man *without* property, is more dangerous to society, than one
who is in the possession of property; and that *poverty* should operate as a
disqualification of civil rights. We are told that money is the very "root of
evil"—that it constitutes the "sinews of war," and the "life blood" of power;
yet the possession of it, no matter to what amount, does not render a man
dangerous to society—no, although he have the revenues of a commonwealth, and be able to subsidize and maintain a whole army of men for his
own purposes.—But the *want* of this 'root' of moral and political evil, renders a man dangerous in society, and disqualifies him of his civil rights—
how preposterous! But it is said that the *poor* are liable to be corrupted or
bought by the wealthy? It was a remark of Sir Robert Walpole, that "every
man had his price," and if this idea is correct, (and it has long been a principle of the English government) not only the poor but also the rich, are
liable to be corrupted; yet perhaps, the "price" of the former would be
somewhat *less* than that of the latter.—But to give this argument all the
force it admits of, let it be supposed that the poor alone are exposed to the
corrupt influence of money—that they can be bribed—that their votes will
be bought like provisions in market. This certainly would be a great corruption. But which party in this corrupt traffic would be most criminal? Is the
one who possesses the means of corruption, and who uses these means for
his *own unlawful purposes*, wholly innocent; and the party who without any
personal design or end in view, but from the *necessity of his situation*, is a
subject of this corrupt influence, wholly guilty? Instead of this being the
fact, the poor are merely the *instruments* of the rich. But it is according to
some men's ideas of moral right, and even of religion, to punish the instrument which is *passive,* and to regard the mind which "conceives and meditates the mischief" as unoffending. Does the security of society require the
poor to be deprived of their civil rights because the rich are disposed to
abuse their wealth? Nothing can exceed the absurdity and iniquity of this
doctrine, unless it is the improvements which have been made upon it in
England, where the government first *make* the people, or the *canaille*[1] as
they call them, poor, and then *punish* them for being so. If property is to be
taken into consideration at all, as it respects the extension of the right of suffrage, the correct principle would be to regard by law, the accumulation of
wealth over a certain amount, as *dangerous to the public security*; which
would be a just cause for a disqualification of civil rights. This would be a
just and important principle; for the accumulation of an "unwieldy mass of

---

[1] French for rabble, mob, or scum of the population.

wealth" is *per se* an evil, in a republican government. Does not the history of the whole world declare that inflated wealth, either from its direct, or indirect influence, has corrupted and destroyed every free government which ever existed.—But if *property* is to form no part of the qualifications of electors, it may be asked what shall be the *principle* of the rights of suffrage? However this right may be extended or restricted, it ought with the exception here noticed, to depend *wholly upon personal considerations*. This is the only correct principle. It would be a juster rule than that of property, to adopt the principle of a man's height, or complexion. Let this right be extended to all who can safely be trusted with it, and let it be withheld from all where its enjoyment would endanger the public security. We are not to suppose that if property is excluded as a test of merit, there can be no qualifications or obstructions to the extension of this privilege.—*Age, residence,* and *character*, form the proper grounds of discrimination.

THE CONSTITUTION—NO. VI. (AUGUST 25)

IN the preceding Numbers we have examined, cursorily, several of the parts, or divisions of our subject—the preamble and declaration of rights; the character, or nominal designation of sovereignty; the executive, appointments, the ratio, or principle of representation, and the qualifications of electors.— The only remaining points which we proposed to consider, are the senatorial branch of the government; the Judiciary, and the rights of conscience, or religion considered with reference to civil governmen[t]s.

We at first proposed to confine our views with respect to the Legislature, to one branch, or the Senate; but now find it convenient to consider the subject more generally.

If our views of the principle of representation were correct, and having some regard to steady habits, the House of Representatives will consist of about the same number of members as at present, and will, perhaps, be organized in a similar manner. It ought, however, to be provided, that it shall be a distinct and *independent* branch of the legislature, which it has scarcely been heretofore. It ought also, from a regard to its dignity, to appoint its own officers, and not be dependent upon the officers of the County or town. It is not the proper business of the Sheriff or Constable, to attend upon the legislature; they are not officers of their appointing, nor accountable to them for their conduct.

In Pennsylvania and several of the other states, the clerks are not elected from the members of the legislature. And when the arduous duties and the drudgery of this office are considered, it seems hardly consistent with the rights of the people, to withdraw the representatives of certain towns from the business of legislation, to which their time and talents ought to be devoted, and which is the right of their constituents, to other services. But these matters are of little consequence, and not deserving of much consideration.—

How shall the other branch of the legislature, or the Senate, be organized, and of what number of members shall it consist? The Senate ought to be organized upon the same principles as the House of Representatives, and its members chosen by the same electors. The principle which makes distinctions between the constituents of one branch of the Government, and those of another, is anti-republican and preposterous in the extreme. This principle has nothing to do with a republican form of government, it belongs to an aristocracy. It is a part of that political system which is founded upon the idea of a *mixed society* consisting of different classes and orders of citizens. It belongs to the creed of Edmund Burke,[2] who considered that "a nobility was the polished corinthian order in the fabric of society." The first principle of our government is, that the sovereign power is vested in the people—the second is, that this power is exercised by delegation, or by authorities constituted for the purpose. The people, then, constitute the authorities of Governments—and have not the people all the same rights and interests? Why then shall they be divided into classes, and one class constitute one branch of the government, and one, another? Why shall the House of Representatives represent one class of citizens, the Senate another, and the Executive a third, when the rights of all are the same? Is it that one may be a check to the other? If it is intended to recognize the principle of the English Government, a "balance of power" you must create the order of society upon which it is founded; a royal family, an agrarian nobility and a "swinish multitude." Politically considered, there is no body of citizens in England, that can be called the "PEOPLE." No, their Society has for its basis, the feudal system, which being opposed to the principles of nature, has given it a character entirely *artificial*—whereas it is the very spirit and life's blood of a republican government, not to oppose, but to *follow nature*.

The number of members of which the Senate ought to consist, is not very important, although it would be well that there should be some proportion between the two branches.—In New-York and Pennsylvania, the representation in the Senate is about one third as numerous as in the House of Representatives.—A number so small as we have had in our

2 A prominent English critic of the French Revolution, who articulated a conservative political philosophy to resist radical change.

Council, or Upper House, can scarcely deserve the character, of a deliberative body.—It is believed that no one would propose to have the senate consist of less than twenty four members, nor more than thirty two.—That the State ought to be districted for their appointment, will not, we think, be made a question. If, then, the state should be divided into eight districts, there would, from what we may suppose to be the present population of the state, be about 34,000 people in each district—and three senators to a district, would make the whole number consist of twenty-four, and there would be one senator to every eleven thousand persons.

What shall be the powers of the Legislature? Shall it possess that "absolute despotic power, which" Judge Blackstone[3] says "in every government, must reside somewhere." As the English political theory gives you no correct idea of a Constitution, so, neither does it contain any just principles of a Legislature.—Their most approved writers speak of the "absolute power," and even of the "omnipotence of parliament"—Blackstone, in treating of the powers of parliament, says, "the power and jurisdiction of parliament, says Sir Edward Coke,[4] is so transcendant and absolute, that it cannot be confined, either for causes or persons, within any bounds. It has sovereign and uncontrollable authority, in the making, confirming, enlarging, abrogating, repealing, reviving and expounding laws, concerning matters of all possible denominations, ecclesiastical or temporal, civil, military, maritime or criminal. This being the place, where that absolute despotic power, which must in all governments reside somewhere, is entrusted by the Constitution of these kingdoms. Parliament can regulate or alter the succession to the crown. It can alter the established religion of the land. It can change, and create afresh, even the *Constitution* of the land, and of parliaments themselves. *It can, in short, do any thing that is not naturally impossible; and therefore some have not scrupled to call its power by a figure rather too bold, the omnipotence of parliament.*" Such is the English theory of a legislature and of a constitution; and such are the absurd and dangerous principles of a legislature whose powers are wholly undefined. But as frightful as this picture may seem, we have something of the same character, nearer home. Yes, the General Assembly of Connecticut, possessing powers equally undefined, can with the same propriety be called an "omnipotent legislature." It can, and we had almost said it has done every thing which is not ["]naturally impossible." In repeated instances, *ex post facto* laws have been passed—and it is notorious that the General Assembly of Connecticut in its "omnipotence" has

---

[3] William Blackstone, a noted English jurist whose *Commentaries on the Laws of England.* 4 vols. (1765-1769) provided a classic digest of English jurisprudence that every American lawyer read.

[4] Edward Coke (1552-1634), a predecessor of Blackstone who championed the supremacy of the common law and Parliament against the prerogative of the Crown.

altered, modified and "created afresh the Constitution" of the state. The constitution (for according to English theory we have a constitution) instead of being a rule of action to the Legislature and binding upon them, in the same manner that an ordinary law is upon the people, has been the creature of their will, and the offspring of their own creation.—

These things shew the necessity of having the powers of the Legislature *defined and limited*[.] If the constituted authority are servants of the people; then let them have authority in what manner to act, and let them not exceed it—let us say to... them, thus far shall you proceed and no further.—A declaration of the rights of the people, we have attempted to show to be unnecessary; but the limitation of the powers of the legislature is all-important[.] It would be proper to enumerate and define these powers, and also to add a prohibitory provision, similar to that in the Constitution of the U.S. that they should exercise no powers not *expressly* granted, or which did not necessarily follow, from the powers that were expressly granted.

How often shall the legislature hold its sessions, and where? We should say once a year, and at Hartford and New-Haven, alternately as heretofore. The circumstance of there being but one session a year, will be no objection to the sessions being held at these two semi capitals of the state; nor do we perceive any reasons for innovating upon our steady habits in this respect. *Judd*

"DAVENPORT," *CONNECTICUT COURANT*, JULY 28, 1818

It took time after the freemen had chosen the delegates to the convention to assess the character of its composition. But it soon became clear that many prominent Federalists had won places there. That emboldened some to urge the convention adopt a conservative course. With a few minor exceptions "Davenport" wanted a codification of existing procedures. John Davenport had been the founding leader of the seventeenth-century New Haven colony. By using this pen name the author sought to underscore a Federalist claim that Connecticut was the oldest and freest republic in Christendom.

THE CONVENTION.

THE result of the late election for members of the Convention to be held in August, for the purpose of deliberating on the expediency of forming a new Constitution for this state, cannot but afford great satisfaction to the sober, reflecting, and judicious inhabitants of Connecticut. However they may have yielded to a momentary delusion, and suffered themselves to become in any degree regardless of the many real substantial blessings which they and their ancestors have enjoyed under the present government, it is apparent that they are not yet prepared to part with them, and to incur the hazard of visionary and fanciful experiments. The freemen have suddenly paused—they have turned their eyes to their old tried friends— to the men who have carried the state through the stormy period of tumult and revolution, and protected them, their families, and their estates, in peace and social enjoyment, whilst the rest of the civilized world has been convulsed to its foundations. This affords the highest evidence, that the people of the state do not mean to part with the old, approved, wise, and excellent principles of their government—that they will reject important and material innovations, and that the convention, let them pursue what course they may, must expect their labours to be rejected, if they attempt to introduce a new, untried, and extravagant set of fundamental principles, in the place of those which have been tested by an experiment of nearly two hundred years duration.

In the first place, the religious institutions of the state must be held sacred. Although the Ark has been shaken for two years past, yet let not the unhallowed hand of Uzzah[1] touch its sacred fabrick. Religious and moral instruction have formed the basis of all the prosperity and social happiness of the people of this state. The corner stone of the civil constitution was laid by pious hands, the edifice was raised by christian liberality and zeal, it was cherished by christian prayers, and was defended by piety and patriotism. When this part of the system shall be removed, the edifice will tumble into ruins. Let no friend to the state be deceived on this subject. Hostility to the religious institutions of the state, proceeds from hostility to its freedom and happiness. Nothing is to be gained by temporising with the spirit that meditates their destruction. It proceeds from the deepest hostility not only to religion itself, but to public virtue, public morals, to literature, and to freedom. Whenever the proposition shall be made for its destruction, look at the quarter from whence it proceeds—search the heart and scan the life of him or them from whom it originates, and draw the conclusion accordingly. Are they characterised by the loosest principles, the foulest immoralities, the most impious scoffings at religion, and the grossest disregard of decency and virtue, beware of imbibing the principles of your government from such a polluted source.

[1] A Biblical figure, who had been struck dead when contrary to divine law he had touched the Ark of the Covenant.

The blessing of God cannot be expected to crown the system which is thus "*conceived in sin and shapen in iniquity.*" The old plan, in this particular cannot be improved—let it then remain inviolate.

The Schools are next in order. To the earliest settlers of New-England, belongs the high honour of making the sublime experiment of inculcating by law universal instruction in the body politic. That experiment succeeded in the fullest measure, and its fruits have been realized in the highest degree of social happiness, and social respectability, that ever existed among civilized nations. Bold and daring must be the head and the hand of the innovator, that would destroy, or even disturb, this part of our system.

The Legislative department required very little amendment. The highest branch of that body, is as nearly perfect, in its organization, as this imperfect state of things can be supposed to admit. Let it then remain. The other branch has been supposed to require alteration, both *with regard to its numbers, and the frequency of elections.* If it were an abstract question merely, it might be said, that the house of representatives is more numerous than would be necessary: but, the principle upon which it is founded, cannot be changed without the substitution of one less equal, and more inconvenient, than the present. If one from a town should be the rule—and less than that would not answer—Hartford, New-Haven, and all the large towns, would stand upon the same footing, in this respect, as Sterling, Marlborough, Sherman, &c. The people are accustomed to the present mode, it is not burdensome, and the numbers can never be much increased; and therefore it is better to let it remain, than to introduce a novelty.

With regard to the half-yearly election of the house of representatives, the necessity of meeting in September to make a Nomination for Assistants, is a satisfactory reason for retaining the habit. And the fact is, that, in one essential particular, the election is not *practically* more frequent than in most other states. In the states generally, there is but one session of their legislatures annually. They, of course, can have but one election. In this state there are constitutionally *two.* The members, therefore, being chosen for each session, last *officially* as long, as they do in other states where there is but a single session.

On the subject of the two sessions a year, it is to be presumed there will be serious attempts to break that practice up, because it is a part of the *old agreement* between the colonies, and the two towns have equal claims to the seat of government. Should there be but one session in a year, a new seat of government must be established, and with it a new State-House, which, at the present time, must be attended with great expense, and at the same time the present buildings in Hartford and New-Haven must be in a great measure lost.

A point of more importance relates to the Courts. A Superior Court must of course, be provided for. According to popular opinion, the Judges should be made *independent*. The best mode of doing this that has hitherto been devised is, to *secure them in their offices during good behavior*. A provision to this effect will be probably thought necessary.

The School Fund law ought to be incorporated in its present form, in the Constitution.

The appointment of officers of the government should be vested in the General Assembly.

The elections should be held just as they now are—reinstate the qualification for freemen—choose your Treasurer and Secretary as at present—provide for choosing members of Congress by nomination, as at present—fix the mode of taxing by lists.

Davenport

"A FREEMAN," I & II, *CONNECTICUT COURANT,* AUGUST 4, 1818

The Federalist desire to preserve as much of the existing structure of Connecticut's government as possible found many proponents, but few were as forceful as the series of essays written by "A Freeman." They stand in contrast to two essays under the pseudonym "Haynes" appearing on August 18 and 25 in the *Connecticut Courant.* The "Haynes" essays emphasize the sanctity of the state's traditions. The series by "A Freeman" Parts I and II first appeared in the *Connecticut Courant* on August 4 and then were reprinted in the *Connecticut Journal* on August 18. Part III of the series appeared in the *Connecticut Courant* on August 11. In it "A Freeman" accuses the "revolutionists" of intending to change the state's existing system of taxation so as to force farmers to bear the principal burden. He also warns that the reformers might abolish the state's school fund. Part three of the series, along with introductory commentary in Part I complaining of the haste with which the Tolerationists were proceeding, are omitted because they address policy rather than constitutional issues.

I (August 4)

The organization of the government of this state was formed, and has been continued, upon the purest principles of popular sovereignty, and is the farthest removed from every semblance of a monarchical, or aristocratical form, of any government of which we have any knowledge. *All the freemen vote* for the gov. lieut. gov. council, treasurer, secretary and members of congress—and the members of the house of representatives of the general assembly are elected by the freemen of the several towns. All the judicial officers of the government, from the highest to the lowest, are appointed by the general assembly. In all, or nearly all, the modern constitutions in the different states, there are features of a much more monarchical description, which there is great reason to believe, will be attempted by our revolutionists to be introduced here. In the first place, it is fashionable in states boastingly called more republican than Connecticut, to make the governour a distinct and separate branch of the government—giving him the power to reject a bill passed by both houses of the legislature. This is borrowed directly from the constitution of Great-Britain, where the king has precisely this power. Our governour has no such authority, and it is to be hoped never will have. We have gone on remarkably well, with two houses composed, one of the governor and council, and the other of the representatives—when they have concurred in passing a bill, it becomes a law, and no single individual has the power to prevent its going into operation. This is Connecticut republicanism, it is founded upon the principles of election, and is more free, and less aristocratical, than the mode adopted by other states. There is no good reason for departing from our present system in this particular; and without a very good reason, the freemen of Connecticut will never voluntarily deprive themselves of power, nor place themselves, and their legislative concerns, in the hands and controul of any individual.

The power of appointing to office in the hands of any man, or magistrate, is the fruitful source of oppression and corruption. We fortunately have never, thus far, made such an experiment. But we have seen it tried, and heard of its effects, in many other states. The magistrate who has the power of appointment to office, or even of nomination, is forever exposed to intrigues, impositions, importunities, and every mischievous and dangerous attack, which the hungry seekers of office can possibly make upon him. It is scarcely possible for him to resist. The fear of losing popularity, and with it his re-election, are strong temptations to him to yield to applications which his judgment would lend [lead] him to reject, and the wealth of the people, and the honours of the government, are squandered upon the worthless, the vicious, the parasite, and the intriguing. It is much more difficult to manage a virtuous and independent legislature—it is hard to corrupt a majority of two houses. Our appointments, *until a very late period*, have been judiciously and fairly made, no charge of corruption has been made against the legislature in this respect. I am decidedly of the opinion, that the power should be retained in the hands of the people, to be exercised by their representatives, in preference to the more monarchical plan of other states.

No. II (August 4)

THE history of elective governments furnishes no instance of the organization of a legislative department so just and equal as that of the General Assembly of Connecticut. All modern legislative bodies are divided into two houses. Such is the case here. Our Council answers for that which is commonly called the senate, and has been found, in practice, as just, upright, independent, and virtuous a body, as perhaps can be found in any country. The manner of electing this house is peculiar to this State, and has advantages over all others. It is *free*, well calculated to promote the best men, and to preclude those of a different character. Long habit has rendered this part of our elections easy and familiar, it is adapted to our feelings, and has acquired the strong attachment of the freemen. There is no good reason that can be urged for changing either that or the organization of the body. If we are to have a Senate, by name, it must be much more numerous, which will, of course, be proportionably more expensive, for they must all be paid—they will introduce, instead of the plain unostentatious manners of the Council, the practice of making formal speeches, oratorical exhibitions, and *eloquent* harangues, calculated more to display the talents of the members, than to forward the public business. Such a change in the Upper house, may naturally be expected to lengthen sessions of the Assembly, take one time with another, at least one week—which, with the pay of twenty additional members, for a Senate must contain not less than *thirty-two* members, will increase the expenses of every session, upon a fair computation, *four or five thousand dollars*—and after all, the organization would be vastly less convenient and beneficial to the State.

It has always been the fact, that there have been two sessions of the legislature annually. This arose from the compact between the two colonies of Connecticut and New-Haven, at the time they became united. Under this usage, houses and accommodations for the General Assembly have been provided in Hartford and New-Haven; and with a strict regard to its spirit and principle, the House of Representatives have been chosen for each stated session. This has been considered a bad theory, though it is well known that the practice has not proved inconvenient, and the habit is so well established, and has continued so long, that it would be unwise to shake or alter it. In most states, there is but one session of their legislatures, of course, they have but one election, in the year. We have, by constitution, founded upon compact, two; therefore, a half yearly election of one branch is really an election for *a session*, and in this point of view no more frequent than where there is only one session, and one election. But the freemen's meeting in September is necessary for the purpose of making a nomination, and when assembled for that object it is no inconvenience to choose [U.S.] representatives. Besides, it is the true republican theory to recur often to the people, where the sovereignty lies, for the purpose of ascertaining their wishes and directions. This also secures the *annual election* of the other house. Very probably, in the rage for innovation, and from a servility of disposition, an attempt may be made not only to render the governor a distinct branch, but, like the state of New-York, and many others, to form a senate to last three, four or five years, instead of an annual council. The freemen of this State are too strictly republican to follow such aristocratic examples—they are accustomed to an annual election of the council—each freeman has the privilege of voting for the whole house, instead of being confined to one or two members in a small district—they can select the most able and respectable men in the State, instead of being confined within small limits as they would be in districts—and they cannot gain, but must inevitably lose, by a change, if in nothing else, in their own influence in the affairs of their government.

A great effort is to be made to destroy the old ecclesiastical laws and institutions of the State. These laws and institutions have existed from the earliest days of the colony, and have been the great source of the respectability, happiness, and prosperity of the State. When the colony was divided into ecclesiastical societies, and the laws were passed for the support of public worship, there was but one denomination of Christians in its limits, and that was congregationalists, or Presbyterians. Episcopalians, baptists, and methodists, were unknown here. The laws, therefore, were made by the congregationalists, for their own regulation and government, and not for the purpose of oppressing other classes of christians. These laws, then, are entitled to the highest respect, and ought to be held inviolate, by other denominations, who have since sprung up, and who, though a small minority, still claim exemptions from their requisitions. Those laws cannot be dispensed with, without laying an axe at the root of the State's dignity, integrity, and highest social, moral, political, and religious interests and character. There is no reason why they should be dispensed with. Those who make this demand of the state, exceed the bounds of modesty and decorum, when they set up their claim. All that they can with justice or decency require is, that themselves may be freed from the provisions of the laws on the subject; they have no right to ask an exemption for others, especially for the congregationalists, who are satisfied with the present state of things, and are willing to remain in the condition in which they were left by their pious and venerable ancestors. This is a point that ought never to be abandoned.

The laws for the support of schools and the school fund, ought to be held sacred. Indeed, the appropriation law should be incorporated into the new constitution, and thus be secured against all future danger. The charter of Yale College, also, should be recognized in the constitution, and placed in the same situation with the school fund.

Provision should be made in the constitution for the election of members of Congress in the manner that has been practised ever since the establishment of the national government—that is, by nomination, and subsequent election.

The independence of the courts is generally considered an object of first importance in the constitution of government. On this subject there will probably not be much difference of opinion—the federalists have always been desirous of it, and as the present chief magistrate has explicitly recommended it, the revolutionists must be considered as approving of the plan. A provision of this sort may therefore meet with a unanimous vote.

With regard to two sessions of the General Assembly, annually, it may be added to what has been already said, that if there should be but one, there must either be a new seat of government, in a more central spot than either Hartford or New-Haven, or the sessions must be held one year at Hartford, and the next at New-Haven. With regard to the first, if there should be a new seat of government found necessary, the State must necessarily in a great measure lose the buildings which they now possess in those towns, and in addition to that, they must build a new state-house—a matter not accomplished without a great and useless expenditure of money. If the Assembly should sit alternately, one year at Hartford, and the next at New-Haven, they must either transport their records from one place to the other, or keep two distinct sets—either of which would be found sufficiently inconvenient, and the transportation sufficiently hazardous.

There are other subjects which might be noticed, but a disposition not to be too prolix induces me to omit several of them. Still there is one which must not be passed totally by. I allude to that of taxation. As part of the revolutionary system relates to this interesting portion of our system, I shall consider it somewhat minutely in my next number.

A Freeman

"A REPUBLICAN," COLUMBIAN REGISTER, AUGUST 8, 1818

"A Republican" was not the first Tolerationist writing in the *Columbian Register* to complain that the government of Connecticut under the charter of Charles II made inadequate provision for a proper separation of powers between the legislative, executive, and judicial branches. But this short, powerful statement, which appeared on August 8, 1818 shortly before the convention assembled, helped put that issue at the front of the convention's agenda.

THE CONSTITUTION.

What are to form the most prominent features of the new Constitution? is a question often asked, and which multiplies upon us, as we draw near the time appointed for the session of the convention. It would be idle if not presumptuous, for any man to attempt to mark out any plan for the government of the Delegates who are about to assemble,—but it is no less the right, than the duty of every individual to lay such facts and opinions before the public, as seem to be necessarily connected with the business for which the convention is to meet.

The charter of Charles the 2d, which forms the basis of our present government, combines, or rather empowers the legislature to combine in their own hands, the three leading branches of the government, to wit—the Executive, Legislative, and Judicial powers. The Governor is not recognized under our present system as an executive branch, distinct from the legislature; and the Judiciary, if it does not in name, constitute a part of the General Assembly, becomes much the same in effect, when we consider that the Judges of our county courts are eligible to, and generally hold seats in both branches of the Legislature,—and those of our higher courts are created by an annual ballot of the Assembly. The charter which authorises the Assembly to clothe itself with these extensive powers, was doubtless a valuable acquisition to our ancestors, situated as they were at the time they received it. They valued it because it professed to make them less dependent on the mother country than the other colonial settlements in America at that time were; it was also valued by the British court, at whose will it was holden, because it enabled the government of the mother country, by th[r]eatening to revoke or curtail the privileges ostensibly secured by the charter, to coerce the colonists into the favorite measures of the crown: hence the good people of Connecticut were deemed after the charter was granted, "the most faithful, obedient and dutiful of his Majesty's leige subjects." The times however have changed since the charter was granted, and it seems to be very generally admitted that the period has arrived, when the government of Connecticut should throw off the trappings of Royalty, and be likened to those monuments of republican wisdom with which it is surrounded. What then should constitute the most prominent features of the new Constitution? Let the Legislative, Executive and Judicial authorities which have been heretofore amalgamated, be first carefully separated, and as carefully protected by constitutional provisions,–let them be so balanced in different hands, as that they may form checks upon each other. Our rights can never be wrested from us if the powers delegated to the Legislature and Executive branches are bro't back to us by frequent elections,—and if our Judiciary is made sufficiently independent to form a barrier against the encroachments of legislative authority, upon those privileges which the people have retained. I cannot better express myself upon this subject than in the language of Mr. Jefferron[sic], in his notes on Virginia. "The concentrating these powers (legislative, executive and judicial,) in the same hands, is precisely the definition of despotic government. It will be no alleviation, that these powers will be exercised by a plurality of hands, and not by a single one; one hundred and seventy-three despots would surely be as oppressive as one. Let those who doubt it, turn their eyes on the republic of Venice. As little will it avail us, that they are chosen by ourselves. An *elective despotism* was not the government we fought for; but one which should not only be founded on free principles, but in which the powers of government should be so divided and balanced among several bodies of magistrates, as that no one could transcend their legal limits without being effectually checked & restrained by the others."

Such were the sentiments of that eminent statesman, even before the formation of most of the Constitutions in this Union.—and such I may add, are the principles which the constitution of the United States, amid all the trials it has encountered, has completely and triumphantly confirmed. But the principles which I advance are not new to the republicans of Connecticut,—they are the same, for the promulgation of which, William Judd and his associates were persecuted and proscribed during the reign of terror. They are the same sentiments which were adopted in the Republican convention of August, 1804.—It was then claimed that a Constitution was necessary for the following reasons, which will be found in the address signed by Mr. Judd.

"If a constitution shall declare *taxation* and *representation* inseperable, the legislator cannot separate them with his breath.

"If a constitution shall declare all men free in the exercise of religion according to conscience, so far as it can be done without violating public order, the legislature cannot bind over one denomination to another.

"If a constitution shall give permanence and independence to Judges, the legislator cannot make Judges annually dependant on his will.

"If a constitution shall establish the qualifications of a freeman, the legislator cannot change them.

"If a constitution shall separate legislative, executive and judicial powers, the legislator cannot unite them in his own person."

Such are the sentiments which have brought down upon Republicans, the intolerance and political persecutions which they have patiently endured for eighteen years,—such were the doctrines of the Convention of August, 1804, and I trust they will not be forgotton in the Convention of August, 1818.

A Republican

"Sidney," *Connecticut Courant*, August 11, 1818

Discourses Concerning Government (1698) by Algernon Sidney (1622-1683) had exerted enormous influence over eighteenth-century American political thinking. His martyrdom in connection with the Rye House plot (1685) to displace Charles II from the English throne helped make "Sidney" almost as popular a pen name as "Freeman" for those commenting on political matters during the revolutionary period. This Federalist essay is noteworthy because it accepted the upcoming convention as necessary but argued vigorously against unduly liberalizing the franchise.

Whatever difference in opinion may have heretofore existed in the minds of the people, as to the expediency of calling a convention of delegates, to form a new constitution of civil government, for this State; yet, as the subject has been pressed upon them by the present ruling party, and delegates chosen, who are soon to meet for the purpose of considering this interesting subject, and as the people have been put to great trouble, and the State is likely to incur no inconsiderable expense, in consequence of it, a pretty general sentiment seems now to prevail, that it will be well to put the subject at rest, by having a constitution framed and presented to the people, embracing the free principles on which the government of the State has rested for nearly two centuries past.

That the delegates, when convened, will proceed to form a constitution of some sort, is hardly to be doubted; and should they be so fortunate as to unite, and frame a system, founded on sound policy, embracing the general principles of freedom and rational liberty, it might, and probably would, prove a lasting blessing to the people of the State. But, if party feelings and prejudices are to prevail; if the wise and wholesome laws, and excellent institutions, which have been made and established by our venerable forefathers, are to give way, or be abandoned, for the purpose of gratifying any particular sect or party, in their wild and discordant theories, or ambitious and selfish designs; then, indeed, the good people of Connecticut may look for bitterness and a curse, instead of a blessing.

How far the convention may deem it expedient to enter into the details of a system of government, will be a question for the delegates, in their wisdom, to determine. Perhaps, sound policy would dictate, that whatever is done on the subject should be made to conform to our present existing laws and regulations, rather than to depart from those principles and usages which both wisdom and experience have sanctioned, with a view of changing those laws and regulations, so as to conform to any new and untried system that may be adopted.

Whatever course may be pursued, the ideas and opinions of individuals, thrown into common stock, may not be altogether useless to those who are chosen to deliberate and act on a subject altogether new and interesting to the people of this State. With these impressions and views, the writer of these remarks, with due deference, offers them to the public.

In framing a constitution of civil government, the important principle of the right of suffrage will naturally come under consideration. In representative governments, the electors may be said, with propriety, to be the materials of which the government is formed, and the foundation on which it rests: If these materials and this foundation be defective, the fabric cannot long endure, but will soon totter and fall into ruins.

Various have been the opinions and speculations of modern theoretical politicians, respecting this subject. Some few have gone so far as to advocate the doctrine of universal suffrage; others have considered it proper that this privilege should be restricted, in a greater or less degree, to those who possess certain qualifications pointed out by law. No uniform rule has, however, been adopted in any two or more States in the nation; Some qualification has, in every State, been thought necessary; that of a certain fixed term of residence previous to exercising the privilege of voting, has been the least requirement. How far it may be deemed good policy to extend the elective franchise in this State may be a doubtful question. Our prudent and discerning ancestors, it seems, did not consider the extension of this privilege to all classes and descriptions of men as being consistent with the genuine principles of civil liberty, or the stability and safety of the government; and experience has taught us, that our forefathers were wiser in this respect than their descendants in later years have been.

Universal suffrage is to be deprecated, not so much on account of the confusion to which it leads, but because, in reality, we should lose the very object which we all ought to be solicitous to obtain. It would, in fact, from its very nature, embarrass and prevent the deliberate voice of the community from being heard. No man of reflection can for a moment believe, that by counting all the heads the deliberate body of the people would be augmented or multiplied. The great serviceable object is to bring into activity the greats numbers of independent electors, and at the same time to exclude the greatest number of those who, from their situation and condition in society, cannot, or will not, exercise the privilege with propriety and sound discretion. The great difficulty is, to find where the line should be drawn, and what qualifications (which always ought to be possessed at the time of voting) distinctly defined, either by the constitution or by law; and so guarded as to prevent frauds and abuses being practised, whereby the privilege of our elections may become corrupted, and our freedom destroyed.

"Civil liberty," (says a celebrated modern writer,) "does not depend on our exercising the privilege of voting; but consists in this, that *every man, while he respects the persons of others, and allows them quietly to enjoy the fruits of their industry, be certain himself likewise to enjoy the produce of his own industry, and that his person be also secure."* We frequently hear it said, by men who have other views than those of the public peace and happiness, that those who are not freemen or (in other words) voters at our elections, are consequently slaves. Such remarks may serve to create uneasiness, and disturbance in society, and answer the purposes of ambitious designing men, but have no foundation in truth; since it is well known by every man who is fit for an elector, that those who are not voters, are equally benefitted and protected by our laws, as those are who exercise the privilege of voting. And the benefits arising from a well regulated system regarding the rights of election are equally felt by all, whether they exercise the right of suffrage, or whether they do not.

Should this subject engage the attention of the convention, it is suggested, whether some more convenient and regular mode of exercising the privilege of election may not be devised to prevent that irregularity, confusion and delay which sometimes occurs at the meetings in populous towns. *Sidney*

"ANOTHER FREEMAN," *CONNECTICUT COURANT,* AUGUST 18, 1818

On the eve of the convention "Another Freeman" put a new twist on the religious issue. "Plato" had already argued (*Connecticut Courant,* August 5, 1817) that toleration was intolerant of the religious majority of Congregationalists. "Another Freeman" carries this idea further by setting the republican majority principle in opposition to religious freedom and equality. By doing so he threatened the spirit of accommodation that had surfaced once the Federalists realized that they would have a significant voice in the constitutional convention. The warning of "Another Freeman" that the Episcopalians would be destroyed by the implementation of Tolerationist principles, which he argues were intrinsically anti-republican, also challenged the cohesion of the coalition that had led the constitutional movement. "Another Freeman" appeared ten days before the Convention assembled.

AS far as I am acquainted with the feelings of the different denominations of christians in the State, who are generally supposed to have had some direct or indirect interest in bringing us into the condition in which we now stand, and which I believe is viewed by many of them in a much more serious light than they at first expected it would be, the disposition to break down all the old ecclesiastical establishments is confined to two only—*the Baptists and Methodists.* I am well persuaded that this part of the revolutionary system cannot be agreeable to the Episcopalians, because it is very apparent that if once carried into effect, it would go very far to destroy all their congregations. They cannot maintain their present standing for numbers and respectability, if the power of taxation should be taken from them. Indeed, the general system of church government, influence, and control—the distinctions of rank and dignity in the priesthood of the Episcopal church, are diametrically and inherently opposed to the Baptist and Methodist establishments; and it is impossible that they should harmonize on many other points, as well as those above alluded to.

I was struck with the reasonableness and force of some remarks of your correspondent who signs himself "A Freeman," relative to the character of the claim set up by the Baptists and Methodists, that the ecclesiastical laws shall all be repealed, and the community at large *be placed on the footing that pleases them.* These denominations are a small minority compared with the Presbyterians and Episcopalians, or, indeed, the Presbyterians alone. With what face can they claim of the majority, that the laws of the State shall be rendered inconvenient and injurious to the interests of *the many,* and made to suit the views or the feelings of *the few.* The fundamental principle of a republican government is, that *the majority shall govern.* THE MINORITY OF THE PEOPLE HAVE NO MORE RIGHT TO INSIST ON MAKING THE LAWS, THAN THE MINORITY IN THE LEGISLATURE. All that they can require, or can request, in either situation is, that any peculiar hardships which they experience, shall be relieved. To go any further is anti-republican; and not only so, but it is indecent and arrogant. Now the hardships which the Baptists and Methodists are subjected to, or imagine themselves subjected to, by the operation of the ancient and venerable ecclesiastical laws of the State, are completely removed by the laws which have long been in force *exempting them from taxation.* Every privilege which in reason, justice, or decency, they can demand, is afforded to them already; and if they are not satisfied with such a state of things, there is no good reason to conclude that they will be satisfied with any thing short of the absolute control of the reins of government. To them they will be entitled *when they become the majority, and not till then*—nor can they be granted to them whilst they are a minority, without subverting the very vital principle of the government under which we live.

In this view of the case, which has been suggested to me by the remarks of your correspondent above referred to, it is impossible for the State, whether they are hereafter to live under their excellent OLD GOVERNMENT, or to try the hazardous experiment of a new-one—under any system, old or new, it is impossible that this extravagant, and unjust demand of the minority can be submitted to by the majority. And it is very apparent from the extreme alarm and anxiety that exists in the State for our future safety if we should be left under the guidance and control of visionary, ignorant, and unprincipled men, that THE FREEMEN INTEND TO ABIDE BY THE GREAT, SACRED, FUNDAMENTAL PRINCIPLES OF THEIR ANCIENT, FREE, AND BENIGN SYSTEM OF GOVERNMENT.

Another Freeman

"B.X.," *CONNECTICUT JOURNAL,*
AUGUST 18, 1818

Further Federalist misgivings about the approaching convention are voiced by "B.X." in a piece that appeared simultaneously in the *Connecticut Courant* and *Connecticut Journal* on August 18, 1818. He questions whether the legislative resolution calling the convention and prescribing the schedule for the submission of the new constitution to the freemen for ratification is consistent either with republican principles or the best interests of the state. Calling into question the legitimacy of the constitutional movement on the eve of the Convention's meeting did not augur well for its success.

We are on the eve probably of the most important change that has ever taken place in the government of Connecticut, a government more venerable for its antiquity, at least, than any other republic on earth. And such has been the wonderful management of *Foot, Channing,* and other patriots of the same water,[1] that with respect to the great change the voice of the people has been scarcely heard, and all public discussion is in effect silenced.—What part, I would ask, have the freemen been permitted to act on this momentous question, except that of mere puppets, pushed on by some of the most hot-headed of the democratic leaders? Under the pretence that about *thirty* towns wished for a Convention, (I say *pretence,* for a majority of the voters in these towns were never brought to act on the subject) our late *illustrious* assembly resolved forthwith to call a Convention; the business was of such "*unimaginable*" importance, that it would not admit of a moment's delay; it could not be postponed beyond the warm and busy months of summer; but the election of delegates must be holden at least as early as July; the Convention must meet at all events in August, and within three weeks after this, every freeman in the State

---

[1] Samuel A. Foote of Cheshire and Henry Channing of New London had been among the most vocal spokesmen for abandoning the joint committees that had given the Council controlling influence over the legislature as well as for constitutional reform in the recent legislative session.

should be compelled to say yea, or nay, to the new Constitution! Within the short period of a month then the whole of this momentous business is to be completed; the Convention are to meet and finish their work, and the people are immediately to pronounce their judgment. This is indeed despatching business *alamode de Francois;* it is calling upon the people of Connecticut to divest themselves at once of a government under which they have enjoyed perfect liberty for nearly two centuries, and to substitute in a moment as it were, a Constitution sketched off by some visionary politician, perhaps in the space of two hours! There is no time to pause, there is no looking backward or forward. We must march directly up to the precipice; we must vote on this question or on that, both as to manner and time, precisely as we have been directed by the chief jugglers who manoeuver behind the scene.

Admitting that the Convention, with all its imperfections, is more respectable than sober men of either party once apprehended, still it does not seem right to transfer more than two hundred and sixty thousand people from one form of government to another without consulting them, and with less ceremony than the legislature would use in setting off a new town, or granting an insolvent's petition. In the legislature even private business is usually postponed from one session to another, to give those concerned a fair opportunity to furnish the legislature with all the information they can, and to make their wants and grievances fully known, and much more we should suppose in a case of this solemn nature, should ample opportunity be afforded both to the Convention and to the people, for their deliberations. It often takes a week, nay, and sometimes repeated sessions of the legislature, both in our state and general governments, to digest and perfect a single law: but here is a whole code of laws, embracing all our dearest rights, and designed to last for ages, upon which, as the matter has been managed, thirty thousand freemen will be compelled to sit in judgment before the one half of them can have had any fair opportunity even to read the code. The people perceive the awkwardness of their situation on this question; that their voice can have very little weight; and this accounts for their astonishing apathy. Wonderful as it may seem it is a fact, that the freemen of this old republican state actually think and talk less about breaking up the foundations of their antient government, and rearing an entirely new political edifice, than they do about the appearance of a Sea Snake off our coast, or the sulkiness of Bonaparte at St. Helena. These things ought not so to be.

Was it for the good of the people that our legislature have so hurried this business as to cut off all fair opportunity of discussion? Or did they calculate upon such an overwhelming majority of democrats in the convention as would carry the constitution by the mere force of party, and thus relieve the people from the trouble of reflecting upon its principles? Did they expect to *gerrymander* the state, prolong the tenure of their own offices, give the whole power of appointment into the hands of their leaders, break down our religious institutions, and destroy the purity of our elections, and that the majority would yield a blind assent to all this because it was done by *their* party? If so they mistook the character of the majority! The people of Connecticut know what their old constitution is, and unless their judgment has indeed "fled to brutish beasts," they will insist upon knowing what their new one is also, before they give it their support. They will never vote for it until they have fully comprehended and maturely weighed all its principles, they will never throw their old government to the winds, until they are perfectly satisfied that they have got a better one to substitute in its place. The vine which has sheltered them and their fathers they will not relinquish for a gourd, of which it may hereafter be said, that like Jonah's, "it sprung up *in* a night and perished in a night."

Were the people all lawyers or statesmen, the momentary interval allowed by the legislature between the drafting and ratification of the new constitution, might suffice, perhaps for forming our opinions, but these are not the only classes of the people that have an interest in this subject. All classes of people will want to read and understand it, and for the legislature to tell them in effect, that it is no matter whether the *common people* have had time to make up their judgment, that their opinions are of no consequence, that their *votes* are all that is required of them, is an insult to their understandings, and a mockery of freedom.

B.X.

POST-CONVENTION COMMENTARIES

"THE CONSTITUTION," HARTFORD *TIMES*, SPETEMBER 22 AND 29, 1818

The Hartford *Times* greeted the release of the draft constitution with two long editorials that appeared on September 22 and 29, 1818 assessing the strengths and weaknesses of the document. The *Times'* endorsement of ratification grew stronger as the date set for the freemen to vote on the document approached.

THE CONSTITUTION (SEPTEMBER 22)

In the preceding columns of this paper, will be found the Constitution, which has been framed by the Convention, and which, according to a resolve thereof, is to be submitted to the people for their consideration, on the first Monday of October. By the resolve of the General Assembly, under which the Convention was organised, it was left with that body to determine what proportion of the freemen should be necessary to the ratification of the Constitution; and they have decided that if it shall be approved by a majority of those who may vote on the occasion, it shall go into operation. It now remains for the people, who, from the theory of our government possess the sovereign power, to decide whether this Constitution shall become the basis of the government of this state or not. This, if we are not mistaken, is the first instance in which a constitution has been submitted, directly to the people, and in which the voice of every elector would have a direct and numerical influence in its rejection or adoption. In Massachusetts their Constitution was submitted to, and adopted by the towns, which was quite a different thing from one's being submitted to the people, in their individual capacity. A question of this description is undoubtedly the most important of any of a political nature, which can ever come before the people; it is bringing their power directly into view; as they are called upon to decide as to what form of government, & what description & character of magistracy shall be constituted & established[.] This is bringing the government home to the people; or rather it is originating from them, the only legitimate source of power[.] This is the first question of this description which was ever submitted to the people of Connecticut, and if the Constitution which has been framed by the Convention, should be adopted, it is not probable that any of us now living shall ever again be called upon to act upon a subject of a similar nature. Its magnitude and importance are apparent, and we hope and trust that it will receive that candid and dispassionate consideration which its nature and importance demand, and which the intelligence and soberness that characterise our citizens, authorise us to expect. As a Constitution has been formed, and is to be submitted to the people, it must be disposed of—Under existing circumstances then, there are but three courses which can be pursued: 1st, To adopt this Constitution, in which case the government will be organized according to its provisions. 2d, To reject this Constitution, and to attempt to cause it to be amended or another to be framed; or 3d, To reject this Constitution and continue our "Steady Habits," or the present form of government. It may perhaps be expected that we should attempt to give a direction to the public mind upon this subject; and to disclose our views as to the merits or demerits of the Constitution. We have no wish to shrink from any responsibility which it may be proper to assume; and we perceive little in the present case, as we cannot believe it at all *doubtful*, as to the result of this subject. The Constitution will doubtless be adopted, and would if it was much less perfect than it is. Such is the character of the human mind, and so indiscriminating are our views of things, that when any subject has long been agitated, and the public mind strongly excited in its favor, if, in its progress, it should undergo an essential change in its character, no matter from what circumstances, it will still proceed from the impulse which it at first received. With respect to our own views of this Constitution, they had been disclosed upon all the important principles which it embraces, except two; the judiciary and the rights of conscience, before it was framed, and we have had no occasion to change them since. Of the two subjects here noticed, the former has not been disposed of according to our ideas, although we would have wished to have given to the judiciary a more permanent and a *different* character from what it has had in this state; but we would not have had it independant of the *people*. The rights of conscience have been settled upon principles more liberal and satisfactory than we expected, considering the situation of the state; it being carved out into religious corporations, many of which have funds and other property, whose rights (however impolitic it might have been to have established them at first) cannot now be invaded. The article relating to this subject is, in our opinion, the most unexceptionable part of the Constitution; besides this, however, it contains many valuable principles. The right of suffrage is established upon a just foundation, and upon more liberal principles than are adopted in any state in the union; although for our own part we should have liked it better if they had been more liberal still. The Executive is to be excluded from the Senatoral branch of the Legislature, and the different powers of the government partially separated and confided to distinct bodies of magistracy: we say partially separated, for the separation of powers is but partial, as all the judicial officers are to be appointed by the Legislature, and with the exception of the supreme judges, all are eligible as members of that body. But we have not room to particularize; and it may suffice to say, that, in our opinion, the Constitution framed by the Convention contains many valuable principles and features, & some which are exceptionable. Our objections to it are, that it "savours too much of the old leaven;" the defects and faults of the old system have not been sufficiently remedied: It exhibits also too much of a spirit of imitation—it pays in some respects, an idolatrous devotion to ancient times, and the venerable institutions of other countries. It is not as we were in hopes it might have been, a mirror of the political science, the experience, the intelligence, and the improvements of modern times. But we are sensible of the situation of the Convention, and of the difficulty which every liberal or novel principle (in the minds of those who never think) met with. We are sensible of the difference in acting upon this subject in the abst[r]act, and under the circumstances which exist in this state—a form of government venerable for its antiquity, and deep rooted and inveterate prejudices, strengthened by associations, consecrated by time, and interwoven into the tissue of the public mind. We are fully sensible of these circumstances, and of the striking difference between what is *proper* and what is *practicable.*

After this succinct and imperfect view of the subject, the question again presents itself: What is the best course to pursue? This question every one must answer for himself, and act accordingly; but we have no hesitation in saying how we shall act, and upon what considerations. *We shall support the Constitution*—not because we deem it a party measure, and in point of fact it is not so, but because we have always considered, and still consider that this state was without a constitution of civil government, and that it is important that it should have one. We wished and hoped that we might have had one more in conformity to our ideas, but it is still problematical, whether the people are prepared for one more perfect than this, or which should be essentially different in its features; and if so, the only question is whether we shall adopt this Constitution or continue the present government without any at all? Upon this view of the subject we cannot hesitate a moment how to act.

THE CONSTITUTION (SEPTEMBER 29)

Shall, or shall it not be ratified by the People? This question is to be decided, on Monday, the 5th of October next. The more we reflect upon this subject, the more we are pursuaded, that it is all-important to ratify the Constitution. The reasons for this measure are derived in part from the Constitution itself, and in part from other considerations.

With respect to the first; although as we observed last week, the Constitution contains some provisions which are exceptionable, it comprises many valuable and important principles. These principles are essential to the security of the rights of the people, and as we have now, for the first time, an opportunity of establishing them forever, it would be extremely unwise to suffer this opportunity to pass by, as it may never occur again. The principles to which we more particularly allude are contained in the 6th and 7th articles, the latter placing upon a just foundation the rights of conscience, and the former establishing the "right of suffrage" upon definite and liberal principles. If the Constitution is ratified these subjects, which have been deemed more important than any other, and which have long agitated the state, will be settled forever, and in the most satisfactory manner. There are other principles which are important; the separation of the powers of government, at least in part; the establishment of the School Fund as a permanent fund, so that it can never be diverted to other purposes, under any pretence whatsoever, the restoring to the towns, or rather to the people, the privilege which they once enjoyed, and of which they are now deprived, of constituting the board for the examination of the qualifications of electors. But in addition to these and other matters, the influence of which is immediate and practical; the great and fundamental principles of civil liberty, and of social rights are recognized and established in the "declaration of rights." These are some of the advantages to be derived from the ratification of this Constitution. Will it be wise then to throw them away? Would not this be the consummation of folly or delirium? There can be but one reason why we should hesitate to secure these principles; which is this: that by sanctioning these we shall of necessity have to sanction others, which are so exceptionable that we shall loose as much upon one hand as we gain upon the other. But is this so; will the people by the ratification of this Constitution, lose any rights which they now possess. We think not. Our objections to the Constitution are, that it has not sufficiently *remedied the defects* which now exist; and that it has too great a conformity to the present system of government. The people can sustain no *loss* by adopting principles which exist at this time, although these principles may be somewhat imperfect. So far as the proposed system is in conformity to the present one, we can lose nothing by adopting it; and if those features and principles which *differ* from the present system, are *better*, and more in conformity to our ideas of Government and civil rights, then so far as this difference extends will the people be gainers by the adoption of this Constitution. Is not this correct? Is it not the greatest objection to the Constitution that it has not gone far enough? But because we cannot obtain all that we wished, shall we obtain nothing? Shall we throw away wholesome nourishment, which would sustain life, because it is not in all respects seasoned to our taste? No, let us secure what we can at this time, and trust to futurity for the rest. All improvements have been slow and gradual, and if we aim at too much we shall get nothing. We must be satisfied with the course and progress of things, and those who are not, repine against Providence. It is true as is here observed, that all the alterations upon the present system are for the better, unless the judiciary be considered as an exception. But the objections to this feature in the Constitution, although we consider them to be just, are in point of fact, confined to abstract principles, for the judges of the Supreme Court always have, and probably always will be, continued in office as long as they *behave well*. And it is proper that *good behavior* should be the tenure of their office, and the only objection is, that the *people* ought to judge as to this. But as the article now stands their representatives can do this; although more than a majority of them is required; which we think incorrect.

We think, therefore, we have established the position which we laid down; that the proposed Constitution, so far as it departs from the present system, is for the *better;* (the judiciary being considered in *point of fact* as it has been heretofore,) and that the objections to it are that it does not go far enough. By adopting it, therefore, we shall *gain* something and *lose* something. Indeed, fellow citizens, we shall gain much; we shall secure some of the most important principles for which we have contended for twenty years. Are not these principles vital to the republican citizens of Connecticut? They must indeed be precious if they are to be estimated according to the sacrifices which have been made to secure them.

What has been the expence of more than 10,000 freemen attending freemen's meeting twice a year for fifteen years past. In the year 1804, there was a Convention of delegates from 97 towns met at New-Haven, for the purpose of considering the subject of procuring a Constitution of Civil Government for the people of this state, the object of which was to secure the right of suffrage, and the other important principles which are provided for in this instrument. It is now fourteen years since that Convention was held, during which time we have been struggling for this object, and for the security of these rights. What has been the expence of this long contest? The time which has been spent in attending freemen's meeting and otherwise, having a relation to this subject, and being calculated to promote these objects, by those who have been friendly to them, for the last fourteen years would, at a fair estimate, amount to an enormous sum. But this is considering merely the pecuniary costs. And it is impossible to estimate the sacrifice of feeling, the reproaches and indignities which the friends of this measure have endured. In addition to all this, there are the sacrifices which individuals have sustained on this account which cannot be estimated, but which must amount to an enormous sum. Such has been the course and the consequences of this measure, such the sacrifices which have been made; and such the difficulties with which it has been attended. But under these difficulties and sacrifices, the friends of a Constitution have remained steadfast; they have remained true to their principles; and from a long and steady perseverance, worthy of a great and good cause, have brought it to its present situation. They have done all they can do, and it now remains for the people to say whether it shall receive its final consummation, or whether all this toil, persevereance and sacrifice, shall be lost, and the subject abandoned forever.

———

We published last week [September 22], connected with the Constitution, the *order* of the Convention, directing the mode of its being submitted to the Freemen, and the number of votes necessary to its ratification. But, neither this order nor the resolution of the General Assembly, relating to this subject, direct, specifically the mode of considering or voting upon the Constitution, by the freemen in the towns.

It is evident, therefore, that the manner of proceeding and voting, is to be regulated by the freemen, themselves, after the meetings are formed. Some gentlemen may wish to discuss the subject; and others having made up their minds, will not wish to be detained. We would propose the following course: After the meetings are formed let the Constitution be read; immediately after which let the votes be called for. The proper mode of voting would be by ballot; each elector who wished to ratify the Constitution, to hand in a piece of paper written upon it "yes," and each who wished to oppose its ratification, to hand in a piece of paper written upon it "no." Although we think it would be proper that the ballot should be opened immediately after the Constitution has been read to the meeting; yet the subject might at the same time be open for discussion. This arrangement would give those who might not wish to be detained, an opportunity to vote and retire; and also would indulge those who may wish to discuss the subject, or to hear it discussed. It would be well to appoint Inspectors of the election, who should receive and count the votes, and make a statement thereof to the presiding officer. It would also be well to have the name of each Elector as he gives in his ballot, written upon a list or alphabet, to guard against frauds. It will be perceived that it is necessary to return the votes which may be given, *both for and against ratifying the Constitution.*

"A FREEMAN," *CONNECTICUT COURANT,*
SEPTEMBER 22, 1818

"A Freeman" drafted these objections to the Constitution of 1818. They appeared first in the *Connecticut Courant* on September 22 and subsequently in the *Connecticut Journal* on September 29, 1818.

Messrs. PRINTERS,
THE Convention having completed their session, and given us a draft of a Constitution, I wish to give you and your readers some of the reasons why I cannot vote to accept it as the constitution of this state.

1. It authorizes universal suffrage. Almost every republic, ancient and modern, has done this in some period of their history. And no one has failed of falling, soon after this measure, into a monarchy. The true qualification for the right of suffrage is character. In a country like ours, every person possessing honesty, prudence, and industry, the principal qualities of good character, may and will acquire a certain portion of property. That, therefore, is the most just qualification for a voter, because it is the surest test of character. And, as such, has been made the necessary qualification for the right of suffrage in all wise and prosperous republics. The qualifications proposed to our new constitution are complicated and perplexing, and amount to nothing. They will make trouble, while they really exclude no man of lawful age. It would be much better if it gave the right of voting to every man of 21 years of age.

2. It makes a mere cypher of the Governor. He is to sign the laws if he approve them. And the acts of the assembly become laws if he does not. He can call them to re-consider their vote, but if a bare majority adheres to the vote his objections are of no avail. What man of honorable feeling would

ever call on the assembly to re-consider a vote under such circumstances? If two thirds of the assembly wish for a dismission of the Judges, the governor must perform the unpleasant task. He has no right to refuse, nor ask for any reasons. During the session of the assembly, the governor must sit at his lodgings, and wait on company, and if he wishes to know something of their deliberations, he must read the newspapers, or go into the gallery. He is to see to the execution of the laws. So is every Justice of Peace and constable. The governor must sign commissions. But he may not refuse to do it, though he has no voice in the appointments. Would Trumbull or Griswold[1] have accepted such an office? I think not.

3. The general assembly are not required to do any thing, by the enactment of laws, or in any other manner, to promote the interest of literature, morals or religion; to afford any encouragement to agriculture, manufactures, or commerce, nor, in short, to make any exertions to promote the improvement, the prosperity, or the happiness of the people of the state. The states around us are making rapid advancements in all the improvements of civil society, while this constitution seems to suppose that we shall remain stationary forever. Indeed the whole spirit of this instrument seems to be to check the enterprise and dampen the energies of the people.

4. Our proposed constitution has no provision whatever on the great and important subject of taxation.

5. It provides for but one session of the general assembly in a year. As the people have constant occasion to present petitions and claims to that body, it must often be very inconvenient to wait for their annual session. As that is to be held in May and June, the most busy season of the year, the representatives will be so anxious to get home, that much business will necessarily be laid over to the following year. Every other year the people in the southern part of the state must come to Hartford for their business with the Assembly, and the people of the northern part must go to New-Haven. The members of the Assembly, sitting so long in May and June, will justly deserve higher wages than they have now. The expense to the state must undoubtedly be increased. I know not how it can be right to take from Hartford the privilege of the general election. I think it would not be right to deprive New-Haven of the benefits of the public commencement. On the proposed plan, the public election must soon come to nothing.

6. The proposed Constitution is designed to *unchristian* a large portion of the community. The young man, on becoming of age, is supposed to belong to no christian denomination, and to have no religion, unless he makes it

---

[1] Jonathan Trumbull and Roger Griswold had been governors of the state, the former during the Revolution and the latter at the beginning of the War of 1812.

known by some public act. This, as is evidently intended, a great number never will do. Why is the young man called upon to take an oath in a court of justice, when the law has no knowledge, and no right to presume that he believes in the existence of God, or an overruling providence, or a future state. The Constitution neither relieves those professing christians who believe it to be wrong to authorize taxes for the support of religion by law, nor answers the wishes of those who believe all ought to bear a part in the support of religious institutions. The existing provisions are sufficient to make trouble and contention, with very little good.

7. An objection equal, almost, to any other, is that a bare majority of the freemen shall be sufficient for the adoption of this Constitution. Of 30,000 voters, the votes of 15,001 shall make this instrument the supreme law of the land; a thing unheard of in the history of constitutions. That of the United States required more than two-thirds of the people for its adoption. Nothing can show more clearly the want of confidence which the Convention had in its merits. Should this instrument be forced into operation by a bare majority of the people, it would produce such dissatisfaction, as would leave no prospect of its continuance, or of peaceable times.

8. The question on the adoption of this Constitution, is not whether we will have this or none; if it were, I should feel differently: for even this would be preferable to no government at all. But we have a form of government, under which the people of this state have enjoyed quietness and prosperity for a long period. I prefer remaining with that system till we have a prospect of something better than the Constitution now proposed.

A Freeman

"A FREEMAN," CONNECTICUT COURANT, SEPTEMBER 29, 1818

On September 29 yet another "A Freeman" offered a more wide-ranging and thoughtful critique of the new constitution in the *Connecticut Courant*. The detailed nature of his objections suggest that he either had been a delegate to the convention himself or had ready access to a delegate. He too urged rejection of the convention's handiwork, arguing that retaining a political system that was sanctioned by more than one hundred fifty years of usage was the wisest course. And he appealed to the religious sentiments of Congregationalists in his effort to have the new constitution rejected.

THE Convention has, at length, closed its labours, and the freemen of this state are to be presented with the fruits of their three weeks deliberation, in the form of a Constitution, on which they are in a few days to act, and either to adopt it as the form of government under which they and their posterity are hereafter to live, or, otherwise to reject it, and resume their old, tried, approved, and excellent system. A very short time is to be allowed us to exercise this solemn duty. It would seem as if the movers of our public disturbances, the fomenters of discord, the voracious spirits, who, hungering and thirsting after offices, had no other means of obtaining them than by throwing the state into confusion and convulsion, were unwilling to trust *us* with the opportunity calmly, coolly, and deliberately to sit down and examine their system, to enumerate their alterations, compare the merits of the old and the new forms, and to duly weigh and estimate the *improvements* in the latter, before we are definitely called upon to adopt or reject them. In this state of things—amidst all the bustle, hurry, and violence, which we have experienced on this subject, it is the duty of every man who feels interested in the happiness and prosperity of the state, to do all in his power to form his own correct opinion, and, as far as possible, to assist his neighbours in making up theirs, that we may act understandingly, firmly, and consistently in the great and solemn duty before us.

We have none of us forgotten the alarming outcries that designing and evil-minded men have made, from time to time, and especially within the last three years, regarding the mischiefs of our old government, and the *intolerable* oppression which it has produced upon a suffering community. Men, whose lives and conversation, have never shewed any serious regard to religion, good order, or good morals, but on the contrary, a deep and practical aversion to them all, have, if we are to believe their own declarations, felt extreme solicitude for their well-being. Thence arose the uproar for "*Toleration*"-and from thence issued that weak and fatal delusion, which has paved the way for the introduction of the threatening calamities which now hang so portentously over our heads. *To turn the attention of my fellow freemen to their present situation, to point out to them the evils with which they are threatened, and to induce them to* EXERCISE THE POWER LODGED IN THEIR HANDS, TO REJECT AN INSTRUMENT POSSESSING SCARCELY ONE MATERIAL ADVANTAGE OVER THEIR OLD GOVERNMENT, BUT UNDER MUCH FORMALITY AND POMP OF UNMEANING LANGUAGE, FRAUGHT WITH EVILS OF A MOST SERIOUS CHARACTER, is the object I have in view. In the execution of this task, I shall use the utmost "*freedom of speech,*" feeling it to be a period in which the exigencies of the state imperiously demand the greatest plainness and frankness of language and sentiment.

In the first place, it will be well for the freemen to estimate the pecuniary expenses which the movers of the Convention have subjected the state to in the execution of their plan. It has heretofore been fashionable in Connecticut to practise the most strict and uniform economy in the expenditure of public money. To this spirit is it owing, that among all the heavy exactions of the last fifteen years—during the period of embargoes, nonintercourses, and other ridiculous and mischievous restrictions on trade and business of every kind, and more especially during a war in which taxes of most unexampled severity were laid upon our houses, lands, trades, furniture, and utensils, that still, the finances of the state have been preserved, no debts incurred, and the treasury has been kept in the most secure and prosperous condition. Would this have been the fact, had there not been the most faithful attention paid by our rulers to rigid economy? But, what has been the conduct of the revolutionary party, since they have had the control of our affairs? This single unnecessary and preposterous measure of a Convention, has cost the people of this state, including the expense of one election past and one to come, no less a sum than $ 40,000.—The expense of the Convention alone is about $11,000. Could such a waste of public money have occurred under the former administration of our government? The answer need scarcely be given—all the friends of that administration look upon the attempt to destroy the old government with abhorrence, and they view the project of making a new one as mischievous in the extreme; of course, they could never have squandered such a large sum of money upon such a needless and pernicious measure.

That the plan of making a new constitution was perfectly unnecessary must be apparent to every friend of the peace, the tranquility, and the happiness of the state, who has been intimately acquainted with its ancient government. But I will endeavor to shew this to be true, by more irrefragable arguments. For this purpose I beg your attention, my fellow freemen, to a few provisions of the constitution, which the convention have formed and submitted to us.

This instrument commences with a long preamble, under the imposing title of a *"Declaration of Rights."* It would seem by the parade with which this article is introduced, that the inhabitants had not heretofore been secured in the enjoyment of their essential privileges. But, is there any honest and intelligent freeman in the state, whose mind is not swayed by passion, resentment, prejudice, or strong selfishness, that will seriously declare this? Every important right which this tedious and prolix article contains, is contained in the "Abstract of Rights," at the head of our venerable statute book,[1] and the people of Connecticut have enjoyed the free and unobstructed exercise of them, ever since that abstract was framed. Nay, this very convention, a great proportion of whom are not greatly accustomed to make their acknowledgements to an overruling Providence, do, in *the very preamble to this their declaration, acknowledge, with gratitude, the good providence of God, in having permitted them to enjoy a free government*—thereby giving the direct lie to their long multiplied complaints of its tyranny and oppression. The "Declaration of Rights," then, with all its pomp and verbiage, is a mere servile copy of similar compositions, drawn up in states whose forms of government are of *yesterday*—the very states themselves having been formed more than a century after Connecticut had enjoyed "the blessing of a free government," administered by her own citizens.

I will now notice some of the alterations in the new form of government. By the old government, we had a General Assembly, formed of a *Council of twelve members,* and a house of representatives, of two hundred. By the new government, we are to have *a Senate of twelve*, and a house of two hundred. The difference, if I understand it, is between the name *Senate*, and that of *Council*. I do not see that any thing is gained by the substitution of this new name. With the old one we are familiar—with the new we are not— and that is all. But there is a change in the mode of electing this branch of the legislature. Heretofore we have first made out a nomination, and from that chosen the council. In order to entitle a man to a seat in that body, he must have received the greatest number of votes at two successive elections, which was considered as equivalent to a single majority. This mode of electing is the wisest and best that was ever devised. In the first place, it prevents a noisy demagogue from suddenly procuring himself to be chosen to an important office, by intrigue, clamour, fraud, and falshood—it gives the freemen an opportunity to select such men as they may prefer, without being impelled by necessity to unite on improper persons, for fear of losing their votes—and, at the same time, it secures the certainty of a choice, because *the double plurality* stands in the stead of *a single majority*. By the new constitution, not only are all the particular advantages, except the last, sacrificed, but a principle is introduced, which runs directly abreast of the fundamental doctrine of republicanism. The senators are to be chosen at a single election; and the *twelve persons having the greatest number of votes are*

---

[1] "A Freeman" was disingenuous in this claim as Hudson & Goodwin were the only printers who regularly issued compilations of the *Acts and Laws of the State of Connecticut*. Their publications of 1796, 1804, and 1808 had begun with a copy of the Charter of 1662, the Declaration of Independence, and the Constitution of the United States, to which the 1808 edition added subsequent amendments to the federal Constitution, including the Federal Bill of Rights. But an individual would have experienced trouble in finding in this maze of documents an "Abstract" of his rights as a citizen of Connecticut.

to be declared chosen. A majority is not necessary. This is monstrous, and ought not to be sanctioned in any well regulated community. The old mode would not be justifiable upon any ground, except that of the double plurality which has been mentioned. By the new, a senator may be elected by a *single hundred votes out of twenty-five thousand.* The votes of the town of Stamford, given to James Stevens, as the case may be, may introduce that man, with all his shining political and moral qualities, into the highest branch of our legislative body! ! !² *This single possibility, is a good ground for the virtuous freemen of this state to reject this constitution.*

But the Governour is to be a separate branch of the legislature—or, in the elegant language of this instrument, before it was amended, a *"separate body of magistracy"*—for what good cause, no human being but the makers of it can determine. The powers that are kindly bestowed upon him are not very copious—being, in no particular of the slightest importance different from what he now enjoys, except that he now belongs to the council and presides at its sessions—by the new he is *to stay at his quarters* during the sessions, and when a bill has passed both houses, it is to be sent to him for examination, and if *he likes it,* it becomes a law—if he dislikes it, he may send it back to the place from whence it came, with the reasons of his disapprobation, giving the two houses a *second opportunity* to examine, discuss, *and pass it, by a bare majority,* and then it becomes a law. If this is not ridiculous in the extreme, what is? The governor is to have three days to deliberate. A large part of the bills are passed the last two days of the session. With regard to these bills, he may, if he should so incline, keep the assembly together three days after their other business had been closed waiting for his answer; and if he should send them back half a dozen bills, with his reasons for not signing them, they must either unanimously pass them over again without debate, a mode of proceeding not consistent with good manners, or they must spend perhaps two or three more days in debating the governor's reasons. Should the governor detain the assembly three days, it would cost the state twelve or fifteen hundred dollars, and if the assembly should spend as much more time in debating, it would double the sum. And this for no possible purpose, but only *to put on the show of having something new in the constitution.* We are also to have only one *stated* session of the assembly in a year. Now it is perfectly clear that this alteration is made merely for the sake of a change; or else for some secret selfish purpose; for it is absolutely certain, that there must and will be two sessions in a year, or the public business will be left unfinished. I say *it is certain,* because I conceive it

² James Stevens, or Stephens, had been elected as a town representative from Stamford to the October 1817 and May 1818 legislatures. There he had vigorously advocated certain "reforms," including the repeal of the "Stand-up Law" and, during the spring of 1818, he insisted that the House and Council act separately rather than through joint committees in making judicial appointments. He also supported repeal of the law that allowed the Governor and Council to appoint sheriffs.

impossible to get through the necessary business, from year to year, under six weeks time; and no man, in his senses, can persuade himself that the general assembly *can be kept together six weeks in May and June*—because *it is the busiest and most important part of the year to the farmers*, of whom that body is principally composed. They will then hold an adjourned session; and the state will, of course be put to all the expense and trouble that would have accrued had there been *two stated sessions*. This change has nothing beneficial in it—it has a hypocritical shew of doing *something*, when in reality *nothing* except mischief takes place.

Another alteration, connected with this, should be noticed, to shew how ridiculously men act, when placed in a situation in which they feel themselves bound to do something to save their credit, and know of nothing which the case required to be done. The Convention have [sic] altered the *time of the annual election, that is the meeting of the General Assembly, from the second Thursday in May, to the first Wednesday in the same month.* Men who were not put to their wits end to know what changes to make in a government, would never have supposed such a ridiculous one as this to be of importance.

The mode of counting the votes is much less secure than the old. Who is desirous of leaving all the questions respecting illegal votes, incorrect returns, and all other matters connected with this subject, in the hands of three executive officers to decide? For myself I can say, and I have no doubt I speak the language of a large proportion of the reflecting part of my fellow freemen, that I consider it far more safe in the hands of the General Assembly, as it has always heretofore been, than in those of any individuals, however respectable.

The convention have [sic] extended the right of suffrage, giving it to every man who has done military duty for a year, or paid a state tax within a year. There is no good reason for extending this privilege thus far, and still stopping short of universal suffrage. If it can be limited any where, and this provision shews that it may be, it is a question of expediency at what point it shall be fixed. Heretofore the laws required a qualification of property, either real or personal. This gave the right of voting to almost every industrious citizen, by the time he arrived at the age of twenty-five years. How few such persons are to be found in our country towns, where party spirit has not raged with such violence as it has in the large ones, who cannot be made freemen, if they choose? In the larger towns, the case may be different. But are we, who live in the country, to be placed in the hands and power of such men as throng the cities for day labor, or with other less meritorious views, who have no stake in the soil, no pledge in their families or property? Let it be borne in mind, that if a man is once a freeman, he is always a freeman, in this State. In other states, voters must possess the qualifications at all times when they offer to exercise the privilege, or they cannot be admitted to it. Now, who would willingly have this right bestowed upon a man who merely shoulders a borrowed musket twice a year, and appears for those times in a militia trainband.

Two other subjects have been made the topics of great debate in the convention, and provisions regarding them have been introduced in the proposed constitution, which remain to be noticed.

    I. THE JUDICIARY.

    II. RELIGION.

Respecting the judiciary, a section is introduced, by which *the judges of the highest courts of law are to hold their offices during good behavior*—or in other words, are, what is called, *rendered independent*. The theoretical principle of this provision is well enough, and if it could be realized, would be a point of importance. But, as the world goes, I have strong doubts of its practicability or usefulness. A similar provision is contained in the constitution of the United States, and in a considerable number of those of the individual states. The independence meant by the theory, altogethere [sic] relate to the tenure of office—that a judge who does his duty, shall not *be liable to be turned out*. It is not the fact, however, that provisions of this kind in constitutions, do always produce the desired effect. It is well known, that in the case of the United States judges, by repealing the law by which the courts were formed, the whole of them were displaced, and were never restored. This has happened *frequently* in *several* of the states; and may happen in all of them, when party and passion run high, and the office of a judge becomes an object for a voracious or an ambitious demagogue. And so it may be in this state. But, by the old practice of annual appointments, the office of judge has been as secure and permanent, and indeed much more so, than in many communities where the office is professedly rendered permanent by constitutional provision. We all know that our judges, *until within a single year*, have been secure of their offices, until disqualified by age or infirmity, or their places have been vacated by death or voluntary relinquishment. Of this stability & independence, we have been in the long use and enjoyment; why should we risque an experiment, with no greater prospect of bettering our condition? I would not object strongly to the constitution, if this were the only difficulty with it; but as there are multitudes of others, it is proper that this should be considered, and be entitled to its due weight.

II. With regard to the provisions of the proposed constitution on the subject of our religious institutions, I have a much stronger and deeper train of feelings and emotions. It is well known to all sensible and well informed people, who are at all conversant with the affairs of this State, and it is acknowledged by all good men of that description, that the laws for the support of the christian religion, lie at the foundation of all that is valuable in the political history of Connecticut. I make this remark without fear, and without reserve, notwithstanding the rude clamor and indecent reproach, to which the declaration may subject me from those who, under the pretence of introducing a more liberal, or more justly called a more licentious system, are aiming a deadly blow at the prosperity of the religion itself. The laws for the support of public worship were formed in the very infancy of the colony—they have upheld and preserved the high reputation of the people for wisdom, sobriety, and virtue; and we have reason humbly to conclude, that they have been the means of bringing upon us the approbation and the blessing of God. Who is it that complains of the operation and severity of these laws? Is it the Baptists and the Methodists? What right have they to clamor? The laws do them no injury. Every member of those societies is freed, by the very laws themselves, from all hardship and injustice. They pay not taxes for the support of presbyterian or congregational worship; and being exempted from them, they cannot possibly experience any other mischief. But, with a degree of assurance that would sit better upon any countenance than that of a christian's, they insist upon it, THAT THEIR WILL SHALL GOVERN THE STATE IN THIS PARTICULAR—*that they, a small minority both in numbers and wealth, shall have the right to subject the great majority to their views and wishes*—that as *they dislike the laws under consideration, they must be abolished, tho' four-fifths of the people of the State are strongly in their favor.* And to this unreasonable, this unjust, this supercilious, this anti-republican dogma, the majority of the convention have yielded; and the question now devolves upon the freemen, in the last resort, to say whether it shall prevail against the highest interests, the strongest convictions, the most ample experience, of the great body of our people.

The original settlers of the colony of Connecticut, viewed it as a wise and just system of policy, that every man in the community should contribute his equitable proportion towards the support of religious instruction—upon the same general principle, that every one is held liable to pay taxes for the support of common schools;—religious and moral instruction being, in their opinion, and in the opinion of all good men who have followed them in the State, of at least equal importance in a christian commonwealth with literary.

Bad men, and men of loose opinions on religious subjects, think otherwise; and with them are joined certain religious sects, whose *individual prosperity*, they seem to think, depends very much on the pursuit of an opposite system. Leaving every man, as our laws do, to worship God in his own mode, they only insist upon it that every man shall bear his share of the expenses of the society to which he belongs. If that society supports religious worship by taxes, he is by law bound to pay taxes—if by voluntary contribution, he is left at liberty to contribute, or not, as he pleases. If he prefers a society that supports public worship without taxes, he is at full liberty to join himself to such society, and relieve himself entirely from the burthen. The baptists and methodists raise no money for public worship by taxes—and the laws exonerate them entirely from taxation for this purpose. Still, they claim that others, whose principles in this respect differ from theirs, and whose practice has been equally varient, shall be also exempted. With what face this arrogance can be justified, it is difficult to imagine. It is surely sufficient for them that they are not subject to taxation; and it is the height of impertinence in them to demand that others who do not desire it, should be placed in the same situation. If episcopalians flatter themselves that they can support their congregations, without the power of taxation, they are undoubtedly at full liberty to make the experiment. About the result, no sensible man can easily mistake. But to presbyterians & congregationalists, the subject comes home with a solemn and emphatic force and interest. They form a large majority of the whole community—they possess an equal proportion of its property—they laid the foundation of the peace, prosperity, and distinguished reputation and happiness, which the people of the state have for nearly two centuries enjoyed—and that at a time when there was not a Baptist nor a Methodist within the limits of the colony, to bestow his labor, either in forwarding the great work in which they were engaged, or in obstructing its progress. They, under the smiles of Providence, and against the exertions of those who now disturb the State, have carried it through all its trials, perplexities, and embarrassments, in peace and in war, in prosperity and adversity, until it had reached a degree of character for wisdom, stability, and happiness, unknown in any other political community. In this state of things, an attack is made by discontented sectaries, in conjunction with men of no religious principle or sentiment, to prostrate the fabrick which they had thus reared and established.

My fellow-citizens, on this subject it is too late to stifle or suppress the truth. If this proposed constitution shall be ratified, Connecticut is in danger of being ruined—her realities as well as her visions, of political and social enjoyment, will be blasted, and the labors of her venerable statesmen will be tumbled to the dust. Be not deceived. A number of highly respectable names, actuated by what motives I cannot say, though I have not a doubt they were such as satisfied their own minds and consciences, appear on the vote in favor of referring this instrument to the freemen. I have confidence in the opinion, that they will join with the opponents of its adoption, and vote for its rejection. The question is to come shortly before us, and must be decided. Let not trifling considerations, or selfish motives, or party passions, influence our conduct on this memorable occasion. We shall be called upon not only to decide the future interests and character of the State, its laws, policy, and institutions, but we shall, at the same moment, necessarily sanction or condemn the characters and virtues of our venerable and pious ancestors. The contest concerns all that they did for our prosperity, happiness, and honour. Shall we part with it without a struggle? Shall the principles and policy which they entertained and pursued, and which the great majority of the State still believe and cherish, fall an easy sacrifice to sectarian ambition, and a spirit of insubordination, united with libertinism and infidelity? Let honor, conscience, common sense, and a regard for all that is valuable in our social institutions forbid—and may the God of our fathers, under whose Providence this Vine was transplanted, and has hitherto been sustained, still protect and succor the heritage which we are now called upon to defend against the attacks of its implacable adversaries.

A Freeman

"Z", *Connecticut Courant*, September 29, 1818

This attempt by "Z" to revive the resentments engendered in Connecticut by the War of 1812 and direct them against the new constitution appeared in the *Connecticut Courant* on September 29, 1818.

PEOPLE OF CONNECTICUT,

What meaneth that clause in the Constitution, viz. "The Governor shall be captain-general of the militia of the state, except when called into the service of the United States:" what reason can be assigned why he may not then also. The object of this provision is, to place the militia of the State into the hands of the officers of the U. States. If the Governor must surrender his rank, as a military officer, to any officer of the United States of the smallest grade, surely every other militia officer must do the same. The officer who has the supreme command of any corps, must be an officer of the U. States; and thus, our young men of the militia, in case of a war with England, will be forced into Canada, to perish by the sword, or fall victims to the diseases incident to camps, and so awfully fatal to those who have never been accustomed to the life of a soldier: or in case of a war with Spain, they will be forced to the deadly climate of Florida, almost infallibly fatal to the life of a northern man. That we are in danger of being thus treated, we know; although the government of the United States has power to raise as large armies as they please, and although the Constitution of the United States has guaranteed to us, that the militia shall not be obliged to march out of the limits of these States, yet the government of the United States demanded the command of the militia for the avowed purpose of marching them into Canada; and this act of a most calamitous despotism would have had a precedent, if the patriotism of Gov. Strong of Massachusetts, and Gov. Griswold of Connecticut, had not prevented it. They firmly withstood the demand, and the claim was given up; but this right, this most important right of not being driven from our homes, secured to us by the Constitution of the United States, and by the United States giving up the demand, is now surrendered to the U. States; whilst the militia of every other State are secured from being forced into foreign lands, the militia of this State may be driven into foreign countries, incurring a loss of domestic comforts, intended to be secured to us by the Constitution of the U. States. You can scarcely conceive of a more desirable privilege than that which has been so complaisantly yielded to the government of the United States. This right which is thus secured to you, the Convention had no more right to grant away, than they had to burn your dwellings.

Z

"An Episcopalian," *Connecticut Journal*, September 29, 1818

The attempt of "An Episcopalian" to argue that the proposed constitution threatened the survival of Christianity in Connecticut received reinforcement neither from the author's pen name nor his attempt to portray himself as a victim of the editor of New Haven's *Columbian Register*.

Republicans of Connecticut—
Being denied the privilege of addressing you in a republican paper, I am compelled to take advantage of the liberality of our opponents, and make my appeal through the columns of the Journal.

The editor of the Register, some time since, engaged that his paper should be open to a free discussion of the merits of the new constitution, on the ground that it was not the instrument of a party, but a public law of momentous concern to every freeman. Relying on this promise, the writer made a respectful, but unsuccessful endeavour, to make known to you his sentiments through the columns of the Register. He has been disappointed. The Register is shut to every communication which does not breathe an unrighteous eulogy over the constitution, and condemn with unmerited and unqualified censure the men who oppose it. Fellow citizens, how perilous is our condition! We have allowed us but little more than one week, to accept or reject a constitution, which must deeply affect the interests and happiness of ourselves and our posterity. The people are hurried forward in this great business, without light and without reflection, and the press, which should be the harbinger of truth and the medium of liberal and manly discussion, is now either compelled to be silent, under the influence of designing men, or at most only permitted to present the bright side of the picture, without that due proportion of light and shade which would enable us to judge of the merits of the whole. I am not able to examine every defect which my mind presents, and, passing over subjects of minor importance, approach the article on the subject of religion.—Here, fellow-citizens, is a place to pause and dwell with interest; and before we take a single step, before we plunge from the exalted condition of moral and political felicity, which we have long maintained, it is wise to bring the subject to the bar of reason and of conscience, and give it a fair and impartial trial.

To what cause is it owing that the citizens of this State have become distinguished in the eyes of the world, for sobriety of manners, obedience to the laws, and an upright moral deportment? To our religious societies undoubtedly. Not a city, or a village, but the spires of our sacred temples remind the serious and contemplative stranger that we are a sober and religious people. The government of the State has not been unmindful of religion, as the most successful means of promoting public happiness, and pointed its subjects to the road to heaven, as the certain course to obtain it. Accordingly the youth of this State (contrary to this constitution) have been taught from their infancy that they belong to some denomination of the christian religion: they have been taught to respect the sabbath, and listen to the preaching of the word of God. The habits of their youth have been confirmed by repetition: if they are wise, in riper years the habit itself is considered to be a duty and a pleasure; and they bless the government which has taught them to be virtuous men and good citizens.—The operation of our religious institutions has been seen and felt, and will not be denied to be salutary by any one who is seeking toleration in religion; but by those only who are seeking a toleration for infidels and blasphemers. What says the constitution? "No person shall be classed with, or associated to any congregation, church, or religious association." If a principle of this kind is adopted in Connecticut, I hesitate not to predict that it will brake up and destroy many well regulated religious societies in the State; and advance the interests of none. It will probably ruin the minor sects.—Under such a law they have but few advantages, of numbers, wealth and influence; and even their own children, upon coming of age, not being classed to any religious denomination, will, most probably, in many instances, leave the society altogether; join themselves to some more numerous association, or live as they were born under this constitution, without being *classed* or *associated* to any denomination of the christian religion. What baptist or methodist parent could in his conscience consent that the government should take his child out of the society in which he was born, without placing him in any other; satisfied only by leaving him out of every "congregation, church or religious association"? Yet this is precisely the object contemplated by the new constitution. It will also destroy many well regulated presbyterian and episcopal societies.—Every one that is disaffected; many who prefer their gold to their God, and many who feel it a burden to be "classed or associated to any congregation, church, or religious association," will leave these societies; and by these means the gospel in very many of them must either be supported by a few, or be given up as insupportable, for want of necessary means. In many instances no doubt we shall see wealthy influential and fashionable men, separating themselves from every christian sect; and thus render it reputable, and perhaps fashionable to follow their example, and thus will be destroyed all distinction between "him who serveth God, and him who serveth him not." Any plan proposed for the benefit of any religious society, as the building of a meeting-house, or the settlement of a clergyman, if attended with the least opposition, must be given up, as unsafe to adopt. And how, I ask, in such a state of things, can new churches, and new societies be formed? how much will the efforts of good and pious men to extend the empire of Jehovah, and build up the waste places of Connecticut be weakened? Who then can fail to predict much evil to civil society, and the cause of religion? But it is said that "a provision of this kind is necessary for the enjoyment of toleration in religion." I maintain that this position is absolutely and palpably false: and the only design of this article is to absolve men from all civil obligation to support the gospel; not that it is intolerant to compel them to do it, or that it is opposed to the dictates of conscience; but because the gospel itself is opposed to the depravity of mankind, and the designs of ambition. Indeed this convention says, "it is the *duty* of all men to worship the supreme being, according to the dictates of their own consciences." And let me ask, would it be intolerant for the government to compel an individual to support, or at least be classed with that denomination or sect of christians, who worship according to the dictates of his conscience? certainly not. Every man, however ignorant and wicked, believes it his duty in the language of the new constitution, "to worship the supreme Being, the great Creator and preserver of the universe." And if he is compelled by law to do it, he is only compelled to do that which his conscience informs him is his duty. It is not probable that there is a man now existing in this State who does not believe in his conscience that it is his duty to worship God according to some of the methods of some of the various sects or denominations of christians in Connecticut; though there are many, no doubt, who would be glad to be excused from such worship, in direct violation of conscience and duty. But if there is no such man to be found, whose conscience would not approve of any of the modes of divine worship adopted by mankind, surely it would not be intolerant to compel him to adopt, or at least associate himself and his family to that sect whose form of worship he did approve of. But lest some wretched being should exist, and his poor conscience be tortured, our wise and philanthropic convention have concluded to absolve all men from any civil obligation to support the gospel, as the shortest and safest method to secure the freedom of the mind. No, fellow citizens, it is not freedom of conscience that this article proposes; but freedom to trample it in the earth: and escape from the most sacred obligation to both God and man, which has been imposed by the wisest government hitherto adopted by mankind. I am confident Connecticut will rue the day she accepts of such a Constitution.

An Episcopalian

TWO FEDERALIST COMMENTS ON THE RATIFICATION PROCESS

On October 13, 1818 the *Connecticut Courant* published the following official account of the yeas and nays on the Constitution together with a summary of Federalist complaints about the ratification procedure.

YEAS: 13,918 / NAYS: 12,364 / MAJ. FOR THE CONSTITUTION: 1,554.

By the return of votes it appears that the good people of this state have ratified a Constitution, which was got up for party purposes, at a time when the two great political parties were nearly equal—which was proposed by a Convention, scarcely a member of which approved it, but voted for it for fear of a worse and which the citizens in general dislike. Only three weeks were allowed to print, circulate, read and understand it—the consequence of this unreasonable haste has been, that thousands in the state never saw it till it was read in town-meeting—In many towns debating on its merits was not allowed—and finally ratified, with all its defects, by a very small majority. How long the people will remain quiet under such a constitution remains to be seen.

From various accounts we have had, it seems as if there was a settled plain in the state to prevent discussion in the several town-meetings called to ratify the constitution. Whether the friends of the constitution were afraid of examination, or whether there was not time, we will not now attempt to determine. As every thing relating to this subject may be of importance, we should be gratified with further information on this subject, that the real facts may be known to the public, and we think a full knowledge of these facts will furnish as curious an history as of the ratification of the constitution which established Napoleon Emperor of France.

The *Connecticut Journal also* summarized the results of the ratification vote on October 13, 1818 in a way that raised doubts about the legitimacy of the lengthy process the state had just completed. This piece was republished by the *Courant* on October 20, 1818.

NEW CONSTITUTION

Our readers will perceive by the proceedings of the Legislature that the Constitution is adopted by a majority of the freemen who voted, of 1554;—26,282 freemen voted on the Constitution—we have more than 30,000 freemen in the State, 13,918 of whom have ratified a form of civil government, for the people; and in addition to this more than 1554 of those who voted in favour of it have come to the polls under the universal suffrage law! let the *majority* hear [sic] *rule*—but at all events let it be the majority!

"ALFRED," *CONNECTICUT COURANT,* OCTOBER 20, 1818

Federalist anxieties about the effect the new constitution would have on the state's future were expressed by "Alfred." The piece appeared in the *Connecticut Courant* on October 20, 1818 and was quoted for the purpose of rebuttal by "Freedom" in the *Times* on November 10, 1818. It is republished here in preference to the six part series" entitled "On the Adoption of the Constitution" by "John Hancock," which appeared in the *Connecticut Journal* between October 27 and December 8, 1818, arguing that the constitution was the expression of "barefaced *injustice, intrigue, & tyranny."*

THE fatal die is cast—The freedom of Connecticut, reared at the expense of the blood and treasures of our venerable forefathers, is prostrated in the dust. An headstrong, unprincipled faction, has at length succeeded in overturning the fair fabrick of our independence, and destroying the most valuable institutions of the state.

Nothing but madness in the extreme, could have induced a majority of the freemen of the state to barter away their best interests, and sell their birth-right, for that which is less valuable than a mess of pottage.

How is it possible that the proprietors of the soil, and the owners of all the real estate in Connecticut, could for a moment consent, that all that numerous class of men, who possess no property whatever, should be placed on an equal footing with them, in selecting our rulers, and in making our laws, when it is well known that almost all our laws have relation to property, and that property liable to be taxed for all the expenses of government, both in peace and war? What safety can there be, for those who own the property of the state, when it is placed at the disposal of those who have none?

Who, that is in the exercise of his rational faculties, would be made to believe, that the Presbyterian and Congregational denomination of Christians, who compose a large majority of the people of this state; who I say could have thought that so large a portion of them, would, without hesitation and without reflection, be made to vote away their just rights and dearest privileges, and to sacrifice their best interests, to gratify an uneasy, railing class of men, who for years back have been striving and exerting every means in their power to undermine and destroy the congregational order, and to break down our located societies: and what is almost equally strange and unaccountable, that so many of the Episcopalian denomination should have lent their aid, in overturning the presbyterian societies, when by so doing, they most assuredly will become immolated on the ruin of their neighbors.

That any number of the citizens of Hartford should have aided in removing the seat of government from themselves, must have been the height of delirium—had an earthquake or a devouring fire destroyed one half of the city, the effects would not have been more fatal or more severely felt. This measure will check the rising prosperity of Hartford, and cannot fail to produce a serious embarrassment to almost every kind of business; nor are the neighboring towns uninterested in this event.

But the fatal instrument is signed, sealed and delivered—and this has been done with less hesitation, care or attention, than most of these same men would exercise, were they called upon to execute a bond concerning the most trivial affairs of life—without knowing what was contained in, or heeding what the effect will be. Thousands have been blindly led to perform an act, by which they have sealed their own destruction, and fastened their children and posterity in bondage.

But to complain at this late hour, would be too much like the course pursued in New-Haven, and attempted in some other towns, to vote in the first instance, and then debate the question!

Alfred

APPENDIX

FUNDAMENTAL ORDERS OF 1639[1]

Forasmuch as it hath pleased the Allmighty God by the wise disposition of his diuyne pruidence so to Order and dispose of things that we the Inhabitants and Residents of Windsor, Harteford and Wethersfield are now cohabiting and dwelling in and vppon the River of Conectecotte and the Lands thereunto adioyneing; And well knowing where a people are gathered togather the word of God requires that to mayntayne the peace and vnion of such a people there should be an orderly and decent Gouerment established according to God, to order and dispose of the affayres of the people at all seasons as occation shall require; doe therefore assotiate and conioyne our selues to be as one Publike State or Com[m]onwelth; and doe, for our selues and our Successors and such as shall be adioyned to vs att any tyme hereafter, enter into Combiation and Confederation togather, to mayntayne and presearue the liberty and purity of the gospell of our Lord Jesus wch we now pr[o]fesse, as also the disciplyne of the Churches, wch according to the truth of the said gospell is now practised amongst vs; As also in or Ciuell Affaires to be guided and gouerned according to such Lawes, Rules, Orders and decrees as shall be made, ordered & decreed, as followeth:—

1. It is Ordered, sentenced and decreed, that there shall be yerely two generall Assemblies or Courts, the on the second thursday in Aprill, the other the second thursday in September, following; the first shall be called the Courte of Election, wherein shall be yerely Chosen fro[m] tyme to tyme soe many Magestrats and other publike Officers as shall be found requisitte: Whereof one to be chosen Gouernour for the yeare ensueing and vntill another be chosen, and noe other Magestrate to be chosen for more than one yeare; pruided allwayes there be six chosen besids the Gouernour; wch being chosen and sworne according to an Oath recorded for that purpose shall haue power to administer iustice according to the Lawes here established, and for want thereof according to the rule of the word of God; wch choise shall be made by all that are admitted freemen and haue taken the Oath of Fidellity, and doe cohabitte wthin this Jurisdiction, (hauing beene admitted Inhabitants by the maior prt of the Towne wherein they liue,)[*] or the mayor p[a]rte of such as shall be then prsent.

2. It is Ordered, sentensed and decreed, that the Election of the aforesaid Magestrats shall be on this manner: euery prson prsent and quallified for choyse shall bring in (to the prsons deputed to recaue the[m]) one single papr wth the name of him written in yt whom he desires to haue Gouernour, and he that hath the greatest nu[m]ber of papers shall be Gouernor for that yeare. And the rest of the Magestrats or publike Officers to be chosen in this manner: The Secretary for the tyme being shall first read the names of all that are to be put to choise and then shall seuerally nominate them distinctly, and euery one that would

* This clause has been interlined in a different hand writing and at a more recent period.

[1] Text from *The Public Records of the Colony of Connecticut*. J Hammond Trumbull et al. eds. (Hartford, 1850-1890), I, 20-25.

haue the prson nominated to be chosen shall bring in one single paper written vppon, and he that would not haue him chosen shall bring in a blanke: and euery one that hath more written papers then blanks shall be a Magestrat for that yeare; wch papers shall be receaued and told by one or more that shall be then chosen by the court and sworne to be faythfull therein ; but in case there should not be sixe chosen as aforesaid, besids the Gouernor, out of those wch are nominated, then he or they wch haue the most written paprs shall be a Magestrate or Magestrats for the ensuing yeare, to make vp the foresaid nu[m]ber.

3. It is Ordered, sentenced and decreed, that the Secretary shall not nominate any prson, nor shall any prson be chosen newly into the Magestracy wch was not prpownded in some Generall Courte before, to be nominated the next Election; and to that end yt shall be lawfull for ech of the Townes aforesaid by their deputyes to nominante any two who[m] they conceaue fitte to be put to Election; and the Courte may ad so many more as they iudge requisitt.

4. It is Ordered, sentenced and decreed that noe prson be chosen Gouernor aboue once in two yeares, and that the Gouernor be alwayes a meber of some approved congregation, and formerly of the Magestracy wthin this Jurisdiction; and all the Magestrats Freemen of this Com[m]onwelth: and that no Magestrate or other publike officer shall execute any prte of his or their Office before they are seuerally sworne, wch shall be done in the face of the Courte if they be prsent, and in case of absence by some deputed for that purpose.

5. It is Ordered, sentenced and decreed, that to the aforesaid Courte of Election the seurall Townes shall send their deputyes, and when the Elections are ended they may prceed in any publike searuice as at other Courts. Also the other Generall courte in September shall be for makeing of laws, and any other publike occation, wch conserns the good of the Com[m]onwelth.

6. It is Ordered, sentenced and decreed, that the Gournor shall, ether by himselfe or by the secretary, send out sum[m]ons to the Constables of eur Towne for the cauleing of these two standing Courts, one month at lest before their seurall tymes: And also if the Gournor and the gretest prte of the Magestrats see cause vppon any spetiall occation to call a generall Courte, they may giue order to the secretary soe to doe wthin fowerteene dayes warneing: and if vrgent necessity so require, vppon a shorter notice, giueing sufficient grownds for yt to the deputyes when they meete, or els be questioned for the same; And if the Gournor and Mayor prte of Magestrats shall ether neglect or refuse to call the two Generall standing Courts or ether of the[m], as also at other tymes when the occations of the Com[m]onwelth require, the Freemen thereof, or the Mayor prte of them, shall petition to them soe to doe: if then yt be ether denyed or neglected the said Freemen or the Mayor prte of them shall haue power to giue order to the Constables of the seuerall Townes to doe the same, and so may meete togather, and chuse to themselues a Moderator, and may prceed to do any Acte of power, wch any other Generall Courte may.

7. It is Ordered, sentenced and decreed that after there are warrants giuen out for any of the said Generall Courts, the Constable or Constables of ech Towne shall forthwth give notice distinctly to the inhabitants of the same, in some Publike Assembly or by goeing or sending fro[m] howse to howse, that at a place and tyme by him or them lymited and sett, they meet and assemble the[m] selues togather to elect and chuse certen deputyes to be att the Generall Courte then following to agistate the afayres of the com[m]onwelth; wch said Deputyes shall be chosen by all that are admitted Inhabitants in the seurall Townes and haue taken the oath of fidellity; pruided that non be chosen a Deputy for any Generall Courte wch is not a Freeman of this Com[m]onwelth.

The foresaid deputyes shall be chosen in manner following: euery prson that is prsent and quallified as before exprssed, shall bring the names of such, written in seurrall papers as they desire to haue chosen for that Imployment, and these 3 or 4, more or lesse, being the nu[m]ber agreed on to be chosen for that tyme, that haue greatest nu[m]ber of papers written for the[m] shall be deputyes for that Courte; whose names shall be endorsed on the backe side of the warrant and returned into the Courte, wth the Constable or Constables hand vnto the same.

8. It is Ordered, sentenced and decreed, that Wyndor, Hartford and Wethersfield shall haue power, ech Towne, to send fower of their freemen as their deputyes to euery Generall Courte; and whatsoeuer other Townes shall be hereafter added to this Jurisdiction, they shall send so many deputyes as the Courte shall judge meete, a resonable prportion to the nu[m]ber of Freemen that are in the said Twones being to be attended therein; wch deputyes shall have the power of the whole Towne to giue their voats and alowance to all such lawes and orders as may be for the publike good, and unto wch the said Townes are to be bownd.

9. It is ordered and decreed, that the deputyes thus chosen shall huae power and liberty to appoynt a tyme and a place of meeting togather before any Generall Courte to aduise and consult of all such things as may concerne the good of the publike, as also to examine their owne Elections, whether according to the order, and if they or the gretest prte of them find any election to be illegall they may seclud such for prsent fro[m] their meeting, and returne the same and their resons to the Courte; and if yt proue true, the Courte may fyne the prty or prtyes so intruding and the Towne, if they see cause, and giue out a warrant to goe to a newe election in a legall way, ether in prte or in whole. Also the said deputyes shall haue power to fyne any that shall be disorderly at their meetings, or for not coming in due tyme or place according to appoyntment; and they may returne the said fynes into the Courte if yt be refused to be paid, and the Tresurer to take notice of yt, and to estreete or levy the same as he doth other fynes.

10. It is Ordered, sentenced and decreed, that euery Generall Courte, except such as through neglecte of the Gournor and the greatest prte of Magestrats the Freemen themselves doe call, shall consist of the Gouernor, or some one chosen to moderate the Court, and

4 other Magestrats at lest, wth the mayor prte of the deputyes of the seuerall Townes legally chosen ; and in case the Freemen or mayor prte of the[m], through neglect or refusall of the Gouernor and mayor prte of the magestrats, shall call a Courte, yt shall consist of the mayor prte of Freemen that are prsent or their deputyes wth a Moderator chosen by the[m]: In wch said Generall Courts shall consist the supreme power of the Com[m]onwelth, and they only shall haue power to make lawes or repeale the[m], to graunt leuyes, to admitt of Freemen, dispose of land vndisposed of, to seuerall Townes or prsons, and also shall haue power to call ether Courte or Magestrate or any other prson whatsoeuer into question for any misdemeanour, and may for just causes displace or deale otherwise according to the nature of the offence; and also may deale in any other matter that concerns the good of this com[m]on welth, excepte election of Magestrats, wch shall be done by the whole boddy of Freemen.

In wch Courte the Gouernour or Moderator shall haue power to order the Courte to giue liberty of spech, and silence vnceasonable and disorderly speakeings, to put all things to voate, and in case the voate be equall to haue the casting voice. But non of these Courts shall be adiorned or dissolued wthout the consent of the maior prte of the Court.

11. It is ordered, sentenced and decreed, that when any Generall Courte vppon the occations of the Com[m]onwelth haue agreed vppon any sume or somes of mony to be leuyed vppon the seuerall Townes wthin this Jurisdiction, that a Com[m]ittee be chosen to sett out and appoynt wt shall be the prportion of euery Towne to pay of the said leuy, prvided the Com[m]ittees be made vp of an equall nu[m]ber out of each Towne.

14th January, 1638, the 11 Orders abouesaid are voted.[2]

---

[2] With the adoption of the Gregorian calendar in 1752, 14 January 1638 became the equivalent of 24 January 1639.

THE CHARTER OF CONNECTICUT (1662).[1]

Charles the Second, By the grace of God, King of England, Scotland, France and Ireland, defender of the Faith, &c.; **To** all whome theis presents shall come, Greetinge: **Whereas,** by the severall Navigaçons, discoveryes and successfull Plantaçons of diverse of our loveing Subjects of this our Realme of England, Severall Lands, Islands, Places, Colonies and Plantaçons have byn obtayned and setled in that parte of the Continent of America called New England, and thereby the Trade and Comerce there hath byn of late yeares much increased, **And whereas,** We have been informed by the humble Petiçon of our Trusty and welbeloved John Winthrop, John Mason, Samuell Willis, Henry Clerke, Mathew Allen, John Tappen, Nathan Gold, Richard Treate, Richard Lord, Henry Woolicott, John Talcott, Daniell Clerke, John Ogden, Thomas Wells, Obedias Brewen, John Clerke, Anthony Haukins, John Deming and Mathew Camfeild, being Persons Principally interested in our Colony or Plantaçon of Conecticut in New England, that the same Colony or the greatest parte there-of was purchased and obteyned for greate and valuable consideraçons, And some other parte thereof gained by Conquest and with much difficulty, and att the onely endeavours, expence and Charge of them and their Associates, and those vnder whome they Clayme, Subdued and improved, and thereby become a considerable enlargement and addiçon of our Dominions and interest there,—**Now Know yea,** that in Consideraçon thereof, and in regard the said Colony is remote from other the English Plantaçons in the Places aforesaid, And to the end the Affaires and Busines which shall from tyme to tyme happen or arise con-cerning the same may bee duely Ordered and managed, **Wee have** thought fitt, and att the humble Petiçon of the Persons aforesaid, and are graciously pleased to Create and Make them a Body Pollitique and Corporate, with the powers and Priviledges herein after mençoned; And accordingly Our Will and pleasure is, and of our especiall grace, certeine knowledge and meere moçon, **wee have** Ordeyned, Constituted and Declared, And by theis presents, for vs, our heires and Successors, **Doe** Ordeine, Constitute and Declare That they, the said John Winthrop, John Mason, Samuell Willis, Henry Clerke, Mathew Allen, John Tappen, Nathan Gold, Richard Treate, Richard Lord, Henry Woollcott, John Talcott, Daniell Clerke, John Ogden, Thomas Wells, Obedias Brewen, John Clerke, Anthony Haukins, John Deming and Mathew Camfeild, and all such others as now are or hereafter shall be Admitted and made free of the Company and Society of our Collony of Conecticut in America, shall from tyme to tyme and for ever hereafter, bee one Body Corporate and Pollitique in fact and name, by the Name of Governour and Company of the English Collony of Conecticut in New England in America; And that by the same name they and their Successors shall and may have perpetuall Succession, and shall and may bee Persons able and capable in the law to Plead and bee Impleaded, to Answere and to bee Answered vnto,

[1] Text from *The Public Records of the Colony of Connecticut.* J. Hammnod Trumbull et al. eds. (Hartford, 1850-1890), II, 3-11.

to Defend and bee Defended in all and singuler Suits, Causes, quarrells, Matters, Accons and things of what kind or nature soever, And alsoe to have, take, possesse, acquire and purchase lands, Tenements or hereditaments, or any goods or Chattells, and the same to Lease, Graunt, Demise, Alien, Bargaine, Sell and dispose of, as other our leige People of this our Realme of England, or any other Corporaçon or Body Pollitique within the same may lawfully doe. **And further,** that the said Governour and Company, and their Successors shall and may for ever hereafter have a Comon Seale to serve and vse for all Causes, matters, things and affaires whatsoever of them and their Successors, and the same Seale to alter, change, breake and make new from tyme to tyme att their wills and pleasures, as they shall thinke fitt. **And** further, wee will and Ordeine, and by theis presents for vs, our heires and Successors **Doe** Declare and appoint, that for the better ordering and manageing of the affaires and businesse of the said Company and their Successors, there shall be one Gouvernor, one Deputy Gouvernor,, and Twelve Assistants, to be from tyme to tyme Constituted, Elected and Chosen out of the Freemen of said Company for the tyme being, in such manner and forme as hereafter in these presents is expressed; which said Officers shall apply themselves to take care for the best disposeing and Ordering of the Generall busines and affaires of and concerning the lands and hereditaments herein after mençoned to bee graunted, and the Plantaçon thereof and the Government of the People thereof. And for the better execuçon of our Royall Pleasure herein, **Wee doe** for vs, our heires and Successors, Assigne, name, Constitute and appoint the aforesaid John Winthrop to bee the first and present Governour of the said Company; And the said John Mason to bee the Deputy Governour; And the said Samuell Willis, Mathew Allen, Nathan Gold, Henry Clerke, Richard Treat, John Ogden, Thomas Tappen, John Talcott, Thomas Wells, Henry Woolcot, Richard Lord and Daniell Clerke to bee the Twelve present Assistants of the said Company; to contynue in the said severall Offices respectively, vntill the second Thursday which shall be in the Moneth of October now next comeing. **And** further, wee will, and by theis presents for vs, our heires and Successors, Doe Ordaine and Graunt that the Governour of the said Company for the tyme being, or, in his absence by occasion of sicknes, or otherwise by his leave or permission, the Deputy Governour for the tyme being, shall and may from tyme to tyme vpon all occasions give Order for the assembling of the said Company and calling them together to Consult and advise of the businesse and Affaires of the said Company, And that for ever hereafter, Twice in every yeare, (That is to say,) on every second Thursday in October and on every second Thursday in May, or oftner, in Case it shall be requisite, The Assistants and freemen of the said Company, or such of them (not exceeding twoe Persons from each place, Towne or Citty) whoe shall bee from tyme to tyme therevnto Elected or Deputed by the maior parte of the freemen of the respective Townes, Cittyes and Places for which they shall be soe elected or Deputed, shall have a generall meeting or Assembly, then and their to Consult and advise in and about the Affairs and businesse of the said Company;

And that the Governour, or in his absence the Deputy Governour of the said Company for the tyme being, and such of the Assistants and freemen of the said Company as shall be soe Elected or Deputed and bee present att such meeting or Assembly, or the greatest number of them, whereof the Governour or Deputy Governour and Six of the Assistants, at least, to bee Seaven, shall be called the Generall Assembly, and shall have full power and authority to alter and change their dayes and tymes of meeting or Generall Assemblies for Electing the Governour, Deputy Governour and Assistants or other Officers, or any other Courts, Assemblies or meetings, and to Choose, Nominate and appoint such and soe many other Persons as they shall thinke fitt and shall bee willing to accept the same, to bee free of the said Company and Body Politique, and them into the same Admitt and to Elect, and Constitute such Officers as they shall thinke fitt and requisite for the so Ordering, manageing and disposing of the Affaires of the said Governour and Company and their Successors. **And wee doe** hereby for vs, our heirs and Successors, Establish and Ordeine, that once in the yeare, for ever hereafter, namely, the said Second Thursday in May, the Governour, Deputy Governour and Assistants of the said Company and other Officers of the said Company, or such of them as the said Generall Assembly shall thinke fitt, shall bee, in the said Generall Court and Assembly to bee held from that day or tyme, newly Chosen for the yeare ensuing, by such greater part of the said Company for the tyme being then and there present. And if the Governour, Deputy Governour and Assistants by these presents appointed, or such as hereafter bee newly Chosen into their Roomes, or any of them, or any other the Officers to be appointed for the said Company shall dye or be removed from his or their severall Offices or Places before the said Generall day of Eleccon, whome we doe hereby Declare for any misdemeanour or default to bee removeable by the Governour, Assistants and Company, or such greater part of them in any of the said publique Courts to be Assembled as is aforesaid, That then and in every such Case itt shall and may be lawfull to and for the Governour, Deputy Governour and Assistants and Company aforesaid, or such greater parte of them soe to bee Assembled as is aforesaid in any of their Assemblies, to Proceede to a New Eleccon of one or more of their Company in the Roome or place, Roomes or Places of such Governour, Deputy Governour, Assistant or other Officer or Officers soe dyeing or removed, according to their discretions; and immediately vpon and after such Eleccon or Eleccons made of such Governour, Deputy Governour, Assistant or Assistants, or any other Officer of the said Company in manner and forme aforesaid, The Authority, Office and Power before given to the former Governour, Deputy Governour or other Officer and Officers soe removed, in whose stead and Place new shall be chosen, shall as to him and them and every of them respectively cease and determine. **Provided,** alsoe, and our will and pleasure is, that as well such as are by theis presents appointed to bee the present Governour, Deputy Governour and Assistants of the said Company as those that shall succeed them, and all other Officers to bee appointed and Chosen as aforesaid, shall, before they vndertake the

Execuçon of their said Offices and Places respectively, take their severall and respective Corporall Oathes for the due and faithfull performance of their dutyes in their severall Offices and Places, before such Person or Persons as are by these presents hereafter appoynted to take and receive the same; That is to say, the said John Winthrop, whoe is herein before nominated and appointed the present Governour of the said Company, shall take the said Oath before one or more of the Masters of our Court of Chancery for the tyme being, vnto which Master of Chancery **wee doe**, by theis presents, give full power and authority to Administer the said Oath to the said John Winthrop accordingly. And the said John Mason, whoe is herein before nominated and appointed the present Deputy Governour of the said Company, shall take the said Oath before the said John Winthrop, or any twoe of the Assistants of the said Company, vnto whome **wee doe** by these presents, give full power and authority to Administer the said Oath to the said John Mason accordingly. **And** the said Samuell Willis, Henry Clerke, Mathew Allen, John Tappen, Nathan Gold, Richard Treate, Richard Lord, Henry Woolcott, John Talcott, Daniell Clerke, John Ogden and Thomas Welles, whoe are herein before Nominated and appointed the present Assistants of the said Company, shall take the Oath before the said John Winthrop and John Mason, or one of them, to whom **wee doe** hereby give full power and authority to Administer the same accordingly. **And** our further will and pleasure is, that all and every Governour or Deputy Governour to bee Elected and Chosen by vertue of theis presents, shall take the said Oath before two or more of the Assistants of the said Company for the tyme being, vnto whome Wee doe, by theis presents, give full power and authority to Administer the said Oath accordingly; And the said Assistants and every of them, and all and every Officer or Officers to bee hereafter Chosen from tyme to tyme, to take the said Oath before the Governour or Deputy Governour for the tyme being, vnto which said Governour or Deputy Governour we doe, by theis presents, give full power and authority to Administer the same accordingly. **And further,** of our more ample grace, certeine knowledge and meere moçon **wee have** given and Graunted, and by theis presents, for vs, our heires and Successors, **Doe** give and Graunt vnto the said Governour and Company of the English Colony of Conecticut in New England in America, and to every Inhabitant there, and to every Person and Persons Tradeing thither, And to every such Person and Persons as are or shall bee free of the said Colony, full power and authority from tyme to tyme and att all tymes hereafter, to take, Ship, Transport and Carry away, for and towards the Plantaçon and defence of the said Collony such of our loveing Subiects and Strangers as shall or will willingly accompany them in and to their said Collony and Plantaçon; (Except such Person and Persons as are or shall be therein restrayned by vs, our heires and Successors;) And alsoe to Ship and Transport all and all manner of goods, Chattells, Merchandizes and other things whatsoever that are or shall be vsefull or necessary for the Inhabitants of the said Collony and may lawfully bee Transported thither; Neverthelesse, not to bee discharged of payment to vs, our heires and Successors, of the Dutyes, Customes and Subsidies which are or ought to bee paid or payable for the same. **And further,** Our will and pleasure is, and **wee doe** for vs, our heirs and Successors, Ordeyne, Declare and Graunt vnto the said Governor and Company and their Successors, That all and every the Subiects of vs, our heires or Successors which shall goe to Inhabite within the said Colony, and every of their Children which shall happen to bee borne there or on the Sea in goeing thither or returneing from thence, shall have and enioye all liberties and Immunities of free and naturall Subiects within any the Dominions of vs, our heires or Successors, to all intents, Construccons and purposes watsoever, as if they and every of them were borne within the Realme of England. **And wee doe** authorise and impower the Governour, or in his absence the Deputy Governor for the tyme being, to appionte two or more of the said Assistants att any of their Courts or Assemblyes to bee held as aforesaid, to have power and authority to Administer the Oath of Supremacy and obedience to all and every Person and Persons which shall att any tyme or tymes hereafter goe or passe into the said Colony of Conecticutt, vnto which said Assistants soe to bee appointed as aforesaid, **wee doe,** by these presents, give full power and authority to Administer the said Oath accordingly. **And wee doe further,** of our especiall grace, certeine knowledge and meere moçon, give and Graunt vnto the said Governor and Company of the English Colony of Conecticutt in New England in America, and their Successors, that itt shall and may bee lawfull to and for the Governor or Deputy Governor and such of the Assistatns of the said Company for the tyme being as shall be Assembled in any of the Generall Courts aforesaid, or in any Courts to be especially Sumoned or Assembled for that purpose, or the greater parte of them, whereof the Governor or Deputy Governor and Six of the Assistants to be all wayes Seaven, to Erect and make such Judicicatories for the heareing and Determining of all Accçons, Causes, matters and thinges happening within the said Colony or Plantaçon and which shall bee in dispute and depending there, as they shall thinke fitt and convenient; And also from tyme to tyme to Make, Ordaine and Establish All manner of wholsome and reasonable Lawes, Statutes, Ordinances, Direccons and Instruccons, not contrary to the lawes of this Realme of England, as well for setling the formes and Ceremonies of Governement and Magestracy fitt and necessary for the said Plantaçon and the Inhabitants there as for nameing and Stileing all sorts of Officers, both superior and inferior, which they shall find needfull for the Governement and Plantaçon of the said Colony, and the distinguishing and setting forth of the severall Dutyes, Powers and Lymitts of every such Office and Place, and the formes of such Oathes, not being contrary to the Lawes and Statutes of this our Realme of England, to bee Administred for the Execuçon of the severall Offices and Places; As alsoe for the disposeing and ordering of the Eleccçon of such of the said Officers as are to bee Annually Chosen, and of such others as shall succeed in case of death or removall, and Administring the said Oath to the new Elected Officers, and Graunting necessary Comissions, and for imposition of lawfull Fines, Mulcts, Imprisonment or other Punishment vpon Offenders and Delinquents, according to the Course of other Corporaçons within this our Kingdome of England, and the same Lawes, fines, Mulcts and Execuçons to alter, change, revoke, adnull, release or Pardon, vnder their Comon Seale, As by the said Generall Assembly or the maior part of them shall bee thought fitt; and for the directing, ruleing and disposeing of all other matters and things whereby our said people, Inhabitants there, may bee soe religiously, peaceably and civilly Governed as their good life and orderly Conversaçon may wynn and invite the Natives of the Country to the knowledge and obedience of the onely true God and Savior of mankind, and the Christian faith, which in our Royall intençons and the Adventurers free profession is the onely and principall end of this Plantaçon; Willing, Commanding and requireing, and by these presents, for vs, our heires and Successors, Ordaineing and appointeing, That all such Lawes, Statutes and Ordinances, Instrucçons, Imposiçons and Direcçons as shall bee soe made by the Governor, Deputy Governor and Assistants, as aforesaid, and published in writeing vnder their Comon Seale, shall carefully and duely bee observed, kept, performed and putt in execuçon, according to the true intent and meaning of the same. **And** these our letters Patents, or the Duplicate or Exemplification thereof, shall bee to all and every such Officers, Superiors and inferiors, from tyme to tyme, for the Putting of the same Orders, Lawes, Statutes, Ordinances, Instrucçons and Direcçons in due Execuçon, against vs, our heires and Successors, a sufficient warrent and discharge. **And wee doe further,** for vs, our heires and Successors, give and Graunt vnto the said Governor and Company and their Successors, by these presents, That itt shall and may bee lawfull to and for the Cheife Commanders, Governors and Officers of the said Company for the tyme being whoe shall bee resident in the parts of New England hereafter mençoned, and others inhabiting there by their leave, admittance, appointment or direcçon, from tyme to tyme and at all tymes hereafter, for their speciall defence and safety, to Assemble, Martiall, Array and putt in Warlike posture the Inhabitants of the said Colony, and to Commissionate, Impower and authorise such Person or Persons as they shall thinke fitt to lead and Conduct the said Inhabitants, and to encounter, expulse, repell and resist by force of Armes, as well by Sea as by land, And alsoe to kill Slay and destroy, by all fitting wayes, enterprizes and meanes whatsoever, all and every such Person or Persons as shall att any tyme hereafter Attempt or enterprize the distruccon, invasion, detriment or annoyance of the said Inhabitants or Plantaçon, And to vse and exercise the Law Martiall, in such Cases onely as occasion shall require, And to take or suprize by all wayes and meanes whatsoever, all and every such Person and Persons, with their Shipps, Armour, Ammuniçon and other goods of such as shall in such hostile manner invade or attempt the defeating of the said Plantaçon or the hurt of the said Company and Inhabitants; and vpon iust Causes to invade and destroy the Natives or other Enemyes of the said Colony. **Neverthelesse,** Our Will and pleasure is, And **wee doe** hereby Declare vnto all Christian Kings, Princes and States, That if any Persons which shall hereafter bee of the said Company or Plantaçon, or any other, by appointment of the said Governor and Company for the tyme being, shall att any tyme or tymes hereafter Robb or Spoile by Sea or by land, and doe any hurt, violence or vnlawfull hostillity to any of the Subiects of vs, our heires or Successors, or any of the Subiects of any Prince or State beinge then in league with vs, our heires or Successors, vpon Complaint of such iniury done to any such Prince or State, or their Subiects, **wee,** our heires and Successors, will make open Proclamaçon within any parts of our Realme of England fitt for that purpose, That the Person or Persons commitinge any such Robbery or Spoile, shall within the tyme lymitted by such Proclamaçon, make full restituçon or satisfacçon of all such iniuries done or committed, Soe as the said Prince or others soe complayneing may bee fully satisfied and contented. And if the said Person or Persons whoe shall committ any such Robbery or Spoile shall not make satisfacçon accordingly, within such tyme soe to bee limitted, That then itt shall and may bee lawfull for vs, our heires and Successors, to putt such Person or Persons out of our Allegiance and Protecçon; And that it shall and may be lawfull and free for all Princes or others to Prosecute with hostility such Offenders and every of them, their and every of their Procurers, ayders, Abettors and Councellors in that behalfe. **Provided,** alsoe, and our express will and pleasure is, **And wee doe** by these presents for vs, our heires and Successors, Ordeyne and appointe that these presents shall not in any manner hinder any of our loveing Subiiects whatsoever to vse and exercise the Trade of Fishinge vpon the Coast of New England in America, but they and every or any of them shall have full and free power and liberty to contynue and vse the said Trade of Fishing vpon the said Coast, in any of the Seas therevnto adioyning, or any Armes of the Seas or Salt Water Rivers where they have byn accustomed to Fish, And to build and sett vpon the wast land belonging to the said Colony of Conecticutt, such Wharfes, Stages and workehouses as shall bee necessary for the Salting, dryeing and keeping of their Fish to bee taken or gotten vpon that Coast, any thinge in these presents conteyned to the contrary notwithstanding. **And Knowe yee further,** That Wee, of our more abundant grace, certaine knowledge and meere moçon **have** given, Graunted and Confirmed, and by theis presents, for vs, our heires and Successors, **Doe** give, Graunt and Confirme vnto the said Governor and Company and their Successors, **All** that parte of our Dominions in Newe England in America bounded on the East by Norrogancett River, comonly called Norrogancett Bay, where the said River falleth into the Sea, and on the North by the lyne of the Massachusetts Plantation, and on the South by the Sea, and in longitude as the lyne of the Massachusetts Colony, runinge from East to West, (that is to say,) from the said Narrogancett Bay on the East to the South Sea on the West parte, with the Islands therevnto adioyneinge, Together with all firme lands, Soyles, Grounds, Havens, Ports, Rivers, Waters, Fishings, Mynes, Mynerals, Precious Stones, Quarries, and all and singular other Comodities, Iurisdicçons, Royalties, Priviledges, Francheses, Preheminences and hereditaments whatsoever within the said Tract, Bounds, lands and Islands aforesaid, or to them or any of them belonging, **To have and to hold** the same vnto the said Governor and Company, their Successors and Assignes, for ever vpon Trust and for the vse and benefitt of themselves and their Associates, freemen of the said Colony, their heires and Assignes, **To bee holden** of vs, our heires and Successors, as of our Mannor of East Greenewich, in Free and Comon Soccage, and not in Capite nor by Knights Service, **Yeilding and Payinge** therefore, to vs, our heires and Successors, onely the Fifth parte of all the Oare of Gold and Silver which from tyme to tyme and att all tymes hereafter shall be there gotten, had or obteyned, in lieu of all Services, Dutyes and Demaunds whatsoever, to bee to vs, our heires or Successors, therefore or thereout rendered, made or paid. **And lastly,** Wee doe for vs, our heires and Successors, Graunt to the said Governor and Company and their Successors, by these presents, that these our Letters Patent shall be firme, good and effectuall in the lawe to all intents, Construccçons and purposes whatsoever, according to our true intent and meaneing herein before Declared, as shall be Construed, reputed and adiudged most favourable on the behalfe and for the best benefitt and behoofe of the said Governor and Company and their Successors, **Although Expresse mençon** of the true yearely value or certeinty of the premises, or of any of them, or of any other Guifts or Graunts by vs or by any of our Progenitors or Predecessors heretofore made to the said Governor and Company of the English Colony of Conecticutt in New England in America aforesaid in theis presents is not made, or any Stateute, Act, Ordinance, Provision, Proclamaçon or Restricçon heretofore had, made, Enacted, Ordeyned or Provided, or any other matter, Cause or thinge whatsoever to the contrary thereof in any wise notwithstanding. **In witnes** whereof wee have caused these our Letters to bee made Patent: **Witnes** our Selfe, att Westminster, the three and Twentieth day of Aprill, in the Fowerteenth yeare of our Reign.

By writt of Privy Seale. **Howard**.

THE CONSTITUTION OF 1818[1]
PREAMBLE.

THE people of Connecticut acknowledging with gratitude, the good providence of God, in having permitted them to enjoy a free government, do, in order more effectually to define, secure, and perpetuate the liberties, rights and privileges which they have derived from their ancestors, hereby, after a careful consideration and revision, ordain and establish the following Constitution and form of Civil Government.

ARTICLE FIRST.
DECLARATION OF RIGHTS.

That the great and essential principles of Liberty and Free Government may be recognized and established,

WE DECLARE.

Sec. 1. That all men when they form a social compact, are equal in rights; and that no man, or set of men, are entitled to exclusive public emoluments or privileges from the community.

Sec. 2. That all political power is inherent in the people, and all free governments are founded on their authority, and instituted for their benefit; and that they have at all times an undeniable and indefeasible right to alter their form of government in such manner as they may think expedient.

Sec. 3. The exercise and enjoyment of religious profession and worship, without discrimination, shall forever be free to all persons in this State, provided that the right hereby declared and established, shall not be so construed as to excuse acts of licentiousness, or to justify practices inconsistent with the peace and safety of the State.

Sec. 4. No preference shall be given by law to any Christian sect or mode of worship.

Sec. 5. **Every citizen may freely speak, write, and publish his sentiments on all subjects, being responsible for the abuse of that liberty.**

Sec. 6. **No law shall ever be passed to curtail or restrain the liberty of speech or of the press.**

Sec. 7. **In all prosecutions or indictments for libels, the truth may be given in evidence and the jury shall have the right to determine the law and the facts, under the direction of the Court.**

Sec. 8. **The people shall be secure in their persons, houses, papers and possessions from unreasonable searches or seizures; and no warrant to search any place, or to seize any person or things, shall issue without describing them as nearly as may be, nor without probable cause supported by oath or affirmation.**

Sec. 9. **In all criminal prosecutions, the accused shall have a right to be heard by**

---

[1] What follows is the text the Convention adopted after amending the draft of the Constitution a committee submitted to it on September 14, 1818. It is taken from Wesley W. Horton, ed., "Annotated Debates of the 1818 Constitutional Convention," *Connecticut Bar Journal* (January 1991)65: 85-10, and republished here with the permission of the Connecticut Bar Association. Wording that also appears in the Constitution of 1965 is rendered in bold, cf. *Connecticut General Statutes Annotated, I*, 567-590.

himself and by counsel; to demand the nature and cause of the accusation; to be confronted by the witnesses against him; to have compulsory process to obtain witnesses in his favor; and in all prosecutions by indictment or information, a speedy public trial by an impartial Jury. He shall not be compelled to give evidence against himself, nor be deprived of life, liberty, or property, but by due course of law. And no person shall be holden to answer for any crime, the punishment of which may be death or imprisonment for life, unless on a presentment or an indictment of a grand jury; except in the land or naval forces, or in the militia, when in actual service in time of war, or public danger.

Sec. 10. **No person shall be arrested, detained or punished, except in cases clearly warranted by law.**

Sec. 11. **The property of no person shall be taken for public use, without just compensation therefor.**

Sec. 12. **All courts shall be open, & every person, for an injury done him in his person, property, or reputation, shall have remedy by due course of law, and right and justice administered without sale, denial or delay.**

Sec. 13. Excessive bail shall not be required, nor excessive fines imposed.

Sec. 14. All prisoners shall, before conviction, be bailable by sufficient sureties **except for capital offences, where the proof is evident, or the presumption great;** and the privileges of the writ of HABEAS CORPUS shall not be suspended, unless when in case of rebellion or invasion the public safety may require it; nor, in any case, but by the legislature.

Sec. 15. **No person shall be attainted of Treason or Felony, by the Legislature.**

Sec. 16. **The citizens have a right, in a peaceable manner to assemble for their common good, and to apply to those invested with the powers of government, for redress of grievances, or other proper purposes, by petition, address or remonstrance.**

Sec. 17. **Every citizen has a right to bear arms in defence of himself and the State.**

Sec. 18. **The military shall in all cases, and at all times, be in strict subordination to the civil power.**

Sec. 19. **No soldier shall in time of peace be quartered in any house, without the consent of the owner; nor in time of war, but in a manner to be prescribed by law.**

Sec. 20. **No hereditary emoluments, privileges, or honors, shall ever be granted or conferred in this state.**

Sec. 21. **The right of trial by jury shall remain inviolate.**

ARTICLE SECOND.
OF THE DISTRIBUTION OF POWERS.

The powers of government shall be divided into three distinct departments, and each of them confided to a separate magistracy—to wit—, those which are legislative, to one; those which are executive to another, and those which are judicial to another.

ARTICLE THIRD.
OF THE LEGISLATIVE DEPARTMENT.

Sec. **1. The Legislative power of this State shall be vested in two distinct houses or branches; the one to be styled THE SENATE, the other THE HOUSE of REPRESENTATIVES, and both together THE GENERAL ASSEMBLY. The style of their laws shall be, *Be it enacted by the Senate and House of Representatives, in General Assembly convened.***

Sec. 2. There shall be one stated session of the General Assembly, to be holden in each year, alternately at Hartford and New Haven, on the first Wednesday of May, and at such other times as the General Assembly shall judge necessary; the first session to be holden at Hartford; but the person administering the office of Governor, may on special emergencies, convene the General Assembly at either of said places, at any other time. And in case of danger from the prevalence of contagious diseases in either of said places, or other circumstances, the person administering the office of Governor may, by Proclamation, convene said Assembly at any other place in this State.

Sec. 3. The House of Representatives shall consist of electors residing in towns from which they are elected. The number of Representatives from each town shall be the same as at present practised and allowed. In case a new town shall hereafter be incorporated, such new town shall be entitled to one Representative only; and if such new town shall be made from one or more towns, the town or towns, from which the same shall be made, shall be entitled to the same number of Representatives as at present allowed, unless the number shall be reduced by the consent of such town or towns.

Sec. 4. The Senate shall consist of twelve members, to be chosen annually by the electors.

Sec. 5. At the meetings of the electors, held in the several towns in this state in April annually, after the election of Representatives, the electors present shall be called upon to bring in their written ballots for Senators. The presiding officer shall receive the votes of the electors, and count and declare them in open meeting. The presiding officer shall also make duplicate lists of the persons voted for, and of the number of votes for each, which shall be certified by the presiding officer; one of which lists shall be delivered to the Town Clerk and the other within ten days after said meeting shall be delivered under seal either to the Secretary, or to the Sheriff of the County in which said town is situated, which list shall be directed to the Secretary, with a superscription expressing the purport of the contents thereof. And each Sheriff who shall receive such votes shall within fifteen days after said meeting, deliver, or cause them to be delivered to the Secretary.

Sec. 6. The Treasurer, Secretary, and Controller, for the time being shall canvass the votes publicly. The twelve persons having the greatest number of votes for Senators, shall be declared to be elected. But in cases where no choice is made by the electors in consequence of an equality of votes, the House of Representatives shall designate by ballot which of the candidates having such equal number of votes, shall be declared to be elected. The return of votes, and the result of the canvass, shall be submitted to the House of Representatives, and also to the Senate, on the first day of the session of the General Assembly, and each house shall be the final judge of the election returns and qualifications of its own members.

Sec. 7. **The House of Representatives when assembled, shall choose a Speaker, Clerk, and other officers. The Senate shall choose its Clerk, and other officers, except the President. A majority of each House shall constitute a quorum to do business; but a smaller number may adjourn from day to day, and compel the attendance of absent members in such manner, and under such penalties as each House may prescribe.**

Sec. 8. **Each house shall determine the rules of its own proceedings, punish members for disorderly conduct, and with the consent of two thirds expel a member, but not a second time for the same cause, and shall have all other powers necessary for a branch of the Legislature of a free and independent State.**

Sec. 9. **Each house shall keep a journal of its proceedings and publish the same when required by one fifth of its members, except such parts as in the judgment of a majority require secrecy. The yeas and nays of the members of either House shall at the desire of one fifth of those present, be entered on the journals.**

Sec. 10. **The Senators and Representatives shall in all cases of civil process, be privileged from arrest during the session of the General Assembly, and for four days before the commencement, and after the termination of any session thereof. And for any speech or debate in either house, they shall not be questioned in any other place.**

Sec. 11. **The debates of each house shall be public except on such occasions as in the opinion of the House may require secrecy.**

ARTICLE FOURTH.
OF THE EXECUTIVE DEPARTMENT.

Sec. 1. The supreme executive power of the State shall be vested in a Governor, who shall be chosen by the electors of the State, and shall hold his office for one year from the first Wednesday of May next succeeding his election, and until his successor be duly qualified. No person who is not an elector of this State and who has not arrived at the age of thirty years shall be eligible.

Sec. 2. At the meetings of the electors in the respective towns, in the month of April, in each year, immediately after the election of senators, the presiding officers shall call upon the electors to bring in their ballots for him whom they would elect to be Governor, with his name fairly written. When such ballots shall have been received and counted, in the presence of the electors, duplicate lists of the persons voted for, and of the number of votes given for each, shall be made and certified by the presiding officer; one of which lists shall be deposited in the office of the town clerk, within three days, and the other within ten days, after said election, shall be transmitted to the secretary, or to the sheriff of the county in which such election shall have been held. The sheriff receiving said votes shall deliver, or cause them to be delivered, to the secretary within fifteen days next after said election. The votes so returned shall be counted by the treasurer, secretary and comptroller, within the month of April. A fair list of the persons, and number of votes given for each, together with the returns of the presiding officers, shall be by the treasurer, secretary and comptroller, made and laid before the General Assembly, then next to be holden, on the first day of the session thereof; and said assembly shall, after examination of the same, declare the person whom they shall find to be legally chosen, and give him notice accordingly. If no person shall have a majority of the whole number of said votes, or if two or more shall have an equal and the greatest number of said votes, then said assembly, on the second day of their session, by joint ballot of both houses, shall proceed, without debate, to choose a governor from a list of the names of the two persons having the greatest number of votes, or of the names of the persons having an equal and highest number of votes, so returned as aforesaid. The general assembly shall, by law, prescribe the manner in which all questions concerning the election of a governor or lieutenant-governor shall be determined.

Sec. 3. At the annual meetings of the electors, immediately after the election of Governor, there shall also be chosen in the same manner as is herein before provided for the election of Governor, a Lieutenant-Governor, who shall continue in office for the same time, and possess the same qualifications.

Sec. 4. The compensations of the Governor, Lieutenant Governor, Senators and Representatives, shall be established by law, and shall not be varied so as to take effect until after an election, which shall next succeed the passage of the law establishing said compensations.

Sec. 5. The Governor shall be Captain General of the Militia of the State, except when called into the service of the United States.

Sec. 6. He may require information in writing from the officers in the executive department on any subject relating to the duties of their respective offices.

Sec. 7. The Governor, in case of a disagreement between the two Houses of the General Assembly, respecting the time of adjournment, may adjourn them to such time as he shall think proper, not beyond the day of the next stated session.

Sec. 8. He shall from time to time, give to the General Assembly, information of the state of the government, and recommend to their consideration, such measures as he shall deem expedient.

Sec. 9. He shall take care that the laws be faithfully executed.

Sec. 10. The Governor shall have power to grant reprieves after conviction, in all cases except those of impeachment, until the end of the next session of the General Assembly, and no longer.

Sec. 11. All Commissions shall be in the name and by authority of the State of Connecticut; shall be sealed with the State Seal, signed by the Governor, and attested by the Secretary.

Sec. 12. Every bill which shall have passed both Houses of the General Assembly, shall be presented to the Governor. If he approves, he shall sign and transmit it to the Secretary, but if not, he shall return it to the House in which it originated, with his objections, which shall be entered on the journals of the house, who shall proceed to reconsider the bill. If, after such reconsideration, that House shall again pass it, it shall be sent with the objections, to the other House, which shall also reconsider it. If approved, it shall become a Law. But in such cases the votes of both Houses shall be determined by Yeas and Nays; and the names of the members voting for and against the Bill, shall be entered on the Journals of each House respectively. If the Bill shall not be returned by the Governor within three days (Sundays excepted) after it shall have been presented to him, the same shall be law in like manner as if he had signed it; unless the General Assembly, by their adjournment, prevents its return, in which case it shall not be a law.

Sec. 13. The Lieutenant Governor shall, by virtue of his office, be President of the Senate, and have, when in committee of the whole, a right to debate, and when the Senate is equally divided, to give the casting vote.

Sec. 14. In case of the death, resignation, refusal to serve, or removal from office of the Governor, or of his impeachment, or absence from the State, the Lieutenant Governor shall exercise the powers and authority appertaining to the office of Governor, until an other be chosen at the next periodical election for Governor, and be duly qualified; or until the Governor impeached or absent shall be acquitted or return.

Sec. 15. When the government shall be administered by the Lieutenant-Governor, or he shall be unable to attend as President of the Senate, the Senate shall elect one of their members, as President, *pro tempore.* And if during the vacancy of the office of Governor, the Lieutenant Governor shall die, resign, refuse to serve, or be removed from office, or if he shall be impeached, or absent from the state, the president of the senate, *pro tempore*, shall in like manner administer the government until he be superseded by a Governor or Lieutenant Governor.

Sec. 16. If the Lieutenant Governor shall be required to administer the government, and shall, while in such administration, die or resign during the recess of the General Assembly, it shall be the duty of the secretary for the time being, to convene the senate for the purpose of choosing a president *pro tempore.*

Sec. 17. A State Treasurer shall annually be chosen by the electors at their meeting in April, and the votes shall be returned, counted, canvassed and declared, in the same manner as is provided for the election of Governor and Lieutenant Governor, but the votes for Treasurer shall be canvassed by the Secretary and Controller only. **He shall receive all monies belonging to the state, and disburse the same only as he may be directed by law. He shall pay no warrant or order for the disbursement of public money until the same has been registered in the office of the Controller.**

Sec. 18. A secretary shall be chosen next after the treasurer and in the same manner; and the votes for secretary shall be returned to, and counted, canvassed, and declared by the Treasurer and Comptroller. **He shall have the safekeeping and custody of the public records and documents, and particularly of the Acts, resolutions and orders of the General Assembly, and record the same, and perform all such duties as shall be prescribed by law. He shall be the keeper of the Seal of the State, which shall not be altered.**

Sec. 19. A Comptroller of the public accounts shall be annually appointed by the General Assembly. **He shall adjust and settle all public accounts and demands, except grants** and orders of the General Assembly. **He shall prescribe the mode of keeping and rendering all public accounts. He shall *ex officio* be one of the auditors of the Accounts of the Treasurer.** The General Assembly may assign to him other duties in relation to his office and to that of the Treasurer, and shall prescribe the manner in which his duties shall be performed.

Sec. 20. A sheriff shall be appointed in each County by the General Assembly, who shall hold his office for three years, removable by said assembly, and shall become bound, with sufficient sureties, to the treasurer of the State, for the faithful discharge of the duties of his office, in such manner as shall be prescribed by law. **In case the Sheriff of any county shall die, or resign, the Governor may fill the vacancy occasioned thereby, until the same shall be filled by the general assembly.**

Sec. 21. **A statement of all receipts, payments, funds and debts of the state, shall be published from time to time, in such manner, and at such periods, as shall be prescribed by law.**

ARTICLE FIFTH.
OF THE JUDICIAL DEPARTMENT.

Sec. 1. **The Judiciary power of the state shall be vested in a Supreme Court** of Errors, **a superior Court and such inferior Courts as the General Assembly shall from time to time ordain and establish. The powers and jurisdiction of which Courts shall be defined by law.**

Sec. 2. There shall be appointed in each county a sufficient number of Justices of the Peace, with such jurisdiction in civil and criminal cases as the General Assembly may prescribe.

Sec. 3. **The Judges of the Supreme Court** of Errors, **of the Superior &** Inferior Courts, and all Justices of the Peace, **shall be appointed by the General Assembly, in such manner as shall by law be prescribed. The Judges of the Supreme Court, and of the Superior Court, shall hold their offices** during good behavior; **but may be removed by impeachment; and the governor shall also remove them on the address of two thirds of the members of each house of the General Assembly;** all other Judges and Justices of the Peace shall be appointed annually. **No judge or justice of the peace shall be capable of holding his office after he shall have arrived to the age of seventy years.**

ARTICLE SIXTH.
OF THE QUALIFICATIONS OF
ELECTORS.

Sec. 1. All persons who have been, or shall hereafter previous to the ratification of this constitution, be admitted Freemen, according to the existing laws of this State, shall be electors.

Sec. 2. Every white male citizen of the United States, who shall have gained a settlement in this state, attained at the age of twenty-one years, and resided in the town in which he may offer himself to be admitted to the privilege of an elector, at least six months preceding; and have a freehold estate of the yearly value of seven dollars in this state; or having been enrolled in the militia, shall have performed military duty therein for the term of one year next preceding the time he shall offer himself for admission, or being liable thereto, shall have been by authority of law excused therefrom; or shall have paid a State tax within the year next preceding the time he shall present himself for such admission, and shall sustain a good moral character, shall on his taking such oath as may be prescribed by law, be an elector.

Sec. 3. The privileges of an elector shall be forfeited by a conviction of bribery, forgery, perjury, duelling, fraudulent bankruptcy, theft, or other offence for which an infamous punishment is inflicted.

Sec. 4. Every elector shall be eligible to any office in this state, except in cases provided for in this Constitution.

Sec. 5. The select men and town clerk, of the several towns shall decide on the qualifications of electors, at such times and in such manner, as may be prescribed by law.

Sec. 6. **Laws shall be made to support the privilege of free suffrage, prescribing the manner of regulating and conducting meetings of the electors, and prohibiting, under adequate penalties, all undue influence therein, from power, bribery, tumult and other improper conduct.**

Sec. 7. In all elections of officers of the state, or members of the General Assembly, the votes of the electors shall be by ballot.

Sec. 8. At all elections of officers of the state, or members of the General Assembly, the electors shall be privileged from arrest during their attendance upon, and going to, and returning, from the same on any civil process.

Sec. 9. The meetings of the electors for the election of the several State officers by law annually to be elected, and members of the General Assembly of this state, shall be holden on the first Monday of April in each year.

ARTICLE SEVETH.
OF RELIGION.

Sec. 1. **It being the duty of all men to worship the Supreme Being, the Great Creator and Preserver of the universe, and their right to render that worship, in the mode most consistent with the dictates of their consciences; no person shall by law be compelled to join or support, nor be classed with, or associated to any congregation, church, or religious association.** But every person now belonging to such congregation, church or religious association, shall remain a member thereof, until he shall have separated himself therefrom, in the manner herinafter provided. And **each and every** society or denomination of christians in this State, **shall have and enjoy the same and equal powers, rights and privileges; and shall have power and authority to support and maintain the Ministers or Teachers of their respective denominations, and to build and repair houses for public worship,** by a tax on the members of any such society only, to be laid by a major vote of legal voters assembled at any society meeting, warned and held according to law, or in any other manner.

Sec. 2. If any person shall choose to separate himself from the society or denomination of christians to which he may belong, and shall leave a written notice thereof with the Clerk of such society he shall thereupon be no longer liable for any future expenses, which may be incurred by said society.

ARTICLE EIGHT.
OF EDUCATION.

Sec. 1. **The charter of Yale College, as modified by agreement with the Corporation thereof, in pursuance of an act of the General Assembly, passed in May 1792, is hereby confirmed.**

Sec. 2. **The fund called the SCHOOL FUND shall remain a perpetual fund, the interest of which shall be inviolably appropriated to the support and encouragement of the public or common schools throughout the state, and for the equal benefit of all the people thereof. The value and amount of said fund, shall, as soon as practicable, be ascertained in such manner as the General Assembly may prescribe, published & recorded in the Controller's office; and no law shall ever be made, authorizing said fund to be diverted to any other use than the encouragement and support of public, or common schools, among the several school societies, as justice and equity shall require.**

ARTICLE NINTH.
OF IMPEACHMENTS.

Sec. 1. **The House of Representatives shall have the sole power of impeaching.**

Sec. 2. **All impeachments shall be tried by the Senate. When sitting for that purpose they shall be on oath or affirmation. No person shall be convicted without the concurrence of two thirds of the members present. When the Governor is impeached, the Chief Justice shall preside.**

Sec. 3. **The Governor, and all other executive, and judicial officers, shall be liable to impeachment; but judgments in such cases shall not extend further than to removal from office, and disqualification to hold any office of honor, trust, or profit under this state. The party convicted shall nevertheless be liable, and subject to indictment, trial, and punishment, according to law.**

Sec. 4. **Treason against the state shall consist only in levying war against it, or, adhering to its enemies, giving them aid and comfort. No person shall be convicted of Treason, unless on the testimony of two witnesses to the same overt act, or on confession in open court. No conviction of Treason, or attainder, shall work corruption of blood, or forfeiture.**

ARTICLE TENTH.
GENERAL PROVISIONS.

Sec. 1. **Members of the General Assembly and all officers, executive and judicial, shall, before they enter on the duties of their respective offices, take the following oath or affirmation, to wit.**

You do solemnly swear (or affirm as the case may be) that you will support the Constitution of the United States, and the Constitution of the state of Connecticut, so long as you continue a citizen thereof; and that you will faithful-

ly discharge according to law, the duties of the office of to the best of your abilities. **So help you God.**

Sec. 2. Each town shall annually elect Select-men, and such officers of local police, as the laws may prescribe.

Sec. 3. The rights and duties of all corporations shall remain as if this Constitution had not been adopted, with the exception of such regulations and restrictions as are contained in this constitution. All judicial and civil officers, now in office, who have been appointed by the general assembly, and commissioned according to law, and all such officers as shall be appointed by said assembly, and commissioned as aforesaid, before the first Wednesday of May next, shall continue to hold their offices until the first day of June next, unless they shall before that time, resign or be removed from office according to law. The treasurer and secretary shall continue in office until a treasurer and secretary shall be appointed under this constitution. All military officers shall continue to hold and exercise their respective offices, until they shall resign, or be removed according to law. **All laws not contrary to, or inconsistent with the provisions of this Constitution, shall remain in force, until they shall expire by their own limitation, or shall be altered or repealed by the General Assembly in pursuance of this Constitution. The validity of all bonds, debts, contracts, as well of individuals as of bodies corporate, or the State, of all suits actions or rights of action both in law and equity, shall continue as if no change had taken place.** The governor, lieutenant-governor, and general assembly which is to be formed in October next, shall have, and possess, all the powers and authorities not repugnant to, or inconsistent with this constitution, which they now have and possess, until the first Wednesday of May next.

Sec. 4. No judge of the superior court, or of the supreme court of errors; no member of Congress; no person holding any office under the authority of the United States; no person holding the office of Treasurer, Secretary, or Controller; no Sheriff or Sheriff's Deputy, shall be a member of the General Assembly.

ARTICLE ELEVENTH.
OF AMENDMENTS OF THE CONSTITUTION.

Whenever a majority of the House of Representatives shall deem it necessary to alter, or amend this Constitution, they may propose such alterations and amendments, which proposed amendments shall be continued to the next General Assembly, and be published with the laws which may have been passed at the same session; and if two thirds of each house at the next session of said Assembly, shall approve the amendments proposed, by yeas and nays, said amendments shall, by the secretary, be transmitted to the town clerk in each town in the state; whose duty it shall be to present the same to the inhabitants thereof for their consideration at a town meeting legally warned and held for that purpose. And if it shall appear, in manner to be provided by law, that a majority of the electors present at such meetings, shall have approved such amendments, the same shall be valid to all intents and purposes as a part of this Constitution.

Done in Convention on the fifteenth day of September, in the year of our Lord, one thousand eight hundred and eighteen, and of the Independence of the United States the forty-third.

By order of the Convention,

OLIVER WOLCOTT, President.

James Lanman,

Clerks,

Robert Fairchild,